D0891922

Bond Markets in Latin America

Bond Markets in Latin America: On the Verge of a Big Bang?

edited by Eduardo
Borensztein, Kevin Cowan,
Barry Eichengreen, and Ugo
Panizza

The MIT Press
Cambridge, Massachusetts
London, England

© 2008 Massachusetts Institute of Technology

All rights reserved. No part of this book may be reproduced in any form by any electronic or mechanical means (including photocopying, recording, or information storage and retrieval) without permission in writing from the publisher.

MIT Press books may be purchased at special quantity discounts for business or sales promotional use. For information, please e-mail special_sales@mitpress.mit.edu or write to Special Sales Department, The MIT Press, 55 Hayward Street, Cambridge, MA 02142.

This book was set in Palatino on 3B2 by Asco Typesetters, Hong Kong and was printed and bound in United States of America.

Library of Congress Cataloging-in-Publication Data

Bond markets in Latin America : on the verge of a big bang? / edited by Eduardo Borensztein ... [et al.].
    p.   cm.
Includes bibliographical references and index.
ISBN 978-0-262-02632-1 (hardcover : alk. paper)
1. Bond market—Latin America. I. Borensztein, Eduardo.
HG5160.5.A3B66   2008
332.63′23098—dc22   2007032263

10 9 8 7 6 5 4 3 2 1

Contents

Contributors

Camila Aguilar
Fedesarrollo

Patrick Bolton
Columbia University, Graduate
School of Business and
Department of Economics

Eduardo Borensztein
International Monetary Fund

Matías Braun
Universidad Adolfo Ibáñez and
UCLA Anderson School of
Management

Ignacio Briones
Universidad Adolfo Ibáñez and
UCLA Anderson School of
Management

Mauricio Cárdenas
Fedesarrollo

Andre L. Carvalhal-da-Silva
Coppead Graduate School of
Business at the Federal University
of Rio de Janeiro

Sara G. Castellanos
Banco de México and Instituto
Tecnológico Autónomo de
México

Kevin Cowan
Central Bank of Chile

Julio de Brun
Universidad ORT, Uruguay

Barry Eichengreen
University of California, Berkeley

Roque B. Fernández
Universidad del CEMA,
Argentina

Xavier Freixas
Universitat Pompeu Fabra,
Barcelona

Néstor Gandelman
Universidad ORT, Uruguay

Herman Kamil
International Monetary Fund

Ricardo P. C. Leal
Coppead Graduate School of
Business at the Federal University
of Rio de Janeiro

Lorenza Martínez
Instituto Tecnológico Autónomo
de México

Marcela Meléndez
Fedesarrollo

Ugo Panizza
UNCTAD

Sergio Pernice
Universidad del CEMA,
Argentina

Arturo C. Porzecanski
American University and
Columbia University

Natalia Salazar
Fedesarrollo

Jorge M. Streb
Universidad del CEMA,
Argentina

Preface

Developing local bond markets and enhancing the capacity of borrowers to issue long-dated, domestic-currency-denominated debt securities is high on the policy agenda in Latin America. Facilitating the efforts of public and private borrowers to issue domestic-currency-denominated, long-term, fixed-rate bonds is a way of insulating them from the rollover and balance sheet risks that have been central elements in financial crises past. Moreover, a robust domestic bond market is rightly seen as an essential spare tire, as a way for non-financial firms to retain their capacity to borrow when the banking system grows reluctant to lend. It is critical to the development of an efficient and well-diversified financial system, with banks specializing in information-impacted segments of the economy while bond markets provide cheap and stable finance for large, well-established borrowers.

Latin American countries have made important progress in developing bond markets in the last decades. But the region's markets —especially in long-duration, local-currency, fixed-interest debt instruments—are still relatively small and illiquid by international standards. The causes, consequences, and remedies for this situation are the focus of the present volume.

The book is the outgrowth of an Inter-American Development Bank research network project on bond market development in Latin America. Without the generous support, both financial and intellectual, of the IDB, none of this would have been possible. We are grateful to Guillermo Calvo, then chief economist of the IDB, for his support for this research. We thank Raquel Gómez for logistical support at every stage of the way. Comments on earlier versions of the papers were provided by readers both inside and outside the Bank. In particular, we would like to thank the following academics, officials, and market participants who acted as discussants at the preliminary conference held in Buenos Aires in December 2005 and at the final conference in Berkeley in July 2006: Sandro Andrade, Michael Dooley, Franco Fornasari, Márcio Garcia, Reuven Glick, Michael Hasenstab, Luis O. Herrera, Kenneth Kletzer, Daniel Marx, Ignacio Munyo, Mark Seasholes, Mark Spiegel, Alfredo Thorne, and Camilo Tovar. Most of all we appreciate the efforts of the contributors, who stuck to their chapter templates, responded to our insistent requests for revisions, met our unreasonable deadlines, and pushed forward the frontier of knowledge on the development of Latin American bond markets.

Bond Markets in Latin America

1 Building Bond Markets in Latin America

Eduardo Borensztein, Kevin Cowan, Barry Eichengreen, and Ugo Panizza

As they recovered from the debt crisis of the 1980s, Latin American countries regained access to international bond markets for foreign financing, while for domestic financial intermediation they relied mainly on banks. This strategy had several drawbacks. Investors in international markets have a preference for bonds denominated in the major international currencies, such as US dollars, rendering borrowers vulnerable to currency mismatches and to disruptions when exchange rates change.[1] Dependence on bank intermediation, for its part, heightens the vulnerability of the economy to systemic banking crises. These drawbacks are reasons why Latin American countries would benefit from better diversified financial systems and specifically deep and liquid bond markets. The corporate bond market plays a key role in the financial system, providing cheap and stable financing for large, well-established corporations, leaving banks to specialize in lending to borrowers for which information asymmetries are greater. Moreover, well-established yield curves for public bonds provide crucial information on market expectations of interest rates, inflation, and sovereign risk.

Yet the development of well-functioning corporate and government bond markets presupposes extensive infrastructure, payments and settlements systems, rating agencies, and networks of brokers to sell bonds. In the case of corporate bonds, it also requires rigorous disclosure standards and effective governance of corporations issuing publicly traded debt securities along with well-developed accounting, legal, and regulatory systems. Finally, it presupposes the existence of corporations that are large enough to defray the fixed costs of placing a bond issue.

These are not conditions that develop overnight. Rather, they are by-products of the larger process of economic and financial development, which is why even in the advanced countries bond markets historically have been late to develop. So long as some of these developmental preconditions remain absent, borrowers may prefer to tap the more extensive and efficient bond market infrastructure that exists in the major financial centers. Or they may find it easier to borrow from banks, which rely on long-term relationships with their clients to obtain information and enforce repayment, thereby enabling them to circumvent imperfections in the information and contracting environments.

Latin American countries have made some progress in bond market development in the course of the last ten years, but the region's bond markets remain small by international standards—particularly the private securities segment. A comparatively low share of both public and corporate bonds is made up of long-duration, local-currency, fixed-interest debt instruments, despite notable progress in a number of countries. This volume asks why and what can be done about this situation.

The work presented in this volume has three main objectives. The first is to document the characteristics of Latin American bond markets and evaluate their "underdevelopment" in absolute terms and relative to other forms of financing. A second objective is identify the factors behind the recent growth (or lack thereof) in these bond markets. In recent years the countries covered in this volume carried out extensive policy reforms, including improvements in market infrastructure and regulation, privatization of utilities and other public enterprises, reforms of pension systems, and a broad enhancement of macroeconomic and financial stability; this raises the question of why there has not been more of a payoff in terms of bond market development. The third and final objective is to discuss whether policies aimed at promoting the growth of Latin American bond markets will have a positive effect on the region's economic performance.

The chapters that follow exploit three approaches to these issues: they analyze conceptual models of the role of bonds in corporate finance, present country case studies, and exploit international comparisons. Chapter 2 presents a framework that addresses the value of bond markets for firms that operate in the typical emerging market environment, namely, in the presence of fragile credit markets and tenuous macroeconomic stability. Chapters 3 through 8 comprise studies of six national cases: Mexico, Argentina, Colombia, Chile, Brazil, and Uruguay. Importantly, these six case studies adopt a common template. All analyze broad historical trends in the development of markets for public and private debt securities, their current state, and the main obstacles and distortions that may impede their fuller development. Focusing on both private and government bonds is necessary because the interactions between the two markets are extensive. Wherever possible, the authors also analyze firm and issue-level data, addressing questions such as what types of firms issue bonds and what sort of investors buy them rather than sticking to national aggregates. Most of these case studies utilize not only micro-data sets but also the results of surveys of issuers and investors specifically commissioned for this volume. Finally, chapter 9 analyzes data on bond market development for a cross-section of emerging markets and advanced countries as a way of summarizing the state of play. It uses evidence from other regions as a yardstick for measuring the principal obstacles to the corporate bond market in Latin America.

An important contribution of the research teams whose work is assembled here has been to gather, for the first time, data on individual corporate bond issues in a number of Latin American countries along with information on the issuing firms and the bond markets of the economies of which they are part. These data sets, which underlie much of the analysis that follows, are made available to the reader through a website hosted by the MIT Press (http://mitpress.mit.edu/9780262026321/webappendix).

The State of the Markets

Latin American bond markets lag along a number of dimensions, not just when compared with the advanced industrial countries, but even when assessed relative to the emerging economies of East Asia, which are similarly seeking to develop their local markets.[2] This is evident from table 1.1, which shows the stocks of public and private bonds relative to GDP. The capitalization of Latin American bond markets, measured as percent of GDP, is markedly lower. Moreover, Latin American bond markets tend to be dominated by government securities, although this feature is also prominent in other emerging market economies, especially those of Europe.

Latin American bond markets also appear to be lagging in dimensions such as the duration of issues (see figure 1.1). The region has made some progress here, but in terms of the share of bonds with a residual maturity of less than one year, for example, it still compares unfavorably with both the advanced economies and emerging East Asia.

Table 1.1
The State of Bond Markets, 2004

	Developed economies	East Asia	Latin America	Other emerging markets
Bonds issued as percent of GDP:				
Private	70.9	22.0	9.0	3.9
Financial	44.6	11.8	4.8	2.6
Corporate	26.3	10.2	4.3	1.2
Government	59.6	29.3	22.3	47.1
Total	130.5	51.3	31.3	50.9

Source: Calculations based on BIS and Dealogic data.

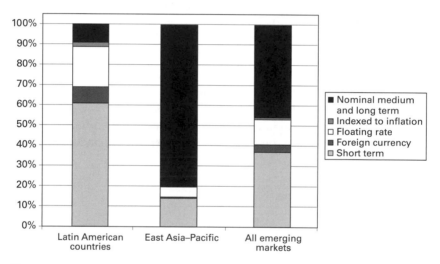

Figure 1.1
Composition of bonds issued, 2000–2005. Source: Chapter 9, based on Dealogic data.

The majority of long-term issues in Latin American markets either have floating interest rates or are indexed to inflation or the exchange rate, in contrast to emerging Asian markets where fixed rates are the norm and indexation is virtually nonexistent. About 80% of all bonds issued in East Asia between 2000 and 2005 (weighted by value) had a maturity above one year and no indexation, whereas the comparable figure for Latin America was less than 10%.

The question is whether these contrasts are likely to be short-lived or enduring. If the problem in Latin America is that years of budget defi-

Table 1.2
Bond Markets in Latin America, 2004

	Argentina	Brazil	Chile	Colombia	Mexico	Peru
Bonds issued as percent of GDP:						
Private	9.8	12.6	23.3	0.6	3.4	4.5
Financial	3.4	12.0	11.1	0.0	0.8	1.3
Corporate	6.3	0.7	12.2	0.6	2.6	3.2
Government	5.0	48.9	21.3	30.4	22.4	5.8
Total	14.7	61.5	44.5	31.0	25.7	10.4
Share of corporate bonds with maturity above 5 years	25.7	21.9	93.0	40.7	4.1	91.6
Turnover of locally issued bonds (percent of stock of bonds)	108.6	123.4	56.7	75.0	463.4	4.8

Source: Calculations based on BIS data, Dealogic data, and 2005 EMTA surveys.

cits have led to excessive government bond issuance that has crowded out private bond issuance, then many years of primary fiscal surpluses may have to pass before the overhang of government bonds is worked down. If the problem is that Latin America's history of macroeconomic and financial instability limits investors' demands to debt securities with interest rates indexed to inflation or the exchange rate, then many years may have to pass before stronger policies produce a demand for longer-term issues. If perceptions of imperfect corporate governance and unreliable contract enforcement currently make investors reluctant to hold corporate bonds at any price, then some time may have to pass before the relevant reforms begin to create a significant demand. If in smaller Latin American and Caribbean countries the local market's lack of scale is the obstacle to spreading the fixed cost of an issue and enhancing secondary-market liquidity, then reasonable questions can be raised about whether this obstacle can ever be overcome. Or perhaps these qualms are overstated: the key reforms could succeed in producing deeper and more liquid bond markets in short order.

Note that bond markets in Latin America are far from homogeneous. This is evident from table 1.2. The table shows, for example, that bond markets in Brazil and Chile are an order of magnitude larger than those of Argentina and Peru, even scaled by GDP. This variation is especially prominent in the case of bonds placed by private issuers (corporations and financial institutions), the market segment of particular concern to many policy makers. Thus, we see that while Brazil and Chile have the two best-capitalized bond markets in the region, those markets are very different in composition: in Brazil private bonds are relatively small, while in Chile they represent a larger share of market capitalization than government bonds. This variation is equally apparent in other dimensions of bond market development, including the maturity of corporate issues and turnover rates.[3]

A substantial and growing literature discusses the benefits and determinants of domestic bond markets in emerging economies. This literature includes both broad cross-country overviews and detailed case studies (see, for example, IFC 2000; Turner 2002; IMF 2002; De la Torre and Schmukler 2004; Mihaljek et al. 2002). There is also an ample collection of studies in connection with recent initiatives to develop local bond markets in Asia. The policy literature has generally endorsed the value of local bond markets as the natural venue for domestic currency securities and for strengthening the soundness of domestic financial markets in emerging economies, where the banking system may not be as robust as in more mature economies. This literature has additionally highlighted measures to improve bond market infrastructure, along with supporting institutions, and has debated the pros and cons of regional integration, international openness, and sequencing of institutional and market development initiatives.

A more limited empirical literature explores the determinants of bond market development at the government and corporate levels. (See chapter 9 for a review.) Existing studies explore the impact of three sets of variables on bond market depth: macroeconomic policies and outcomes, including interest rates, fiscal deficits, inflation and the exchange rate regime; institutional quality, as measured directly by indices of the rule of law and corruption, or more indirectly by geographical and legal origin variables; and structural variables, such as country size. Because of lack of comparable cross-country data, none of these studies analyzes the impact of the bond market "infrastructure" discussed above. Furthermore, several potentially important reforms implemented recently in Latin America, including the role of pension reform, tax changes, and the privatization of public companies, are not evaluated. In sum, many important policy questions remain unanswered.

With these limitations in mind, we turn next to the main results presented in the chapters of this volume.

Findings of the Country Studies

The case studies of six Latin American bond markets included in this volume help us to better understand the constraints on the development of local bond markets. It is noteworthy that there is broad variation across the region on several dimensions. The size of the economy, the size of potential corporate issuers, macroeconomic stability, institutional shortcomings, the development of institutional investors such as pension funds, and the extent of openness and of international integration—all of these factors, among others, play a role in explaining contrasts among countries.

Government Bond Markets

Five of the six countries considered in this volume had strikingly small domestic government bond markets for most of the 1990s (less than 15 percent of GDP). Indeed, Argentina and Uruguay saw very little growth in the market (again, relative to GDP) as late as 1999. On the other hand, in Brazil, Colombia, and Mexico, 1995 marks the beginning of a period of rapid growth in domestic government bond markets that continued until 2005. Issuance was particularly large in Brazil, which in 2003 overtook Chile as the Latin American country with the largest government bond market. Unlike the other five countries covered in this volume, Chile started the period with government bond market capitalization above 60 percent of GDP but experienced a reduction in bond market capitalization (relative to GDP) over the 1990–2005 period as a result of continuous fiscal surpluses (figure 1.2, panel A).

The evolution of the share of bonds in total public debt has also differed across the region (figure 1.2, panel B). Broadly speaking, the countries fall into three groups. In the case of Chile, the evolution of the share of domestic government bonds in total public debt has the appearance of an inverted U. This is due to the fact that the Chilean authorities increased their reliance on the domestic market until 1999 but then started issuing international sovereign debt in order to provide a benchmark for private issuers. A second group, comprised of Argentina and Uruguay, displays a steady fall in the share of domestic government bonds in total debt since the late 1990s. This implies that the increase in domestic government bonds relative to GDP that took place after 1999 was due to higher levels of debt and not to a shift toward more domestic bonded debt.[4] And in the third group of

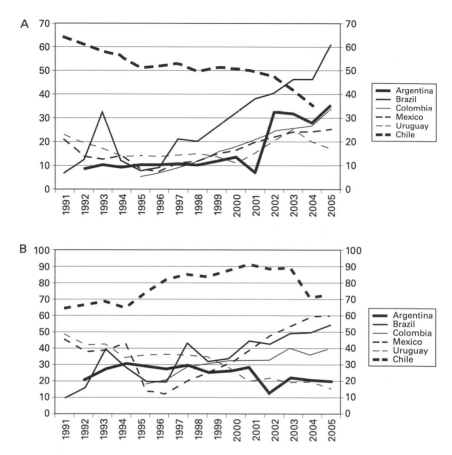

Figure 1.2
(Panel A): Stock of domestic government bonds relative to GDP (%). (Panel B): Domestic government bonds as a share of total public debt (%). Source: Chapters 3 to 8, as described in the appendix to chapter 9.

countries—Brazil, Colombia, and Mexico—the increase in the stock of domestic government bonds over GDP was due to a shift toward domestic issuance that led to an increase in the share of domestic government bonds in total public debt.

The turnaround in the pattern of government debt financing in this last group of countries coincided with the international financial crises that started in Mexico in 1995, followed by East Asia in 1997, and Russia in 1998. These crises limited access to international capital markets and convinced policy makers of the importance of developing reliable domestic sources of funding. To be sure, this was not the first time that a crisis, either domestic or international, had served as a catalyst for the development of government bond markets. Mexico and Uruguay, for instance, started issuing domestic government bonds when the debt crisis of 1982 prevented them from accessing international capital markets. The Argentine bond market restarted in 1990–1991 in the wake of that country's inflationary crisis, when the government issued bonds to consolidate Central Bank debt with commercial bank debt and to consolidate existing liabilities to pensioners, government contractors, and victims of the military regime. In Chile, a significant fraction of outstanding government bonds (mostly those issued by the Central Bank) is a legacy of the banking crisis that hit the country in the early 1980s.[5,6] To be sure, this relationship between crisis and development of the local bond market is not only a Latin American phenomenon: Bordo, Meissner, and Redish (2005) show that several former British colonies started developing their domestic markets when external events such as World War II prevented them from accessing international capital markets.

Another theme of the country studies is the role played by macroeconomic factors in the development of sovereign debt markets. In Brazil, the government bond market started growing when the government implemented the Real Plan and stopped monetizing fiscal deficits. Likewise, in Mexico falling inflation and greater macroeconomic stability played a key role in the growth of the stock of sovereign bonds. In Colombia, in contrast, large and persistent fiscal deficits, rather than stabilization, spurred growth in the stock of government bonds since the mid-1990s.

A further theme is the role of pension reform. Five of our six countries undertook some form of pension reform in the last 25 years, moving from pay-as-you-go to individual capitalization systems. In four countries, private pension funds (PPFs) directly held more than 20% of total domestic public debt as of 2004 (see table 1.3). While official data suggest that Brazilian pension funds do not have large holdings of government debt, these figures may underestimate the actual share of Brazilian pension fund assets invested in government securities. Leal and Lustosa (2004) show that in 2004 Brazilian pension funds had only 12% of their portfolios directly invested in treasury securities, but their indirect holdings were much larger. A full 62% of their portfolios were invested in fixed-income funds and hedge funds, which invest most of their assets in securities issued by the Brazilian Treasury. Leal and Lustosa (2004) suggest that aggregate pension fund holdings of

Table 1.3
The Importance of Private Pension Funds (PPF) in Bond Markets

Country	Year of implementation of the pension reform	Year	PPF holdings of public debt as a percent of:		
			Total public debt	Total domestic public debt	Total PPF assets
Argentina	1994	1994	1	3	98
		1999	6	23	46
		2004	5	14	59
Brazil	No pension reform	1994	1	2	4
		1999	1	2	6
		2004	2	3	11
Chile	1981	1994	18	22	40
		1999	28	30	35
		2004	25	28	19
Colombia	1999	1994	0	0	
		1999	3	6	45
		2004	15	27	83
Mexico	1996	1994	0	0	
		1999	5	9	95
		2004	14	20	85
Uruguay	1996	1994	0	0	
		1999	4	9	60
		2004	9	36	79

Source: Asociación Internacional de Organismos de Supervisión de Fondos de Pensiones; Associação Brasileira de Fundos de Pensão.

treasury securities may be well above 60% of total assets (12% in direct holdings and more than 50% indirectly through other funds). This would suggest that the only country in which public debt accounts for less than 50% of PPFs' assets is Chile, where it is only about 20%.

Placing public debt is a necessity for governments during the transition from a public to a private pension system. During this transition, social security contributions cease to accrue to the government, which is still responsible for pension payments to the currently retired population, and this results in an increase in the government's financing needs.[7] This explanation for the dominance of public debt in PPFs' assets is consistent with the gradual reduction of the share of government bonds in the total assets of pension funds in Chile (where government bonds fell from 40% to 20% of assets over the 1994–2004 period) and, to a lesser extent, in Mexico. However, it does not fit with the rising importance of public debt in the assets of PPFs in Colombia, Argentina, and Uruguay.

In these countries other factors are apparently at work. As discussed in chapters 4 and 8, during Argentina and Uruguay's financial crises, institutional investors were forced by their governments to increase their holdings of public bonds. Although in the case of Colombia the causes of the upward trend are unclear, the need to finance large public deficits with domestic bond issuances, discussed in chapter 5, probably played a role.

Several chapters conclude on the basis of such observations that pension reforms are a mixed blessing for bond market development. On the one hand, PPFs are a captive source of demand for public bonds, particularly long-term bonds, leading to the growth of the stock of outstanding instruments.[8] On the other hand, PPFs often follow buy-and-hold strategies, limiting liquidity and the usefulness of the bond market as a pricing device. This is a point emphasized in both the Chilean and Uruguayan chapters. Chapter 8, for instance, emphasizes that in Uruguay PPFs' transactions are closer to private placements than public issuance, with almost no secondary market activity.

Significant changes have also occurred over the last decade in the maturity, currency composition, and indexation of domestic government bonds (table 1.4). For most countries, the shift has been toward "safer" forms of debt.[9] Argentina and Uruguay decreased the share of foreign-currency denominated bonds and increased the share of inflation-indexed and long-term bonds. Brazil all but eliminated foreign currency bonds, decreased the share of bonds indexed to the

Table 1.4
Composition of Domestic Government Bonds

Country	Year	Government domestic bonded debt (%)						GDP total (%)
		Foreign currency	Prices	Interest rate	Nominal	Short term	Long term	
Argentina	1994	66	0	0	34	0	100	8
	2000	90	0	0	10	16	84	12
	2005	28	71	0	1	0	100	30
Brazil	1990	0	0	87	13	13	0	7
	1994	44	32	22	2	2	76	10
	2000	5	2	68	25	27	6	28
	2005	1	15	54	30	18	27	52
Chile	1990	0	84	16	0	0	84	68
	1994	0	86	14	0	0	86	56
	2000	0	74	26	0	0	74	51
	2004	0	92	8	0	0	100	35
Colombia	1995	0	0	0	100	0	100	5
	2000	7	20	0	73	0	100	15
	2005	1	20	0	79	3	97	29
Mexico	1990	2	9	42	47	48	10	22
	1994	55	17	5	24	79	17	12
	2000	0	11	55	34	23	23	14
	2005	0	5	43	52	17	40	22
Uruguay	1990	93	0	0	7	59	41	24
	1994	98	0	0	2	41	59	12
	2000	97	0	0	3	10	90	9
	2005	72	27	0	1	20	80	15

Source: Web Appendix to this volume (http://mitpress.mit.edu/9780262026321/webappendix).

overnight interest rate, and increased the share of nominal bonds, bonds indexed to inflation, and long-term bonds. Mexico increased the share of long-term, nominal bonds while maintaining the share of debt indexed to inflation broadly unchanged.

Although there was no clear shift toward "safer" financing in Colombia and Chile, these countries started the 1990s with a debt structure that was already relatively safe. Colombia had low levels of dollarization of public sector domestic bonds and a high reliance on nominal and inflation-indexed instruments. Similarly, Chile had a large share of its public debt in long-term bonds indexed to inflation, almost no domestic bonds indexed to foreign currency, and only a small share of bonds indexed to the short-term interest rate.

Private Bond Markets

All the countries considered in this volume except Chile had essentially no private domestic bond market at the beginning of the 1990s, although regulatory reforms allowing or fostering private bond issuance had been carried out during the 1970s and 1980s.[10] Most of the case studies attribute the lack of a significant corporate bond market to macroeconomic instability, particularly high inflation, which in the absence of credible indexation mechanisms heightened the risk of holding long-term instruments.[11] Investors' reluctance to hold long-term instruments placed bonds at a disadvantage relative to bank credit because of the larger fixed-issuance costs of bonds, which become cost-effective only when those costs can be spread both over a large issuance and a long maturity. As Chile had enjoyed relative macroeconomic stability since the mid-1980s, it is not surprising that Chilean private bond markets were earlier to develop, reaching 5% of GDP by 1990—below developed country standards but substantially above the other five countries studied in this volume.

During the 1990s, the development of the private bond market in the six countries studied in this volume followed different paths (figure 1.3). Chapter 4 describes how in Argentina, issuance began in 1991 and continued until the 1998 recession, following the reduction of inflation and a tax reform that leveled the playing field between bank and bond finance. Although the market for Mexican bonds grew continuously (if slowly) during the 1990s, chapter 3 argues that new regulations approved in 2001, especially the creation of a new flexible debt instrument (the *certificados bursátiles*) and improvement in corporate

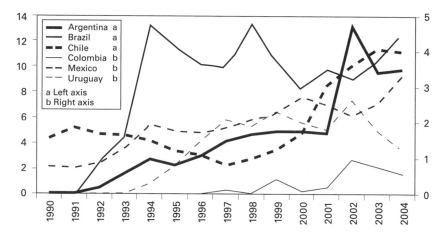

Figure 1.3
Private bonds as a share of GDP. Source: Chapters 3 to 8, as described in the appendix to
chapter 9.

governance laws, stimulated growth in bond issuance in recent years.[12]
The Uruguayan market had a brief renaissance following the enactment of the Securities Market Law in 1996, but financial scandals that
erupted in 1998 halted issuance of new bonds. Generalizing from this
experience, chapter 8 argues that lack of transparency and poor corporate governance are two of the chief obstacles to the development of
the Uruguayan private bond market.

Brazil and Chile are the two countries where the corporate bond
market grew the fastest. In Brazil, growth was concentrated in the
years that followed the reduction in inflation brought about by the
Real Plan. Starting from less than 1% of GDP in 1990, the stock of private bonds reached 10% of GDP by 1994 and then remained stable at
that level until 2004. In Chile, the private bond market started expanding after 1998; chapter 6 argues that this recent growth is due to factors
affecting both the demand and supply of corporate bonds. On the supply side, the Central Bank's defense of the peso exchange rate in the
aftermath of the Russian crisis in 1998 led to a sharp increase in short-
term rates and a credit crunch, which increased the attractiveness of
long-term, non-bank finance and encouraged borrowers to turn to the
bond market. Also contributing to an increase in the supply of private
bonds were the financial requirements of the large private infrastructure programs that were undertaken in the 1990s. On the demand
side, placement of these bonds was facilitated by large institutional

investors who were forced by regulation to buy domestic assets and, in an environment of decreasing public debt, needed to find alternatives to their traditional strategy of investing most of their assets in government bonds.[13]

Colombia is the outlier in this group, as its private market experienced essentially no growth over the period. Chapter 5 argues that crowding out by increasing public debt played a key role in stunting demand for corporate bonds. In this sense, the poor performance of the corporate bond market is the counterpart of the growth of the government bond market documented in the previous section. We return to this point below.

Even though the countries surveyed in this volume differ with respect to recent experience, private bond finance remains small by international standards for all of them. In Argentina, Colombia, Mexico, and Uruguay, 2005 data reveal that private bond market capitalization is below 5% of GDP; in Brazil and Chile, outstanding private bonds barely exceed 10% of GDP. These values are considerably lower than the averages for East Asia and the advanced economies which, according to Bank for International Settlements (BIS) data, reach 28% and 70% of GDP, respectively.

Table 1.5 summarizes additional characteristics of the private debt instruments issued in each market. Nominal, fixed-rate debt is still rare. Chile has issued most of its debt in a unit indexed to inflation; Brazil and Colombia tend to issue debt indexed to the interest rate; and Argentina and Uruguay issue debt indexed to the dollar.[14] In contrast to the government bond market, there is no clear movement toward more reliable forms of private debt, with the sole exception of Mexico. The divergence between public and private instruments is starkest in Argentina, where the dollarization of the private bond market increased at a time when government debt dollarization fell. This may be explained by the fact that the underlying factors affecting dollarization in Argentina have not changed. Perceptions of volatile inflation still persist, making dollar debt a more reliable form of financing than nominal contracts (see Levy Yeyati 2006), and new issues in the private market reflect those fears. In the public sector, in contrast, de-dollarization has been boosted in a series of debt restructuring operations that followed the default of 2001 (see chapter 4).

The country studies suggest important regularities in the characteristics of firms that issue bonds. Larger firms substitute domestic bonds for bank credit, and the largest firms also rely on offshore bond

Table 1.5
Composition of Corporate Bonds

Country	Year	Share of private domestic debt indexed to:				As a percent of GDP
		Foreign currency	Prices	Interest rate	Nominal	
Argentina[1]	1991	84	0	0	16	0
	1994	97	0	0	3	1
	2000	97	0	0	3	5
	2005	98	0	0	2	6
Brazil	1992	2	22	76	0	3
	1994	2	22	76	0	13
	2000	2	17	78	3	8
	2005	3	12	84	0	16
Chile	1990	7	93	0	0	4
	1994	12	88	0	0	4
	2000	24	76	0	0	5
	2004	3	96	0	1	11
Colombia	1997	0	0	100	0	0
	2000	0	54	36	10	0
	2004	0	0	100	0	1
Mexico	1990	0	0	100	0	1
	1994	0	0	100	0	2
	2000	0	0	100	0	3
	2004	0	0	57	43	3
Uruguay	1994	100	0	0	0	0
	2000	100	0	0	0	2
	2005	100	0	0	0	1

[1] Includes private domestic and foreign bonds.
Source: Web Appendix to this volume (http://mitpress.mit.edu/9780262026321/webappendix).

Table 1.6
Characteristics of Bond Issuers and Issue Size

	Mean size of issuance	Minimum size of issuance	Mean size of issuers (assets)	Minimum size of issuer	Number of issued bonds	Number of firms issuing bonds	Period
	US dollars (thousands)						
Domestic issuances							
Argentina	141,900	NA	NA	NA	568	NA	1994–2001
Brazil	85,590	753	3,813,668	4,146	319	111	2004
Chile	61,833	NA	694,612	NA	186	125	1994–2004
Colombia	23,438	10,000	86,851	NA	NA	67	1994–2004
Mexico	109,545	NA	NA	NA	NA	185	1994–2004
Uruguay	17,867	NA	NA	NA	71	67	1994–2004
International issuances							
Brazil	199,435	20,000	10,161,450	130,528	117	57	2004
Chile	352,500	NA	3,170,697	NA	29	14	1994–2004

Source: Web Appendix to this volume (http://mitpress.mit.edu/9780262026321/webappendix).

Table 1.7
Firm-Level Survey

Country	Number of firms surveyed	Percentage that have issued bonds	Percentage with some experience with bonds[1]	Average size (no. of employees)	
				Issuers	Nonissuers
Argentina	56	16	25	4,762	1,416
Brazil	30	83	83	8,777	308
Chile	40	75	NA	4,264	345
Colombia	274	6	9	653	316
Uruguay	463	2	5	NA	NA

[1] Have issued in the past or plan to issue in the future.
Source: This volume.

issuance. In addition, in most countries the firms that are most likely to issue bonds are those with more tangible assets, higher profitability, and greater-than-average leverage.

Another reason why bond markets are dominated by a select group of large firms that issue large bonds (table 1.6) is the significant fixed cost of issuance. Moreover, the fact that many firms are repeat issuers suggests the existence of two forms of fixed costs: those related to becoming an issuer (disclosure costs and required accounting changes) and those related to each specific issuance (such as underwriting fees). In some countries, high issuance costs also help to explain the growth of alternative short-term debt instruments such as the "checks of deferred payment" that have become an increasingly common form of financing for firms in Argentina (see chapter 4).

The importance of issuance costs is further supported by the firm-level survey results summarized in tables 1.7 and 1.8. A sizable fraction of the firms that had in the past placed bonds but no longer do so identifies high issuance costs as a reason for shunning the market. They also identify high fees and issue requirements as impediments to bond financing. Additional factors frequently cited as making bonds less attractive than bank financing include minimum size, information requirements, and lengthy procedures, all of which are related to fixed costs.

Another commonly cited obstacle to bond issuance is market size—in line with the cross-section evidence in chapter 9, which finds that country size is one of the few variables that have a significant and robust correlation with the size of the private bond market.[15] Interestingly, size matters when bond stocks are scaled either by GDP or by a measure of broad financial development, indicating that, in larger countries, bond markets are not only larger but are also relatively more important within the financial system.

An obvious question is whether the fixed costs of issuance and disclosure that make bonds attractive to only a small group of large firms are particularly high in the region. Table 1.9 shows issuance costs as a percentage of the value of the issue for four of the countries in this volume. Domestic issuance is almost three times as expensive in Uruguay as in Mexico, perhaps reflecting the importance of market size and the consequently greater ease of spreading fixed costs over larger issues. Moreover, in Brazil, Chile, and Uruguay, issuance costs for debt placed offshore are lower than for domestic debt. It is not clear whether these differences are due to the existence of fixed costs associated with the development of market infrastructure—which should therefore fall as bond markets expand—or whether they are due to differences in regulation and financial market structure that would lead to higher costs for a given size of total issuance (see Zervos 2004 for a discussion of this point).

Private and Sovereign Debt Market Interactions

A large and liquid government bond market can have a positive effect on the development of the corporate bond market by creating the necessary infrastructure for trading, producing information about the future path of interest rates, and providing a benchmark yield curve (see, for example, McCauley and Remolona 2000). However, it has been noted that "bigger is not always better" and that the benefits related to the creation of pricing and hedging instruments can be annulled if excessive government issuance "crowds out" market access by private borrowers.

It is not easy to determine the net effect of government bonds on the private segment of the market. Efforts to identify these linkages through econometric methods—and to measure which effect dominates—have yielded mixed results. Eichengreen and Leungnaruemitchai (2004) found no impact of the size of the government bond market on corporate bond market capitalization in a panel of 41 countries. They conjecture that this may reflect the fact that the benefits of greater liquidity and more highly developed market infrastructure are offset by the crowding out of corporate bonds by government bonds.

Table 1.8
Why Do Firms Issue Bonds?

Answers to the question: "If you issued in the past and you are no longer issuing, what is the main reason?"

Argentina	High issuance costs (25%), issuance requirements (19%), low demand (13%)
Brazil	High issuance costs (30%)
Colombia	Issuance requirements (26%), high interest rate (23%), high issuance costs (19%)
Uruguay	Low investor demand (33%), high issuance costs (25%)

Answers to the question: "What are the most important problems with domestic bond financing?"

	All firms	Firms with experience issuing bonds	Firms without experience issuing bonds
Argentina	Small market (51%), disclosure requirements (46%)	Small market (71%), high fees (29%)	Disclosure requirements (53%), small market (47%)
Brazil	Fees (50%), low liquidity (43%), small market (40%)	Fees (40%), small market (36%), other regulatory requirements (28%)	Fees (100%), minimum issue requirement (60%), low liquidity (60%), small market (60%), no junk bond market (60%)
Chile	Small market (23%), high fees (15%)	NA	NA
Colombia	No junk bond market, small market, minimum issue requirements	NA	NA
Uruguay	Small market (62%), no junk bond market (55%), high fees (50%)	NA	NA

Relative advantages of bond and bank financing

	Bonds dominate loans in terms of:	Loans dominate bonds in terms of:
Argentina	Maturity, interest rate	Speed of access to finance, minimum amount, guarantee requirements, information requirements
Brazil	Maturity, interest rate	Speed of access to finance, guarantee requirements, information requirements, minimum amount
Chile	Maturity	Speed of access to finance, information requirements
Colombia	Maturity, interest rate, guarantee requirements	Speed of access to finance, minimum amount, information requirements
Uruguay	Maturity, guarantees	Speed of access to finance, minimum amount, information requirements

Source: Web Appendix to this volume (http://mitpress.mit.edu/9780262026321/webappendix).

Table 1.9
Total Issuance Costs as Percent of Issue Size (for Issues of US$100 Million)

	Brazil	Chile	Mexico	Uruguay[1]
Domestic debt	2.39	2.74	1.18	2.88
Domestic equity	4.39	1.62	3.93	NA
International debt	2.22	2.22	2.22	2.22

[1] Cost for issuing a bond with a value of US$50 million.
Source: Zervos (2004) and chapter 8, this volume.

In principle, the crowding out effect should stem from all types of government debt, and not just bonded debt, implying that the method of financing the government deficit (through bonds or bank loans for example) should not matter. Only in the extreme case that the different financial markets are completely segmented would it be the case that only bonded debt mattered. Chapter 9 in this volume pursues this reasoning and finds that, after controlling for total public debt, the higher the share of public domestic bond financing, the greater the development of the private bond market. This is consistent with the market creation effect of government bonds, regardless of whether government debt exerts a crowding out effect (which is generally not significant).

In practice, however, most countries experience simultaneous changes in the level of total public debt and its breakdown between domestic bonded debt and other forms, making it difficult to disentangle the market development effect of a larger government bond market from the crowding-out effect of total public debt. For example, chapter 5 argues that rising domestic government bonded debt contributed to the weak performance of the private bond market in Colombia, and chapter 6 points out that the reduction of total domestic government debt played a key role in stimulating the rapid growth of the Chilean private bond market after 1999.

The country studies also provide a different perspective on this issue by directly gauging the views of institutional investors through opinion surveys. In view of the discussion above, it is perhaps not surprising that several of the questions that address the issue yield mixed results. Investors in Chile, Colombia, Mexico, and Uruguay agree with the idea that a large stock of public debt is important for the development of the corporate bond market. Investors in Brazil strongly disagree, while Argentine investors have mixed feelings about the role of the government bond market (figure 1.4). However, investors in all six

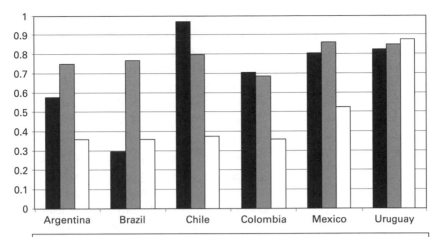

Figure 1.4
Investors' perception of the interaction between government and corporate bond markets. The figure reports average answers to the following three questions: (1) a large stock of public sector bonds is important for the development of the corporate bond market; (2) the yield curve provided by public bonds is crucial for pricing corporate bonds; (3) government and corporate bonds are substitutes in your portfolio. In the original questionnaire 1 meant that the respondent strongly agreed with the statement and 5 that the responded strongly disagreed. The answers have been rescaled so that 1 means strongly agree and 0 strongly disagree.

countries agree that a yield curve is a crucial element for pricing corporate bonds, a key developmental function of government bonded debt. The surveys also asked a direct question of whether government and corporate bonds were substitutes in portfolios. Judging from the survey responses, government and corporate bonds compete in the portfolios of institutional investors in Uruguay and to a lesser extent Mexico (a fact consistent with crowding out), while investors located in Argentina, Brazil, Chile, and Colombia disagreed with the statement that corporate and government bonds are substitutes in their portfolios.

What about spillover effects from the composition and maturity of public debt to the composition and maturity of private debt? No clear pattern emerges from the six studies considered in this volume. Whereas in Mexico, "safer" public bonded debt has been accompanied by "safer" private bonds, this was not the case in the other countries. This is not surprising, as the theoretical effects are ambiguous. On the one hand, having a CPI-indexed or nominal yield curve for public debt should make the pricing of similar types of private debt easier. On the other hand, a government balance sheet with a larger share of nominal debt could lead private investors to renew their historical concerns regarding opportunistic government behavior, such as using higher inflation to dilute debts; those investors may therefore demand more, rather than fewer, dollar-denominated contracts.

Finally, there may be a "credit risk spillover" from government debt to private debt. Credit rating agencies have for years followed a "sovereign ceiling" policy in assigning ratings on foreign debt that implied that private borrowers could not attain a credit rating higher than that of the government.[16] The rationale for sovereign ceilings was that, in a situation of debt default, the government would impose capital controls that would make servicing private external debts impossible. But more generally, a government debt default tends to have a strong negative impact on domestic financial markets and banks and on the credit quality of the whole private sector in the country. Although credit ratings for the government's domestic bonds denominated in domestic currency are usually at the top of the scale, the credit risk premiums that markets require can be significant, and they do spill over from the public to the private sector.

Conclusions

The first objective of this volume is to document the characteristics of Latin American bond markets and to evaluate their level of "underdevelopment" relative to other forms of financing. The studies included here paint a mixed picture. On the one hand, government bond markets have been growing substantially and are increasingly characterized by longer-term nominal instruments. Private bond markets, on the other hand, remain small—well below those of the industrial countries but also smaller than those of the emerging economies of East Asia.

The second objective is to determine the factors behind the recent growth (or lack thereof) in the bond markets. On the positive side, macroeconomic stabilization and the privatization of pension systems have played an important role in the development of domestic bond markets. Interestingly, crisis episodes have also helped to kick-start public bond markets. On the negative side, inflation fears, default episodes, corporate scandals, and the relatively small number of large firms (in the case of private bonds) are among the main obstacles to the development of the Latin American bond markets. Regulatory restrictions and regulatory reforms are also found to be important for hindering or promoting private bond financing. Of particular interest are the development of the flexible *certificados bursátiles* in Mexico and the deferred payment checks in Argentina as tradable debt instruments.

The third objective of the volume is to describe whether policies aimed at promoting the growth of the Latin American bond market can have a positive effect on the economic performance of the region. The studies published in this book show that many countries now have a government yield curve, which is gradually pushing out its maturity, providing market interest rates for the pricing of private instruments and facilitating the conduct of monetary policy. Holding total public debt constant, these developments are also likely to benefit the private bond market and the domestic financial sector more generally. In contrast, in most countries covered, private bond financing is so small that aggregate benefits are likely to be marginal and concentrated in the largest firms. Furthermore, both firm and market size seem to be important obstacles to the development of this market, so it is not clear whether policies aimed at promoting the issuance of traditional instruments will be sufficient to foster private bond markets in all countries of the region. Addressing the issue of small firm participation may require policies aimed at developing innovative instruments with low fixed costs or instruments that allow the pooling of costs over a broad number of issuers (for instance, asset-backed securities and collateralized debt obligations). Addressing the issue of small market size may also require cross-country coordination—especially amongst the smaller countries of the region—and possibly establishing strong links with regional and global bond markets as well.[17]

Notes

1. See Goldstein and Turner (2004). There has been some progress recently in placing on international markets bonds denominated in Latin American currencies but not enough to change this fundamental fact. See Tovar (2005).

2. Asian efforts revolve around the Asian Bond Fund (ABF) and Asian Bond Market Initiative (ABMI). Launched by the Executives' Meeting of East Asia–Pacific Central Banks (EMEAP) in June 2003, the ABF is designed to catalyze the growth of Asian bond markets by allocating a portion of the reserves of regional central banks to purchases of

government and quasi-government securities. The initial US$1 billion of investments, known as ABF-I, was devoted exclusively to Asian sovereign and quasi-sovereign issues of dollar-denominated bonds. ABF-II is twice as large and includes bonds denominated in regional currencies. It has two components: a $1 billion central bank reserve pool to be overseen by professional managers for local bond allocation, and a $1 billion index unit designed to list on eight stock exchanges beginning with Hong Kong in 2005. The latter is designed to facilitate one-stop entry for retail and institutional buyers as well as providing a benchmark structure for tracking pan-Asian performance. The ABMI, endorsed by ASEAN+3 finance ministers at their meeting in Manila in August 2003, is designed to foster an active and liquid secondary market in local-currency bonds and to develop the infrastructure needed for the growth of local bond markets, mainly through the activity of six working groups and a focal group intended to coordinate their activities. See Ito and Park (2004).

3. Note that the turnover rates reported in table 1.2 correspond to data reported by international investors. The data are obtained from monthly surveys of members of the EMTA—Trade Association for the Emerging Markets, an industry association located in New York; thus, it may not provide a full picture of the liquidity of the local markets.

4. In Argentina, after the collapse of convertibility, bonds held domestically were converted into guaranteed loans (*préstamos garantizados*), which we do not classify as bonds because they are not tradable. This led to a sudden drop in government bonds in 2001 and to recovery in 2002 when some of these loans were turned back into bonds. The alternative—to consider guaranteed loans as bonds (as in Cowan et al. 2006)—leads to a different pattern for the behavior of the domestic government bond market.

5. Chile is the only country in which the Central Bank is a major issuer of bonds; in fact, several countries prohibit the Central Bank from issuing bonds. Colombia's Central Bank was the main bond issuer within the public sector until 1991, when a new law revoked its bond-issuing authority. Argentina has moved in the opposite direction. The Central Bank could not issue bonds under the convertibility regime, which was abandoned in 2001, but now the Central Bank is becoming an important issuer in the market for short-term notes.

6. Caprio and Klingebiel (2003) estimate that over 1982–1985 the Chilean government spent the equivalent of 42% of GDP to resolve the banking crisis.

7. In the case of Chile, for instance, the transition was financed by issuing *bonos de reconocimiento* ("acknowledgement" bonds that capitalized past pension contributions), which now amount to about 15% of GDP. These bonds tend to be mostly held to maturity by institutional investors, and hence they have effectively no role in contributing to market development.

8. This fact is also confirmed by chapter 9, which finds econometric evidence of the positive correlation between the presence of PPFs and the size of the domestic bond market based on a broad cross-section of countries.

9. From the borrower's point of view, long-term domestic currency nominal debt is safer than short-term debt or debt indexed to foreign currencies or interest rates. Although not as safe as long-term nominal debt, debt indexed to inflation is probably safer than short-term debt or debt indexed to the exchange rate. A crisis that causes inflation to accelerate can undermine fiscal solvency, but inflation is a slowly moving variable, in contrast to the exchange rate or short-term interest rates.

10. In Argentina corporate bonds (*obligaciones negociables*) were authorized in 1988. Brazil carried out several reforms aimed at developing the domestic financial system in the 1980s, although rules aimed at promoting the commercial paper market were passed

only in 1991. Chile implemented several regulatory changes after the financial crisis of 1982, and Mexico authorized the issuance of corporate bonds in 1982.

11. This is in line with cross-country evidence on this issue. Braun and Briones (2006) find that inflation and budget deficits have a negative impact on the maturity of bonds. In turn, Burger and Warnock (2005) find that inflation volatility negatively impacts the capitalization of local bond markets. Argentina and Brazil endured episodes of hyperinflation in the early 1990s that essentially wiped out the wealth of private bondholders. In Mexico and Uruguay, inflation only fell below 100% per annum as late as 1989 and 1992, respectively.

12. The reforms improved the rights of minority shareholders and information disclosure (see chapter 2).

13. For an alternative explanation that focuses on the role of international financial markets see Cifuentes, Desormeaux, and González (2002).

14. In fact, the bond market mimics the maturity and indexation structure of other forms of corporate debt in the region (Kamil 2004).

15. Similar results are obtained by Eichengreen and Leungnaruemitchai (2004). Their interpretation, however, is slightly different. They argue that country size matters because of fixed costs in developing the relevant bond market infrastructure, whereas the firm-level evidence reported here emphasizes fixed costs for each individual firm.

16. While this policy has been relaxed considerably, research shows that sovereign ratings still exert a strong influence on the ratings obtained by private corporations and banks (Borensztein, Cowan, and Valenzuela 2007).

17. See Eichengreen, Borensztein, and Panizza (2006) for a discussion of the costs and benefits of this approach and a comparison of the Latin American and Asian strategies for the development of their bond markets.

References

Bordo, Michael, Christopher Meissner, and Angela Redish (2005). "How Original Sin Was Overcome." In B. Eichengreen and R. Hausmann, eds., *Other People's Money*. Chicago: University of Chicago Press.

Borensztein, Eduardo, Kevin Cowan, and Patricio Valenzuela (2007). "Sovereign Ceilings 'Lite'? The Impact of Sovereign Ratings on Corporate Ratings in Emerging Market Economies." IMF Working Paper No. 07/75.

Braun, Matías, and Ignacio Briones (2006). "The Development of Bond Markets around the World." Mimeo, Anderson School, UCLA.

Burger, John, and Francis Warnock (2005). "Foreign Participation in Local-Currency Bond Markets." International Finance Discussion Paper No. 794. Washington, D.C.: Board of Governors of the Federal Reserve System.

Caprio, Gerard, and Daniela Klingebiel (2003). "Episodes of Systemic and Borderline Financial Crises." Unpublished paper, World Bank.

Cifuentes, Rodrigo, Jorge Desormeaux, and Claudio González (2002). "Capital Markets in Chile: From Financial Repression to Financial Deepening." In BIS Papers No. 11, "The Development of Bond Markets in Emerging Markets."

Cowan, Kevin, Eduardo Levy-Yeyati, Ugo Panizza, and Federico Sturzenegger (2006). "Public Debt in the Americas." Working Paper No. 577, Research Department, Inter-American Development Bank.

De la Torre, Augusto, and Sergio Schmukler (2004). *Whither Latin American Capital Markets?* Washington, D.C.: World Bank.

Eichengreen, Barry, Eduardo Borensztein, and Ugo Panizza (2006). "A Tale of Two Markets: Bond Market Development in East Asia and Latin America." Hong Kong Institute for Monetary Research, Occasional Papers No. 3.

Eichengreen, Barry, and Pipat Luengnaruemitchai (2004). "Why Doesn't Asia Have Bigger Bond Markets?" NBER Working Paper No. 10576.

Goldstein, Morris, and Paul Turner (2004). *Controlling Currency Mismatches in Emerging Markets.* Washington, D.C.: Institute for International Economics.

International Finance Corporation (2000). "Building Local Bond Markets: An Asian Perspective." World Bank, Washington D.C.

International Monetary Fund (2002). *Financial Stability Report,* Chapter IV.

Ito, Takatoshi, and Yung Chul Park, eds. (2004). *Developing Asian Bond Markets.* Canberra: Asia Pacific Press at Australian National University.

Kamil, Herman (2004). "A Database of Currency Composition of Firms in Latin America." Database Paper DBA-001, Research Department, Inter-American Development Bank.

Leal, Ricardo P. C., and Eliane Lustosa (2004). "Institutional Investors and Corporate Governance in Brazil." Unpublished paper, Coppead Business School, Rio de Janeiro.

Levy Yeyati, E. (2006). "Optimal Debt? On the Insurance Value of International Debt Flows." Working Paper No. 574, Research Department, Inter-American Development Bank.

McCauley, Robert, and Eli Remolona (2000). "Size and Liquidity of Government Bond Markets." *BIS Quarterly Review* (November), 52–60.

Mihaljek, Dubravko, Michela Scatigna, and Agustin Vilar (2002). "Recent Trends in Bond Markets." In BIS Papers No. 11, "The Development of Bond Markets in Emerging Markets."

Tovar, Camilo (2005). "International Government Debt Denominated in Local Currency: Recent Developments for Latin America." *BIS Quarterly Review,* December 2005.

Turner, Philip (2002). "Bond Markets in Emerging Economies: An Overview of Policy Issues." In BIS Papers No. 11, "The Development of Bond Markets in Emerging Markets."

Zervos, Sarah (2004). "The Transaction Costs of Primary Market Issuances: The Case of Brazil, Chile, and Mexico." World Bank, Policy Working Paper No. 3424.

2

How Can Emerging Market Economies Benefit from a Corporate Bond Market?

Patrick Bolton and Xavier Freixas

The aim of this chapter is to explore the effect of the creation of a corporate bond market in emerging market economies (EMEs) on the efficiency of capital allocation. That corporate bond markets improve the allocation of resources in developed economies is a well-established fact, with a strong theoretical foundation and abundant empirical evidence establishing that financial development fosters growth. Still, when we consider an EME several standard assumptions of the main models appear to be violated, the main one being that sovereign debt default risk is far from being negligible as reflected in the spreads on EME government debt quoted in international financial markets.

In the years since the Asia crisis, we have witnessed the rapid growth of corporate bond markets in EMEs, especially in Malaysia and South Korea, which mirrors the explosion of debt securitization around the world. Nonetheless, this growth in securitization and corporate bond financing has taken place only in some EMEs. In particular, the development of a wide corporate bond market seems to follow the expansion of the market for Treasuries with a sufficiently wide range of maturities. Casual empirical evidence suggests that countries with larger outstanding government debt securities tend to have larger corporate bond markets. The contributions in the present volume show this is indeed the case in the major Latin American markets.

We base our analysis on existing models that allow for the coexistence of bank lending and a bond market, such as Diamond (1991), Holmstrom and Tirole (1997), Boot and Thakor (1997), and Bolton and Freixas (2000, 2005). We extend these theories by introducing both aggregate output shocks and risky government debt. Indeed, in our view, a key characteristic of EME countries is the risk of government debt defaults; therefore, a key issue for financial market architecture in EMEs is how a government debt crisis affects the financial sector.

Specifically, we base our discussion in this chapter on a formal model developed in Bolton and Freixas (2006) in which there is always a joint government debt and banking crisis. In this context a corporate bond market provides a basic benefit, which is to shield bond-issuing firms from the consequences of government debt defaults. We refer to this as the "spare-tire" benefit of bond financing. An added benefit of the creation of a corporate bond market is that it induces the government to shift away from bank debt to government bond issues. This, in turn, may reduce the banking sector's exposure to government debt if government bonds are ultimately held by private investors rather than banks. We refer to this latter effect as the benefit of decoupling banking activities from public finances—a benefit that may require regulatory intervention in the form of separation of commercial banking from the financing of government debt.

In summary, this chapter argues that the main benefit of the creation of a corporate bond market and of decoupling the banking sector from public finances is that the fragility of the banking sector is reduced and a greater proportion of corporations is shielded from the consequences of government debt crises. We also use the formal model in Bolton and Freixas (2006) to evaluate the effects of different types of policies, such as financial liberalization or the creation of a market for collateralized debt obligations (CDOs) on the efficient allocation of capital and the incidence of debt crises.

Our paper is related to two separate strands of literature. One is the literature on financial architecture, which includes, among others, Besanko and Kanatas (1993); Hoshi, Kashyap, Scharfstein (1993); Holmstrom and Tirole (1997); Chemmanur and Fulghieri (1994); Repullo and Suarez (1997); and Boot and Thakor (1997). As noted above, we contribute to this literature by considering the implications of both risky government debt and aggregate shocks. The other strand of literature our paper is concerned with is emerging market crises and includes, among others, Caballero and Krishnamurthy (2001); Corsetti, Pesenti, Roubini (1999); Chang and Velasco (1998); Diamond and Rajan (2000); and Schneider and Tornell (2004). In contrast to this literature, which emphasizes so-called twin crises characterized by the simultaneous balance of payments and banking crises, we emphasize government debt crises in conjunction with banking crises and analyze the potential benefits of reducing the role of banks in EMEs as both lenders to the corporate sector and to the government.

The Difference between Bond Financing and Bank Loans

Regarding the common distinction between "bank-based" and "market-based" financial systems (see, for example, Allen and Gale 2000), it is worth acknowledging that most EME financial systems are thought to be mainly bank-based systems. Another common observation in the financial development literature is that bank-based systems are better suited for EMEs, as they require less widely spread financial sophistication by market participants. Although we generally accept this distinction and agree with the observation of the basic suitability of bank-based financial systems for EMEs,[1] we believe that the distinction between financial systems has often been oversimplified and that the reality is often that both market and bank financing coexist in any given EME. Thus, in our view a more useful starting point for the analysis of financial systems in EMEs is to consider a framework that allows for the coexistence of bank and bond financing.

Three Approaches to Modeling the Benefits of Each Mode of Financing

The literature on the coexistence of bonds and bank loans is based on two observations. First, these two financial instruments offer different financial services. Second, firms are heterogeneous in their financial needs, so that in equilibrium, some firms prefer to issue bonds while others prefer to be financed by a bank loan.

We distinguish among three broad approaches to modeling mixed financial systems. A first approach, pioneered by Diamond (1991), focuses on firm heterogeneity in terms of different observable probabilities of repayment or ratings. Diamond considers a dynamic model where firms begin by taking out bank loans and, subsequently, when successful loan repayments are observed, market participants revise upward their estimates of the firm's creditworthiness and switch to a less monitoring-intensive form of financing by issuing bonds. Bolton and Freixas (2000) also focus on this key heterogeneity across firms, allowing for both observable and unobservable repayment risk, but take a different view on the main distinguishing features of bank loans and bond issues. Indeed, we believe that monitoring intensity is not necessarily greater with bank loans than with bonds, as bond issuers are intensely scrutinized when a bond issue is placed in the market and subsequently are closely followed by credit rating agencies and other financial analysts. Thus, the key distinction we focus on is between the greater flexibility of bank loans and credit line commitments over bond issues, which typically require unanimity or a supermajority of bondholders to agree to a restructuring when the issuer is in financial distress.

A second, complementary approach, advocated by Holmstrom and Tirole (1997), assumes that firms do not differ in terms of observable probabilities of repayment, but introduces firm heterogeneity through differences in collateral that firms can post or pledge. In their model, when firms can pledge a large amount of collateral, they do not need to be monitored closely and, therefore, turn to bond financing. In contrast, firms with low collateral require closer monitoring, which is provided by banks.

Finally, a third approach proposed by Boot and Thakor (1997) focuses on firms' different propensities toward moral hazard or likelihood to engage in asset substitution, or more generally in corporate malfeasance. Thus, in their model, as in Diamond (1991), firms with lower observable malfeasance risk turn to market financing while firms with greater risk of moral hazard require closer monitoring through bank lending. Moreover, as the economy improves, there is a gradual shift toward market financing as the average quality of borrowers then also increases.

The Costs of Each Mode of Financing

Most of the theoretical literature on financial systems tends to ignore the resource costs involved in allocating funds to investment projects. The reason is not so much that these costs are unimportant in reality, but that it is not very appealing to develop a theory where the results are directly driven by ad hoc cost assumptions. When addressing the policy question of the potential benefits of fostering the growth of corporate bond markets in EMEs, however, it is no longer reasonable to ignore financial intermediation and bond issuing costs.

At an aggregate level, bank-based systems arguably involve higher total costs of allocating funds than market-based systems because banks incur an additional intermediation cost. It is true that banks may be able to reduce duplication in monitoring costs, as Diamond (1984) has argued, but so can underwriters of bond issues and credit rating agencies. Thus, it is not obvious that banks have lower overall monitoring costs. Banks also incur costs in keeping an equity capital base (either because of regulatory restrictions or to signal their soundness to depositors) and in maintaining a branch network to attract deposits and other sources of funding. This is why some of the finance literature assumes that bank financing involves higher costs than market financing.

At an individual firm level, however, it is less clear which mode of financing is more expensive, because taking out a bank loan or issuing a bond involves different fixed and marginal costs. The fixed cost of organizing a bond issue is likely to be higher than the fixed cost of taking out a bank loan. In terms of variable or marginal costs, however, the ranking between bank loans and bond issues is likely reversed in practice. In addition, the fixed costs of setting up a bank of a viable size are likely to be smaller than the fixed costs of setting up a bond market with sufficient critical mass.

In sum, it seems reasonable to make two assumptions. First, the creation of a bond market involves a nonnegligible, fixed start-up cost, and each individual bond issue also involves a fixed issuing cost, but a marginal increase in the size of an issue is virtually costless. Second, to the extent that bank lending involves lower fixed costs and positive marginal costs, and to the extent that any individual bank loan is typically of a relatively small size, the cost structure of an individual bank loan can be taken to be approximately a constant proportional cost, which we shall refer to subsequently as the (unit) intermediation cost.

Besides considering the relative benefits of bond and bank financing, we also discuss another increasingly popular form of hybrid financing, that of securitization and collateralized debt obligations (CDOs), which involve both intermediation and market-based finance. The cost structure of this type of finance involves both an intermediation cost on the portion of loans retained by the originating bank and a bond issuing cost on the securitized portion. However, to the extent that multiple loans can be pooled to form the collateral for a single CDO issue, the unit costs of securitization for any given firm can be substantially reduced relative to the costs of undertaking a direct bond issue.

The Mix of Bank and Bond Financing in EMEs

As explained above, the existing literature on the determinants of the equilibrium mix between bond and bank financing in an economy focuses on the special role of banks as providers of more expensive funds with "higher-quality financial services," which may take the form of either more intensive monitoring or more flexible financing. But this representation of bank financing does not necessarily apply in EMEs, where bank financing cannot always be accurately described as providing any form of high-quality financial services. For the purposes of our analysis, however, we shall not focus on this particular issue. Instead, our main focus is that the key missing characteristic of an EME's financial system in the existing literature is the absence of any form of government debt default risk. In Bolton and Freixas (2006) we have developed a more general model of the equilibrium mix of bank and market financing than is available in the existing literature, incorporating the possibility of default by the EME's government on its debt. Our discussion of the desirability of corporate bond financing in EMEs is based to a large extent on the framework developed in Bolton and Freixas (2006). It is therefore helpful, as a first step, to informally outline the main building blocks of our framework. We begin by describing the corporate sector (firms), the household sector, and the government before turning to the financial side of our representation of a stylized EME.

Firms

All firms' cash flows in our framework will be affected by aggregate shocks, but we think of firms differing in an observable way in their overall creditworthiness. Thus, only the more creditworthy firms will obtain investment funding with the most creditworthy firms preferring bond financing (if available) and the less creditworthy firms preferring the more flexible financing provided by banks. In our formal framework (Bolton and Freixas 2006), we simplify things by taking all firms to be of equal size and differing only in their probability of failure. More generally, though, firms' creditworthiness is affected by both their size (and the size of their collateral, as in Holmstrom and Tirole 1997) and the underlying cash flow risk of their investments. In our discussion here, we shall not be explicit about what drives overall creditworthiness as our analysis requires only that firms differ in their default risk and that credit ratings reflect these differences in risk.

Households

Through their consumption demands, households provide firms with cash flow revenues and through their savings provide investment funds to banks, firms, and the government. The model developed in Bolton and Freixas (2006) focuses on the equilibrium allocation of household savings (and foreign investment flows) to corporations and the government in a static model and does not attempt to fully close the model by equating aggregate consumption with aggregate output or revenues of firms. Although there is no difficulty in fully closing the model, there is also no major insight to be obtained from this final step. In addition, to keep the analysis tractable, we assume that households are risk-neutral and are therefore indifferent as to how they allocate their savings among bank deposit accounts, bonds issued by firms, or government bonds, as long as all these instruments provide the same expected return. The assumption of risk-neutrality is a strong one, and the full policy implications of the development of corporate bond markets may not be identified in a model based on risk-neutral preferences. As we shall discuss below, however, it is likely that the benefits of developing a corporate bond market are even higher when one takes into account the added risk-diversification benefits.

Government

How efficiently and honestly EME governments work is an enormously important question for economic development and one which goes far beyond the much narrower scope of this chapter. Accordingly, we take a highly simplified and mechanical view of how an EME government operates, focusing only on the government's borrowing decisions. Thus, in our model, tax policy is exogenously given and the role of government is limited to choosing the level of spending, which directly determines government borrowing, default risk, and the government's cost of funds (whether government debt is in the form of bank loans or government bonds). The government is assumed to seek to maximize welfare of a representative citizen and determines the level of spending by trading off the benefits of public goods provision and infrastructure investment against the potential costs of a financial crisis triggered by a default. To allow for the possibility of a default, we introduce aggregate shocks to the economy, which affect firm profitability and tax revenues. Thus, in the event of a sufficiently negative shock, tax receipts will be too low to meet the government's debt obligations. In such an event, the government will be forced to default.[2]

Note that our approach is not meant to reflect any mismanagement of public finances by EME governments. We only assume that welfare-maximizing levels of public spending may be such that there is a positive risk of default, as reflected in EME sovereign bonds spreads. Our discussion, therefore, cannot shed any light on crises brought about by public overspending or on how to improve EME financial soundness by introducing more discipline and efficiency in the operation of government. This is not to say that we think that excessive borrowing and runaway budget deficits are not a problem in some EMEs. Rather, our analysis of whether it is desirable to foster the development of a corporate bond market is largely independent of the view one takes of the soundness of the governments' management of public finances.

Also, note that in a closed economy, government spending and borrowing will have a crowding-out effect as the government competes with the private sector for a given total amount of savings (net of intermediation costs).

Bank and Bond Financing

As is standard in the banking literature (since Diamond and Dybvig 1983), the model we consider in Bolton and Freixas (2006) allows depositors to withdraw their deposits from banks at any time. Thus, the model allows for the possibility of bank runs and captures the idea that bank-based financial systems are inherently fragile as they are always under the potential threat of a bank run.

In contrast to much of the existing literature on bank runs, however, we abstract from purely speculative bank runs (which are not very realistic) and focus on situations where a government debt default triggers a fundamental bank run because the banking sector holds too large a fraction of government debt. Thus, a central scenario in our analysis is one where banks hold an amount of government debt greater than their equity capital base, and where, following a government default, depositors realize that banks' total liabilities exceed their assets, and they cause a bank run by attempting to be first in line to get their deposit claims. As a way of reducing the maturity gap between deposits and loans, we also assume that bank loans mostly take the form of short-term revolving credit. This is quite realistic and, due to the revolving credit structure of bank lending to corporations, firms themselves are critically exposed to bank runs. Indeed, when there is a run on banks, firms are denied new short-term bank lending. As a result of the unexpected shortage in liquidity they then face, they may be forced into financial distress even when their operations are fundamentally sound.

Unlike bank financing, which creates a source of endogenous fragility due to the asset-liability mismatch, bond financing as a form of long-term finance does not expose firms to the same risks of bank runs and systemic crises. This is, in our view, the main benefit of bond financing in EMEs. By isolating firms from government debt defaults, bond financing provides a "spare tire" to firms and thus reduces the amplitude of the crisis that inevitably follows a government debt default. However, as we have stressed in our earlier writing (Bolton and Freixas 2000, 2005), bond financing is inherently less flexible and may result in higher costs of financial distress. In addition, in EMEs with a relatively small base of investment-grade firms that would issue bonds, bond financing may at least initially be a very costly form of financing.

To summarize, in our analysis the advantage of banks over bonds is that banks are able to restructure firms in financial distress. On the other hand, when banks face a bank run their liquidity dries up and restructuring becomes impossible. Thus, while bank-financed firms are fully exposed to the risk of bank runs, bond-financed firms are shielded from the direct effects of a financial crisis.

When Is It Desirable to Create a Bond Market?

Having outlined the basic building blocks of our analytical framework, we are now in a position to explore the general policy question of when and why it might be desirable to foster corporate bond financing in EMEs.

Under laissez-faire a corporate bond market can emerge only if the number and size of issuers is large enough so that the cost per issue is not out of proportion with the cost of obtaining financing from a bank. More precisely, the following key economic considerations determine whether a corporate bond market will be set up without any intervention and whether its creation is desirable:

1. As there is a major fixed-cost component to the creation of a bond market, there is a fundamental coordination problem involved in the creation of a bond market. It is thus entirely conceivable that some EMEs do not develop bond markets mainly because of a coordination

failure. In such a situation government intervention may be justified to kick-start the market.

2. As we have alluded to above, only safer and larger firms will generally be willing to seek financing through bond issues. Consequently, for a bond market to emerge, a necessary condition is a sufficient number of large and safe (investment-grade) firms.

3. The form of government borrowing can play a critical role in fostering the emergence of a corporate bond market. First, and perhaps most importantly, as the fixed costs of the creation and maintenance of a bond market are shared among all issuers, raising government debt by issuing government bonds will have the effect of decreasing the share of fixed-cost firms have to pay when they themselves issue bonds. Second, when investors' risk aversion is taken into account, then, as Yuan and Dittmar (2005) have shown, another benefit for corporate bond issuers of the presence of a government bond market is that it allows investors in corporate bonds to hedge country macroeconomic risks and thus lowers the cost of capital for corporate bond issuers. In addition, it may be argued that quite often the government is the first to issue and that, in this way, it sets a term structure benchmark that will subsequently be used by other market participants.

4. When the measure of firms preferring bond finance is large enough, so that the bond market is feasible, then it is also efficient to kick-start a bond market. This is so because all the safer firms benefit from the better terms in funding that are made available by the bond market. In other words, all the firms who end up choosing bond financing then simply internalize the direct welfare gains obtained by switching to a cheaper source of funds (or better mode of financing). This lower cost of funds is akin to an increase in investors' savings and implies, ceteris paribus, a decrease in interest rates and an increase in the number of firms that can be financed.

5. In addition, in comparison with the benchmark situation where all funding goes through the banking sector, an indirect positive externality of the existence of the bond market is to insulate those firms financed by bonds from some of the effects of a government debt default.

Interestingly, our analysis suggests that the benefit of creating a corporate bond market in EMEs is even greater than in advanced economies, where the risk of a banking crisis is negligible. However, because of the large fixed costs in setting up a bond market, only larger EMEs will benefit from the creation of a domestic corporate bond market. For smaller economies, the alternative is either to turn to an international bond market—with the drawback of exposing the country to currency risk—or to develop securitization and a market of CDOs, which can tap a bigger set of issuing firms because of the pooling of small loans into a single CDO issue.

But the creation of a bond market and the spare-tire benefits it brings could paradoxically have the perverse effect of increasing the incidence of government debt crises. Indeed, in the model we analyze in Bolton and Freixas (2006), the government determines its level of spending and the amount it borrows by trading off the expected costs of a debt crisis against the benefits of higher public good provision (e.g., greater infrastructure investment). Thus, in this model, the effect of reducing the cost of a financial crisis through the spare-tire effect might encourage the government to borrow more and thus paradoxically increases the incidence of debt crises.

Securitization

A complement to the development of a corporate bond market is to foster securitization and the market for CDOs. There has been very rapid growth in the market for asset-backed securities (ABS) in the United States and other developed economies in recent years, to the point that now the ABS market in the United States is larger than the corporate bond market. We expect the ABS market to grow in similar proportion in other developed economies and also in EMEs.

Such growth is expected because ABS and CDO instruments have two advantages over direct bond issues. The first is that, unlike direct bond issues, indirect securitization through special-purpose vehicles (the typical form of most CDOs) is a more flexible form of financing, to the extent that originating banks tend to retain the junior portion of the issue and therefore have strong incentives to facilitate loan restructuring in financially distressed firms (see Bolton and Freixas 2000 for a formal analysis of this point). The second benefit is that through indirect securitization it is possible to offer some of the benefits of direct bond financing to a larger pool of firms, which, because of their smaller size or their riskier cash flows, would otherwise choose a bank loan over a bond issue.

Securitization also offers benefits relative to intermediated bank lending. Most importantly, in the event of a banking crisis the entity issuing the CDOs is shielded from the recovery actions of depositors running on the bank. In other words, securitization brings about a reduction in financial fragility by switching households out of short-term demand deposits into long-term security (CDO) holdings. Thus, through securitization, it is possible to obtain some indirect spare-tire benefits by reducing the fraction of household savings that can be withdrawn at any time. This means that the amount of cash banks need to hold in proportion to total savings in anticipation of deposit withdrawals can be reduced.

When we introduce the possibility of securitization in our model (see Bolton and Freixas 2006) we are able to compare the relative performance of bonds, bank loans, and securitized bank loans and to characterize the new equilibrium financial structure of an EME. To see how securitization fits in with other financial alternatives such as unsecuritized bank loans and bond issues, it is useful to start with the observation that securitization actually involves duplication of transactions costs. Indeed, to produce a one dollar CDO, a bank must first incur an intermediation cost by extending a loan to a firm. In order to securitize that loan, the bank must incur again issuing costs that are comparable to bond issuing costs. Given this duplication in costs, one might ask how this hybrid form of financing could ever dominate both full (unsecuritized) bank lending and direct bond financing? As we noted earlier, the answer is that securitization also brings special benefits. If these exceed the higher costs of financing, then securitization will emerge in equilibrium.

It is straightforward to see how securitization might emerge in equilibrium by focusing on the marginal firm that is otherwise indifferent between bank lending (without securitization) and bond financing and to investigate when this firm might strictly prefer securitized bank lending. The marginal firm values the restructuring benefits of bank financing at exactly the cost differential between a bank loan and a bond issue. By securitizing the bank loan, the marginal firm will incur duplicated costs (both intermediation and security issuing costs), but it will also realize double benefits to the extent that it obtains a shield against the consequences of a bank run while retaining the restructuring service that banks provide in the event of financial distress (and no bank run).[3] The firms that tend to benefit more from securitization are those with higher cash flow risks, which therefore value the restructuring services provided by banks. However, very risky firms may not be able to afford the duplicated costs of securitization as they are already close to being credit-rationed and have a smaller portion of safe cash flows they can securitize. In summary, it is possible to obtain an equilibrium outcome where the safest (investment-grade) firms issue bonds directly and do not take out a substantial portion of their funding in the form of securitized bank loans; firms with intermediate cash flow risk take out securitized bank loans; and very risky firms obtain bank loans, which are not securitized.

Note that the presence of a risk of a government debt and banking crisis has ambiguous effects on the desirability of securitization and the creation of a CDO market. On the one hand, an increase in risk of government debt default increases the benefits of securitization, as there is a greater demand for the spare-tire benefits it provides. On the other hand, a greater risk of a bank run reduces the expected benefits of bank restructuring services. Thus, the scope for securitization may be higher or lower in EMEs depending on the structure of the economy.

Decoupling the Banking Sector and Public Finances

As noted above, an important added benefit of the existence of a bond market in an EME is that it shields bond-financed firms from government debt default crises. In addition, by shifting government debt away from banks and into the hands of bond holders, the creation of a bond market also makes possible the decoupling of banking from public finances. Namely, funding of the Treasury through the bond market makes possible the removal of government debt from the balance sheet of banks and thus reduces the exposure of banks to government debt default crises. A bank run need not develop if the portfolio of banks is such that the share of government bond holdings is low in proportion to the banks' capital. This opens the door for the possibility that banks themselves may be able to survive a government debt crisis.

Currently, under Basel I regulations, banks have incentives to hold government debt as it is considered a safe asset and therefore requires no equity capital. However, as Basel II acknowledges, EMEs' government debt is typically risky and should require either sufficient provisions (for expected losses) or sufficient capital (for unexpected losses). Our analysis suggests that it might be desirable to completely prevent banks from holding their country's government debt, whether it takes the form of bank loans or treasury bonds and, by the same token, banks should not be in the business of underwriting government bond issues, as is generally the case.

Banks would then be shielded from the direct effects of a government debt default crisis. This may increase the safety of the banking system and make deposits more attractive. Nevertheless, in practice, this is seldom the case, as banks typically invest a large fraction of their portfolios in their own country's treasuries.[4]

Thus, for banks to be shielded from a government default, the existence of a corporate bond market is necessary but not sufficient. It is not obvious that the market itself provides the right incentives for banks to achieve decoupling as a way to increase their market value, by either attracting additional depositors or by decreasing their probability of failure and therefore increasing their expected charter value. One reason is that there may be coordination failures in the creation of a separate market or institution to purchase government debt. Another reason is that it may be difficult for depositors or other market participants to know the exact exposure of a bank to government debt. Thus, it is likely that decoupling can only be achieved through regulatory intervention. If decoupling enhances the financial system's efficiency by avoiding bank runs, then regulation may be the right way to achieve it.

Still, it may be argued that even if banks are theoretically decoupled from government debt, this will not be sufficient to prevent government debt default from triggering a banking crisis through indirect effects of default on aggregate economic activity and firms' profitability.

While it is plausible that some degree of contagion always exists between government default and banks' defaults, the magnitude of contagion depends on the specific characteristics of the economy. For instance, whether the country is a large exporter may be a key issue in determining the level of indirect contagion. For large exporters like Korea, there may be relatively low contagion and the spare-tire role of corporate bond markets may be fully effective; while for low exporters like Argentina, indirect contagion may be so high that the spare-tire effect may have no impact on the banking sector.

Besides the effect of a government default on aggregate demand, there are also other possible channels of indirect contagion, as for example through economic sanctions imposed on a defaulting sovereign. When indirect contagion has a high impact on banks' profitability decoupling is impossible and bank-financed firms will be hit by the effects of the banking crisis, although bond-financed firms remain unaffected. In such a situation trying to limit government debt holdings in banks' portfolios is pointless.

Equilibrium in an Open Economy

It is theoretically obvious, and also empirically documented, that financial openness provides access to finance at a lower cost of funds and therefore increases the number of projects that can be implemented (see Henry 2000, 2001).

Still, several dimensions of the effects of liberalization depend on a country's financial architecture. To analyze them, we consider a scenario of full liberalization where both domestic banks and bond markets compete in order to obtain foreign funds, deposits, or investments, and where the government is able to obtain funding either from foreign banks or by tapping the foreign bond market. We shall not take into account here the possibility that domestic depositors can diversify their savings by opening deposit accounts in both domestic and foreign banks, as our analysis is based on a model where households are assumed to be risk-neutral and therefore would not benefit from international diversification. That is not to deny, however, that in reality the international diversification of household savings may be an important aspect of financial liberalization.

Effect of Liberalization on Decoupling

Because of the lower cost of funds it implies, liberalization will allow an increase in the equilibrium level of public spending. Nevertheless, this need not imply that it will lead, per se, to a higher level of government default risk, as a higher level of spending may be compensated for by a lower interest rate and an increase in the tax base due to the increase in the number of domestic firms that will obtain funding.

Direct Contagion and Decoupling Effect

Foreign investment can have different effects and implications depending on whether a domestic bond market exists or not. Indeed, if a bond market exists, it allows for additional channels of foreign investment.

When the financial system is entirely dominated by banks, foreign investors—especially foreign banks—have only two broad investment options in sovereign debt: either lend directly to the government or lend to the domestic banks, who in turn will channel the funds to the government. In our framework these two channels of funding the government will have different effects. Through the first channel (direct lending by foreign investors to the government), it is possible to decouple to some extent the domestic banking sector from public finances. Through the second channel, domestic banks are fully exposed to a default and are more likely to face a run and go bankrupt.

When the financial system has both a banking sector and a bond market, the government can issue treasury bonds, and, in an open-economy equilibrium, these will also be held by foreign investors. Consequently, decoupling can then be obtained much more immediately through bond issues and indirect contagion may be much more limited.

To summarize, except when foreign banks lend to EME banks that in turn lend to the government, financial openness and liberalization tend to foster a greater decoupling of government finances and the banking sector. However, one important obstacle to the decoupling effect is that, because of monitoring reasons akin to those modeled in Bolton and Scharfstein (1990), foreign lending to the government through the domestic banking system is likely to be short-term liquid lending while direct lending by foreign investors to the government is generally longer-term illiquid lending, which means that foreigners lending directly to the government could be disadvantaged relative to domestic banks in the event of a crisis. This may be one reason why foreigners may still choose to channel their funds to the government through the domestic banking system, thus limiting the possibilities of decoupling.

Indirect Contagion

As mentioned before, the impact of government debt default on economic growth, on loan losses, and on banks' profitability constitutes an important channel of indirect contagion, from government default to banking crisis. Financial liberalization will provide access to foreign investors with well-diversified portfolios. This will reduce the impact of a government debt default. Nevertheless, if debt defaults generate economic sanctions that will lead to a reduction of economic growth, the effect is the opposite and indirect contagion is increased by financial openness.

Sudden Stop

In a closed economy, it seems reasonable to assume that banking regulation is able to cope with a bank run by using a number of mechanisms such as adequate monetary policy and the intervention of the lender of last resort. In an open economy, bank runs may occur on deposits held by foreign investors denominated in foreign currency. This corresponds to a sudden stop, defined as the sudden stopping of any source of financing by foreign investors. This sudden stop, which is now well documented (see Calvo and Talvi 2005 and its references), is known to be a key issue in EMEs' financial fragility (Becker and Mauro 2006), and it is directly related to EMEs' banks being funded through short-term deposits.

Consequently, financial openness and the risk of sudden stop it implies create an additional trigger for a bank run, which combines with government debt default risk. Thus, although financial liberalization decreases indirect contagion, a sudden stop will increase contagion, and the net effect is a priori ambiguous.

Because both indirect contagion and sudden stop affect only banks and therefore bank-financed firms, they affect the cost-benefit of the creation of a bond market. The higher the probability of a sudden stop, the higher the benefits of the creation of a bond market that is shielded from the effects of a sudden stop.

Effect of Liberalization on the Bond Market

A second point that our model allows us to study is the effect of financial openness on the bond market. Because we assume that the creation of a bond market requires a large fixed cost to be shared among different issuers, the efficient solution implies that only one bond market is created when we consider two countries. This requires coordination among all countries, which would thus issue in a unique market. To the extent that firms can still issue bonds, this should be beneficial for the country as costs decrease. Still, if there are additional costs (such as regulatory, auditing, and disclosing costs) that make it impossible or extremely costly for some firms to issue bonds abroad, then the creation of a domestic bond market complementing the foreign market may be efficient. In this case, it seems reasonable to assume that larger, international, and more transparent firms will issue abroad while smaller, national, and opaque firms will issue bonds in the domestic market. Of course, the existing cost duplication may imply that it is not efficient to create a bond market. This will be the case because large firms that could have shared in the total cost of the creation of the market are funded abroad.

The interpretation of this cost of duplication in terms of liquidity is straightforward: liquidity is obviously decreased when firms issue in different markets.

Conclusion

This chapter discusses the benefits of the creation of a bond market in an EME characterized by sovereign risk and the existence of banking crises caused by government default. The main conclusion of our chapter is that financial architecture will play a key role in economic development for two reasons. First, as in developed economies, an extensive financial architecture decreases the cost of funds to firms by allowing them to choose between bond finance and bank finance. Second, such architecture provides the economy with a "spare tire," as the corporate bond market need not be affected by a banking crisis. In fact, a well-developed corporate bond market may partially insulate firms against sovereign default risk and the associated bank credit crunch risk. This effect can have a greater impact if it increases the banking sector's resilience by insulating it from government debt crises. This can happen because government debt is held outside the banking sector, whether by domestic nonbank investors, foreign banks, or nonbank financial institutions.

There are important limits to this effect when the government debt default has a large impact on firms' profitability. This indirect contagion will occur because government debt affects economic growth, which affects the level of nonperforming loans and, in turn, banks' level of solvency. If indirect contagion is important, banks might go bankrupt in case of a government debt default even if they do not hold government debt in their portfolios, simply because of the indirect contagion channel.

Financial openness will aid EME development not only by providing access to international financial markets at lower rates but also by taking government debt out of banks' portfolios; this will allow for decoupling. Still, the risk of "sudden stop" with foreign depositors causing a run on the bank should be accounted for as a possible negative effect. From this perspective, accessing the international financial market through a bond market that is not vulnerable to "sudden stop" makes it all the more attractive to create a bond market.

Acknowledgments

The authors are thankful to the Fonds français de coopération technique pour les services de conseil et la formation and the Interamerican Development Bank for financial support. They have benefited from comments by participants at the second workshop of the project "The Development of Latin American Bond Markets," sponsored by the IDB's Latin American Research Network. They also acknowledge the excellent research assistance of Milos Bozovic. The usual disclaimer applies: any remaining errors are their own.

Notes

1. As shown by Tadesse (2002), the empirical evidence seems to give some support to this view, as bank-based systems in EMEs have higher growth rates.

2. This may lead to a minor complication as the tax rate might depend upon the economic environment. In Bolton and Freixas (2006), we simplify the analysis by assuming that the government sets a fixed tax rate, which we justify by the serious obstacles in collecting taxes that EMEs face. In the event that total tax receipts exceed total government debt obligations, we assume that the government balances the budget by providing a lump sum transfer to households equal to the amount of excess tax receipts.

3. In the event of a bank run, the restructuring services of bank financing are not available.

4. In some countries, like India or Colombia, government bonds represent the main investment in the portfolio of banks. Holding a large proportion of government bonds may be mandatory in some countries. When this is the case, decoupling is not feasible except if banks hold a sufficient amount of capital.

References

Allen, F., and D. Gale (2000). *Comparing Financial Systems*. Cambridge, MA: MIT Press.

Becker, T., and P. Mauro (2006). "Output Drops and the Shocks that Matter." International Monetary Fund, Research Department.

Besanko, D., and G. Kanatas (1993). "Credit Market Equilibrium with Bank Monitoring and Moral Hazard." *Review of Financial Studies* 6: 213–232.

Bolton, P., and X. Freixas (2000). "Equity, Bonds and Bank Debt: Capital Structure and Financial Market Equilibrium under Asymmetric Information." *Journal of Political Economy* 108: 324–351.

Bolton, P., and X. Freixas (2005). "Corporate Finance and the Monetary Transmission Mechanism." *Review of Financial Studies* 19: 829–870.

Bolton, P., and X. Freixas (2006). "Financial Architecture in Emerging Market Economies." Mimeo.

Bolton, P., and D. Scharfstein (1990). "A Theory of Predation Based on Agency Problems in Financial Contracting." *American Economic Review* 80(1): 93–106.

Boot, A., and A. Thakor (1997). "Financial System Architecture." *Review of Financial Studies* 10: 693–733.

Caballero, Ricardo, and Arvind Krishnamurthy (2001). "International and Domestic Collateral Constraints in a Model of Emerging Market Crises." *Journal of Monetary Economics* 48: 513–548.

Calvo, Guillermo, and Ernesto Talvi (2005). "Sudden Stop, Financial Factors and Economic Collpase in Latin America: Learning from Argentina and Chile." NBER Working Paper No. 11153.

Chang, Roberto, and Andres Velasco (1998). "Financial Crises in Emerging Markets: A Canonical Model." NBER Working Paper No. 6606.

Chemmanur, T., and P. Fulghieri (1994). "Reputation, Renegotiation and the Choice between Bank Loans and Publicly Traded Debt." *Review of Financial Studies* 7: 475–506.

Corsetti, Giancarlo, Paolo Pesenti, and Nouriel Roubini (1999). "Paper Tigers: A Model of the Asian Crisis." *European Economic Review* 43: 1211–1236.

Diamond, D. W. (1984). "Financial Intermediation and Delegated Monitoring." *Review of Economic Studies* 51: 393–414.

Diamond, D. W. (1991). "Monitoring and Reputation: The Choice between Bank Loans and Directly Placed Debt." *Journal of Political Economy* 99: 689–721.

Diamond, D., and P. Dybvig (1983). "Bank Runs, Deposit Insurance and Liquidity." *Journal of Political Economy* 91: 401–419.

Diamond, Douglas, and Raghuram Rajan (2000). "Banks, Short Term Debt and Financial Crises." NBER Working Paper No. 7764.

Henry, Peter Blair (2000). "Stock Market Liberalization, Economic Reform, and Emerging Market Equity Prices." *Journal of Finance* 55: 529–564.

Henry, Peter Blair (2001). "Do Stock Market Liberalizations Cause Investment Booms?" *Journal of Financial Economics* 58: 301–334.

Holmstrom, B., and J. Tirole (1997). "Financial Intermediation, Loanable Funds and the Real Sector." *Quarterly Journal of Economics* 113: 663–692.

Hoshi, T., A. Kashyap, and D. Scharfstein (1993). "The Choice between Public and Private Debt: An Analysis of Post-Deregulation Corporate Financing in Japan." Mimeo, MIT.

Repullo, R., and J. Suarez (1997). "Entrepreneurial Moral Hazard and Bank Monitoring: A Model of the Credit Channel." Mimeo, CEMFI, Madrid.

Schneider, Martin, and Aaron Tornell (2004). "Balance Sheet Effects, Bailout Guarantees and Financial Crises." *Review of Economic Studies* 71: 883–913.

Tadesse, S. (2002). "Financial Architecture and Economic Performance: International Evidence." *Journal of Financial Intermediation* 11: 429–454.

Yuan, Kathy, and Robert Dittmar (2005). "The Price Impact of Sovereign Bonds." Mimeo, University of Michigan, http://webuser.bus.umich.edu/kyuan/.

3 Development of the Mexican Bond Market

Sara G. Castellanos and
Lorenza Martínez

The Mexican bond market, like other capital markets in Latin America, remains underdeveloped. For instance, the BIS International Financial Statistics show that markets of private, public, and international bonds still constitute a lower share of GDP in Mexico than in other Latin American countries at the same level of development.[1]

As in other countries of the region, macroeconomic instability may have been a major impediment to the development of Mexico's financial markets. But other elements have constrained these markets as well, such as weak legal and judicial systems, which hinder the recovery of guarantees in case of financial distress, and very high transaction costs for issuing and trading bonds.[2] All these factors may have created a trap by inhibiting liquidity, which is the worst deterrent for market participants.

During the last 15 years, capital markets, particularly bond markets, have been improving in terms of their size, liquidity, and other indicators. For instance, between 1990 and 2005, total domestic bonds issued by the central government remained around 21% of GDP, but the average maturity of the debt increased from less than one year in 1990 to more than 5 years in 2005. The decline in the 91-day interest rate was more dramatic—from 35% in 1990 to slightly above 5% by mid-2003, before the central bank started a round of restrictive monetary policy—especially considering the peak of 90% reached during the 1995 Tequila Crisis. For the private sector, however, improvements have been more modest. In the 1990–2005 period total domestic bonds issued by the private sector[3] grew from 0.78% to 3.3% of GDP, and the annual issuance of medium- and long-term debt remained below 1% of GDP. Therefore, despite the current market growth and turnover, private sector capital markets are still at an incipient stage.

In this chapter we describe some of the policy actions that may have contributed to fostering capital markets and analyze how much of the recent performance of the corporate debt market in Mexico can be attributed to them. The following section describes some macroeconomic aspects and legal reforms that may be influencing the development of bond markets. The third section explains the government debt management strategics and the extension of the yield curve that may have contributed to expanding the corporate debt market. The fourth section portrays in more detail the recent growth trend of the corporate bond market. The fifth section is dedicated to empirical analysis, using two different approaches: we estimated probit and tobit regressions to determine the impact of macroeconomic and legal factors on the probability of issuing corporate debt and the conditions of issuances. These exercises try to assess the contribution of these domestic reforms, taking into account foreign market conditions and other factors. We think that this distinction is particularly important because, under the abundant liquidity that characterizes international financial markets during the analysis period and the expansion of mandatory pension funds, the recent bond market trend cannot be fully attributed to the policy actions that have been implemented. On the other hand, because several of these developments occurred at about the same time and because it may still be too soon for the reforms' effects to be felt, we complement this analysis through another approach. We surveyed a set of banks, brokerage exchange houses, pension funds, mutual funds, and insurance companies that invest in the domestic bond market to learn their perceptions of what reforms have accomplished and what they have not. Lastly, in the sixth section, we identify additional ways to encourage the deepening of bond markets, and we present some final remarks.

The Development of the Mexican Financial System (1978–2005)

Emergence of the Money Market (1978–1982)

Mexican bond markets' short history starts with the creation of the money market in Mexico. A well-functioning money market represents a critical factor in the development of deep, liquid corporate debt markets because it provides an anchor for the short end of the yield curve and thus serves as a benchmark for pricing other fixed-income securities that differ in terms of liquidity, credit quality, and maturity (Luengnaruemitchai and Ong 2005).

As a prerequisite to launching this money market, a rather soft liberalization process started in the 1970s, aiming to make the intensely regulated financial system more adaptable to higher interest rates and stagflation throughout the world as well as to higher inflation rates and larger financial necessities of the country's public sector. Monetary policy's main objective during the period known as "shared development" (*desarrollo compartido*, 1971–1976) switched from maintaining price stability to financing fiscal expansion.[4] This brought about an exchange rate devaluation in 1976 after several years of economic stability and high growth rates.[5]

A formal debt market was born with the first Securities Market Act (Ley del Mercado de Valores, LMV) in 1975, allowing corporate debt instruments to be issued without any guarantee (*obligaciones quirografarias*).[6] The most important development at that time was the introduction of treasury bills (Certificados de la Tesorería de la Federación, known as Cetes) in 1978. This became the main instrument used by the government to satisfy its increasing financing requirements and to carry out open market operations for monetary policy purposes. Although these bills expanded the limited supply of saving instruments and contributed to the emergence of the corporate debt market, it is very likely that surging macroeconomic instability constrained demand for any instrument with maturity longer than a few months. Moreover, the exchange rate devaluations and financial crises in the 1980s, as well as the nationalization of the commercial banks and the closing of foreign financial resources, worsened Mexico's macroeconomic instability, which in turn frustrated the creation of other securities.[7] Under these circumstances, short-term Cetes achieved levels of liquidity unparalleled by other instruments, and its yield provided the benchmark for pricing other financial instruments.

Financial Liberalization (1983–2000)

Although the 1982 foreign debt crisis led to fiscal adjustment and a stringent monetary policy to stabilize the recently devaluated peso, a second drop in the international oil price in 1986, through its effect on public finances and the collapse of the Mexican Stock Market (Bolsa Mexicana de Valores, BMV) in 1987, caused another exchange-rate devaluation. As a result, in 1987 the annual inflation rate reached a maximum of 160%, and total private and public sector debt added up to 95% of GDP. That December, a heterodox stabilization program (the Pacto de Solidaridad Económica) based on freezing prices, wages, and the exchange rate was launched to control inflation (Aspe 1993).

By the end of 1988, annual inflation fell to 52%. As the economy became more stable, the financial system reforms were accelerated. Among them, perhaps the most salient are the following: the complete abandonment of credit quotas and minimum reserve requirement in September 1989; a more limited intervention by the monetary authorities in determining the interest rates, which aimed at improving the secondary market for Cetes; the elimination of restrictions on foreign capital; the strengthening of financial intermediaries through the Credit Institutions Act (Ley de Instituciones de Crédito, LIC) of 1990, which established how financial intermediaries and groups would be constituted and how the government would screen their operations; a constitutional reform in 1993 granting the Central Bank of Mexico (Banco de México, BM) complete independence in operations and administration; congressional approval of an initiative to privatize commercial banks; and, most importantly, the shift in government deficit financing from compulsory reserve requirements to the allocation of noninflationary debt instruments through credit markets.[8]

An expansion of real credit to the private sector followed the new financial arrangements.[9] This expansion, which by 1994 represented 40% of GDP, was partly financed by foreign investors, whose confidence in the Mexican economy was probably boosted by the signing of the North America Free Trade Agreement (NAFTA), the acceptance of Mexico into the Organization for Economic Cooperation and Development (OECD), and privatization of some state enterpises.[10] But as Lustig (2001) points out, the large capital inflows were both a blessing and a curse. On one hand, they meant more resources to invest in productive activities. On the other, they placed pressure on the exchange rate through asset appreciation and fueled a large surge of domestic credit for which the banking system's poor regulatory framework was unprepared. In fact, many analysts point out that one area of reform received relatively little attention from Mexican authorities: prudential regulation and supervision. Autonomous supervisory agencies for various financial activities had to be created in order to provide clarity and confidence for those who participated in the system. But in Mexico those agencies were created only after the direct control instruments were dismantled. The country's rapid financial liberalization, in an environment of scanty prudential regulation and supervision, may have deepened asymmetric information problems in the banking system.[11]

These weak fundamentals, along with the domestic political turmoil and the increase of international interest rates experienced in 1994, produced capital outflows and an increase in country risk.[12] To defend the exchange rate peg while avoiding a further increase in domestic interest, Mexican authorities increased the issuance of Tesobonos (dollar-denominated treasury bonds) to roll over short-term debt. Several months later, a sharp increase in dollar-denominated debt added fragility to the system. Eventually, the Mexican government had to abandon the peso peg to the US dollar in December 1994, and Mexico experienced the so-called first crisis of the twenty-first century.[13]

Perhaps the most important reform for financial markets in the six years that followed was the transition from a pay-as-you-go pension fund system to a fully funded one in 1997. The new system of individual capitalization generated a significant and more stable demand for long-term saving instruments, contributing to the development of a long-term debt market in pesos.

Expansion of the Long-Term Bond Market (2001–2005)

After 2001, efforts increased to achieve more efficient financial markets in Mexico and to foster a more rapid expansion of the corporate debt market. We can identify six features of the Mexican economy that experienced substantial changes:

• *Macroeconomic stability and low interest rates.* Strict monetary and fiscal discipline may allow the government to increase the size and average maturity of its domestic debt and decrease its dependence on foreign debt. As macroeconomic conditions have become more stable, market participants are becoming more willing to hold longer maturities and nominal yield securities. During this period the government was able to issue 3-, 5-, 10- and 20-year fixed coupon bonds, and to decrease the share of floating rate issues in the outstanding stock of government debt.[14]

• *Fiscal discipline.* Fiscal discipline may have a crucial role in this process by reducing the crowding out of private sector issuers. Net government debt has been stable at around 20% of GDP since 1997. Moreover, a reduced share of foreign debt has strengthened the government's financial position. Thus the cost and maturity of foreign debt have also improved noticeably since 2000, and this has allowed other private issuers to obtain resources at more competitive rates.[15]

• *The mandatory private pension system reform.* Some authors consider the rapid growth of assets under the management of institutional investors, both domestic and foreign, as one of the key factors behind the rapid development of domestic corporate bond markets in Latin America.[16] In Mexico this growth has been spurred mainly by the pensions reform of 1997. Pension fund assets under management have grown from 1% of GDP in 1998 to around 6% of GDP in 2005; at the end of 2004, private bonds managed by mandatory pension fund administrators (*administradoras de fondos para el retiro*, AFOREs) represented 20% of outstanding bonds.[17] However, in Mexico portfolios managed by AFOREs are mainly invested in central government securities. By December 2005 this figure was 82%, which seems very high even when compared to other Latin American countries (figure 3.1). Let us point out that this difference does not seem to be fully explained by differences in investment regime regulations. When the capitalized pension system initiated its operations, AFOREs faced an investment regime for their funds that imposed quantitative limits for each group

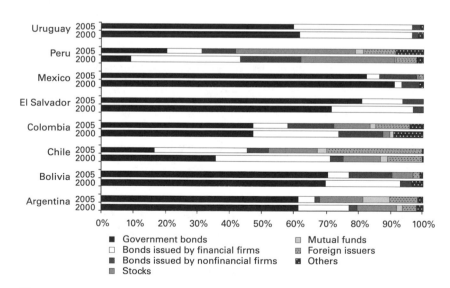

Figure 3.1
Portfolios of mandatory private pension funds in Latin American countries. Source: Asociación Internacional de Organismos de Supervisión de Fondos de Pensiones (AIOS).

of instruments. In particular, at least 65% of a pension fund's portfolio had to be invested in government bonds, leaving a maximum investment of 35% in private instruments, of which only 10% could be invested in instruments issued by financial firms. Nevertheless, investment in government bonds has always exceeded the legal minimum. In fact, the impact on the concentration of investments in government debt is barely discernible, even after the 2002 and 2003 changes to eliminate the quantitative limits by instruments, broaden the range of eligible issuers, and introduce limits for credit rating.

· *Deepening and development of the exchange-rate market.* During the last decade the introduction of instruments to hedge exchange rate risk, such as the currency futures and options on the Mexican peso, may have improved investors' access to financial markets denominated in this currency. Mexican peso futures at the Chicago Mercantile Exchange began trading in April 1995, just four months after the December 1994 peso crisis, and were the first emerging market currency products to be traded on the exchange. At present there are liquid financial markets for such instruments both in Mexico and abroad, including organized and over-the-counter (OTC) markets. The volume of contracts traded in the market has increased steadily; by 2004 the Mexican peso became, after the South Korean won, the most actively traded currency among emerging market economies, both in spot and derivatives markets, according to the survey of Foreign Exchange and Derivative Market Activity of the BIS (BIS 2005).

· *Development of the derivatives market.* The relationship between the development of underlying cash markets and derivatives markets is complex. In the absence of sufficient instruments to hedge against interest rate reversals, investors are reluctant to participate in the original securities markets, although an underdeveloped market for original securities is itself one of the main reasons for having underdeveloped local derivatives. Mexican peso derivatives have been traded internationally on and off since the 1980s. On the fixed-income securities side, such markets started to develop in the early 1990s, with the creation of an interbank nonregulated forward market for inflation-indexed securities. However, the lack of regulation and internal controls in financial institutions led some of them to take large positions, causing large losses to some banks and brokerage exchange houses (BEHs).[18] Since then, the BM began to issue risk management and reporting regulations for banks and BEHs and to monitor derivative markets more closely, so that only institutions in compliance could trade derivatives in Mexico. At the end of 1998, a derivatives exchange specialized in the trading of contracts on financial assets was launched (Mercado Mexicano de Derivados, S.A. de C.V., MexDer). There is a liquid market for foreign exchange futures and options although most of the operations on Mexican derivatives take place OTC around the world. The most liquid security traded in MexDer is the 28-day interbank equilibrium interest rate (*tasa de interés interbancaria de equilibrio*, TIIE), which represents almost 100% of transactions in fixed-income contracts.[19] Prospects for this market are encouraging as in August 2006 it received the approval from the Commodity Futures Trading Commission (CFTC) to offer several securities on the Mexican Stock Exchange Index.

• *Reforms of financial market legislation.* Particularly notable among Mexico's financial reforms was that of the LMV in 2001, which sought to improve the corporate governance of public firms, the rights of minority shareholders, and information disclosure; with the purpose of stimulating the development of the stock market.[20] Another significant aspect of the LMV reform was the introduction of corporate certificates (*certificados bursátiles*, CBs). This instrument has become the dominant debt instrument for corporations, accounting for all medium- and long-term issues since 2004. CBs are credit titles for circulation in the BMV that can be issued by private companies, public companies, and local governments. They can be issued with any maturity and return; their coupons can be negotiated separately; they are operated in the debt market rather than in the capital market; and their issuance does not require a protocol, thus reducing costs.[21] So far many corporations, state and municipal governments, other government entities, and investment societies have tendered issues.[22] In December 2005 an additional LMV reform was undertaken to provide incentives for enhancing capital market development. In more specific terms, the reform sought to promote medium-sized firms' access to the BMV by means of stock investment promotion societies (*sociedades anónimas promotoras de inversión*, or SAPIs). SAPIs are required to comply with higher corporate governance and information revelation standards than traditional corporations (*sociedades anónimas*) in exchange for some exceptions to the Law of Merchant Societies (Ley General de Sociedades Mercantiles, LGSM) that will allow them to perform several risk management operations. This seeks to bring small and medium firms closer to the financial and structural arrangements of large public firms. However, perhaps the gist of this reform is redefining the functions and responsibilities of corporate bodies in public firms, especially the regimes for counselors, directors, auditors, and control shareholders. These definitions are also accompanied by a more precise definition of white collar felonies and crimes. All of these measures are intended to induce a shift toward a more transparent management in all enterprises by means of enforcing accounting, auditory, and control systems as a legal obligation.

These developments coincide with a more diversified holding pattern of government domestic bonds. While during the 1980s and early 1990s these securities were held mainly by banking institutions and some foreign investors, since the late 1990s the share held by pension funds has been growing, in contrast with that of the other domestic investors. However, the proportion of long-term fixed-yield bonds has been higher among mutual funds and insurance companies than among pension funds in recent years.

While foreign investors' participation in local debt markets in Asia and Latin America remains limited despite efforts to open up their markets to foreign investment, foreign interest in Mexico's longer-term government bonds has risen sharply since 2004 (figure 3.2). Since that year, foreign investors' holdings of long-term fixed-yield bonds have made them even more important investors in those securities than the

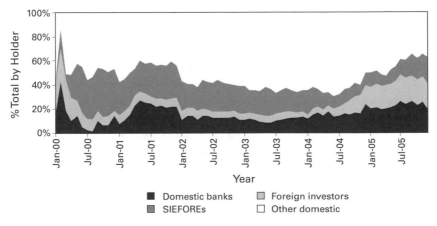

Figure 3.2
Domestic public bonds by holder: long-term fixed-yield bonds. Source: Banco de México.

pension funds: foreign investors now buy more than 80% of the new issuances of long-term fixed-yield government bonds.[23]

Development of the Government Bond Market

The statistics produced by many international financial market institutions show that the size, duration, and liquidity offered by the Mexican government bond market as of 2005 is difficult for any other emerging market to match (Tovar and Jeanneau 2006). This seems quite remarkable when we consider that a one-year fixed coupon bond in pesos was first issued only in 1990 and that longer maturity bonds were first issued only in 2000. Total government bond debt as a percentage of GDP grew from around 6% in 1996 to 26% in 2005. The issuance of debt instruments by BM to perform monetary operations was the major source of this growth, but the increase can also be attributed to the participation of local governments and government agencies in bond markets. In contrast, the outstanding stock of federal government domestic debt has remained below 15% of GDP since the early 1990s.

A distinctive development of government indebtedness in recent years involves its domestic and foreign components. Until the late 1990s, the bulk of government financing came from foreign sources.[24] But after the Tequila Crisis of 1994 that led to the sudden devaluation of the peso, the share of domestic debt increased while foreign-held debt continuously fell. By 2000 the local market had gained depth and it was no longer necessary for the government to resort to international markets, making its liquidity position resilient to emerging market debt volatility. This enabled the federal government to attain an investment grade on its debt in 2002. It should be noted, though, that this strategy could have opened up other vulnerabilities had the federal government not been able to sharply raise the tenor and duration of its domestic debt. Nonetheless, introducing and developing the market for long-term securities may have created a virtuous circle of reducing the government liquidity position's vulnerability. This phenomenon would be increased by an improved confidence of local and foreign investors that allows reducing dependency on external debt and increasing the duration of domestic debt. So far, the increase in the duration of government debt has not resulted in a more vulnerable financial system as it is distributed among different types of investors.

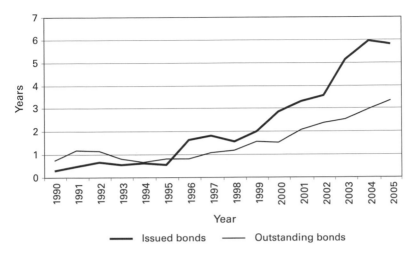

Figure 3.3
Average maturity of federal government bonds. Issued bonds: Average maturity weighted by amount issued. Outstanding bonds: Average years to maturity. Source: Banco de México.

The growth of the government bond market has been accompanied by decreasing interest rates and increasing maturities. Since 2002, the leading interest rate of the 91-day Cetes has remained below 10%. Improvements in domestic government debt maturity are even more visible, as the average maturity of federal government bonds issued rose from less than one year in 1994 to almost 6 years in 2004 (figure 3.3). The long-term maturity of the government yield curve was only 91 days in 1995, but by 2004, the longest maturity date of government bonds had reached 20 years. Because of the government bond yield curve's role as pricing benchmark for other domestic debt instruments, it is not surprising that the expansion of private bonds accelerated only after 2000.

Since 2000 the government has also shifted its domestic bonds from long-term variable rate to long-term fixed rate. Until 1987 all domestic public bonds were short term. Between 1987 and 1995, long-term bonds were issued only with a variable rate. The first long term bonds with an interest rate indexed to inflation were issued in 1995, and these bonds grew noticeably until 1999. Meanwhile, the share of bonds with long-term fixed rates has expanded. By 2005, fixed-rate long-term public bonds had become the most common type, representing almost half of the total outstanding (figure 3.4).

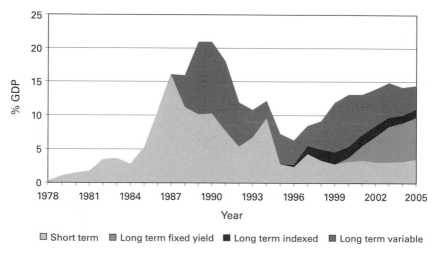

Figure 3.4
Composition of outstanding federal government domestic bonds (percent of GDP). Short-term bonds include Cetes, Tesobonos, Pagafes, and Petrobonos. Long-term with fixed yields are Bonos or Ms. Long-term indexed are Udibonos and with variable rate are Bondes and Ajustabonos. Source: Bolsa Mexicana de Valores and SHCP.

In regard to issuance and management of state and municipal debt, the Mexican government introduced regulatory reforms in 1996 in order to decentralize spending responsibilities. The new framework sought to introduce market discipline through the imposition of a ratings-based investor assessment of the credit quality of state and municipal debt, and the elimination of federal bailouts. These reforms, together with the 2001 LMV reform, also intended to lower the entry cost to the domestic bond market. They enabled states and municipalities to finance themselves through CBs that are sold through master trusts, which are revolving issuance structures that provide a degree of collateralization of debt-servicing obligations. These entities have been able to issue at fairly long periods (between 5 and 12 years), but most bonds issued so far have been indexed to short-term interest rates or inflation. In spite of these modifications, however, the stock of local government debt issued is relatively low, amounting to less than 5.7% of GDP in 2005.

Since 2000, there has been a noticeable increase in securities available for the public through issuance by the broader public sector. BM started to issue its own securities, called Bonos de Regulación Monetaria (money regulation bonds, BREMs), to impede the increasing accumulation of foreign reserves translating into increases of the monetary base. These securities consist of 1- and 3-year floating rate bonds with coupons linked to overnight rates. By the end of 2005, BREMs amounted to 3.21% of GDP.[25] At the same time, the Deposit Insurance Agency (Instituto para la Protección del Ahorro Bancario, IPAB) started issuing floating rate debt with government guarantees and a maturity between 3 and 7 years. However, these securities have been largely indexed to short-term interest rates, so their duration has remained very low (between 30 and 50 days in 2004). Presently, IPAB is the second-largest public sector issuer in Mexico.[26] Among decentralized debt-issuing public entities, the oil company Petróleos Mexicanos (Pemex) is the most important, representing 77% of placements. The nominal value of outstanding stocks issued by these decentralized entities reached US$10 billion in 2005, only three years after the first issue.

In 2005 the government launched a "Strips Market Operation Program" that allows government bond market participants to strip and reconstitute any Bonos (fixed-coupon bonds denominated in pesos) and Udibonos (fixed-coupon bonds denominated in inflation-indexed units), with the purpose of enhancing the depth of the secondary market. The extent of stripping activity has been limited so far by the need to resolve some pending issues such as the tax treatment of income accruing from strips. The availability of long-dated zero coupon bonds, however, may prove attractive to institutional investors with long investment horizons (such as pension funds and insurance companies).

All of these actions may have produced a relatively large and liquid market. The bid-ask spread of the most traded issue, the 10-year federal government bond, has been declining steadily since 2003; in 2005, it was only 5 basis points. The same trend has been experienced by several other bonds. Annual turnover as a percentage of the previous year's outstanding stock of the specified instrument has been in the range of 800% since 2003.

Development of the Private Bond Market

As mentioned above, the unstable conditions of the Mexican economy since the introduction of a formal private debt market in 1982 seem to have constantly hindered its development. However, the recent stabilization of the economy, the expansion of the government yield curve, and the introduction of the CBs and other financial reforms may have contributed to the dramatic change in bond issues observed since 2001.

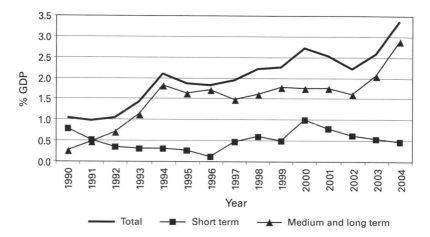

Figure 3.5
Outstanding domestic bonds of private sector (percent of GDP). Source: Bolsa Mexicana de Valores.

The domestic market has continued to increase in outstanding value, rising from 1% to 3.34% of GDP between 1990 and 2004 (figure 3.5). This increase corresponds with both an increase in issuances and an increase in these issuances' maturity. The value of issuing debt as a percentage of GDP began to increase in 2002 after seven years of stagnation, reaching a maximum of 1.2% of GDP in 2004.

Even though corporations have increased the amount of medium- and long-term issues in recent years, most securities issued are floating-rate and inflation-indexed bonds. Issuing is still concentrated among the largest and most credit-worthy firms: almost 80% of issued bonds are still rated AA− or higher.[27] Moreover, some of these firms have found it more convenient to tap the international markets for funds. Thus, the market continues to be very small.

In contrast to their appetite for government debt, foreign investors have for the most part shunned corporate bonds. There are at least three possible explanations. First, the small size of these markets means that it is costly for investors to dedicate the time and effort needed to evaluate every issuer. This same problem makes the market for those securities relatively illiquid and even more costly to investors. Second, investors may still be skeptical about how much could be recovered in case of defaults, even in light of the reformed Bankruptcy Law (Ley de Concursos Mercantiles, LCM) enacted in 2000, that seems to have decreased the average time spent in bankruptcy and the frequency of absolute priority rule violations (APR), as well as raised average recovery rates (Gamboa and Schneider 2006).[28] This reluctance may be based on some bankruptcies of Mexican firms where large international institutional investors had exposure and were involved in ensuing legal battles under the old bankruptcy law, namely Altos Hornos de México S. A. (AHMSA) and Grupo Mexicano de Desarrollo (GMD). On the other hand, the issuance of CBs is more closely linked with the possibility of designing trust funds as a way to avoid bankruptcy procedures, and this type of contract was already permitted by Mexican law long before the insolvency regime reform.[29] Third, most foreigners are subject to a 4.9% withholding tax on interest paid by corporate securities, unlike federal government bonds, which are tax free.

Since 2003 the financial sector has been a major source of this boom, especially in medium- and long-term issuances. In turn, issuance of nonfinancial or corporate firms has experienced a more modest expansion; this sector's placements increased from 0.23% to 0.55% of GDP between 1994 and 2003, and only 0.34% of GDP in 2004. The number of firms issuing this type of debt has recovered since the sharp decline experienced during the 1994–1995 crisis. However, it is still below the peak of 48 issuing firms reached in 1993. Between 2000 and 2004, the annual average number of issuing firms was 21.

These basic statistics suggest that the increased demand for long-term instruments has not contributed significantly to improving more firms' access to financing. For the firms already accessing this market, however, the conditions and available resources seem to have improved, as the average value per issue has risen from around US$30 million in the mid-1990s to more than US$100 million since 2000. This may indicate either that issuing firms are now larger or that the same firms can obtain greater resources.

The average maturity of corporate debt issues has also increased. It stayed below 3 years until 1999 but has reached levels above 5 years since 2002. At the same time the average cost of financing has declined significantly from an average annual yield of 20% between 1991 and 1994 to 10% or below from 2002 onward. This corresponds with the declining trend of inflation after the crisis, remaining below 6% since late 2001. The demand for long-term instruments by various intermediaries, the result of AFOREs and excess international liquidity may also have contributed to keeping interest rates low. Foreign investors have additionally shown interest in Mexican companies, not only in Mexican markets but also in foreign markets, in spite of issuing in

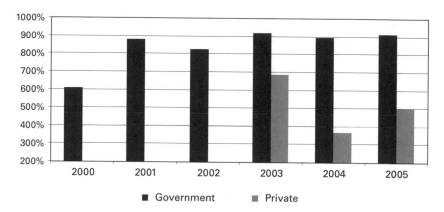

Figure 3.6
Annual turnover as percentage of previous year outstanding stock. Source: Banco de México.

pesos. Although the Europesos securities have been growing, it is still a small and very concentrated market. By June 2006, market value was close to US$6 billion; 32 Europesos bonds were issued by 16 companies, of which 5 of them had 70% of the market. Moreover, not all of these were Mexican companies.

These indicators notwithstanding, corporate debt is lagging behind the government bond market and other corporate Latin American markets, especially in terms of liquidity. While the average turnover for government securities has remained above 800% since 2002, the average turnover for private securities has stayed below 700%. Moreover, the number of traded private instruments does not even include half of the outstanding ones.

Another recent development of the bond market in Mexico is securitization. The emergence of a domestic market for securitized assets and expected future flows can be largely attributed to the creation of the CBs, because it provided an easy way to build trusts with this type of instrument. The first issue of asset-backed securities (ABS) was in 2001, backed with construction bridge loans. The largest and most dynamic type, and the one with the highest potential, is that of mortgage-backed securities (MBS). These two segments comprise 60% of total issues. The rest of the market includes the securitization of toll road revenues, of federal transfers to states and municipalities, and of consumer loans for home improvements issued by the Fund for Promoting and Guaranteeing the Workers' Consumption (Fondo de Fomento y Garantía para el Consumo de los Trabajadores, FONACOT).[30]

The first domestic residential MBS was for MXN600 million; it was underwritten by Credit Suisse First Boston (CSFB) in December 2003 on the basis of mortgages originated by Hipotecaria su Casita and GMAC Hipotecaria, both special purpose financing firms (*sociedades financieras de objeto limitado*, SOFOLs). Since then, this market has grown steadily, with most structures securitizing pools of mortgages to low- and middle-income borrowers. The Sociedad Hipotecaria Federal (SHF), a state-owned development bank, began operations in late 2001 with the objective of promoting a more cohesive and sound market for MBSs.[31] It has encouraged the issuance of bonds with homogeneous characteristics, including the standardization of documentation, the use of mortgage credit insurance, and the reopening of issues. It has also played a role as intermediary and liquidity provider in developing a nascent MBSs secondary market.

At present securitization still accounts for a very small part of total credit to the private sector. But several market segments have a strong growth potential, such as the mortgage credit one. The reason for this is the severe shortage of housing for low- and middle-income families and the growing demand for commercial office space. SOFOLs have been very active in providing mortgages for low-income families and financing bridge loans to developers of low-income housing projects. Because SOFOLs can only fund themselves through government lending agencies or in wholesale markets, securitization of their receivables has been a welcome alternative fundraising source.

Empirical Analysis

First-Time Issuing Firms

In this section we analyze the contribution of the previously mentioned factors to the growth of the corporate bond market in Mexico. In particular, we are interested in identifying the importance of changes in three types of variables:

1. Changes in firm characteristics: size, leverage, growth or investment opportunities, liquidity, growth of more capital demanding sectors, previous investment, and so forth.

2. Changes in the economy: lower international interest rates, a more stable economy (inflation, government debt), and funds managed by AFOREs.

3. Other financial reforms, including the creation of CBs and the development of a long-term fixed-yield government debt market.

We think this distinction is relevant to understanding the impact of the reforms and this market's future prospects. As noted above, the positive trend in the activity of the corporate debt market since 2001 coincides with a very liquid international economy, more stable macroeconomic conditions in Mexico and improvements in certain characteristics of firms that make them more reliable. In order to evaluate the impact of the financial reforms, it is crucial to estimate whether a positive trend persists even after controlling for macroeconomic conditions and firms' characteristics. Moreover, it is interesting to learn which of these variables could best explain the positive trend not only in number of issues but also in their conditions.

The data for firms' characteristics and issues was built from the financial statements of firms listed at the BMV combined with information from the stock market yearbooks (*anuarios bursátiles*). The database includes nonfinancial firms that are either public or that have issued debt; however, it covers only a fraction of the population, ranging from 11% in 1994 to 100% in 2004. The lack of information in either financial statements or the yearbooks reduced the possibility of a complete matching between these sources. Data for macroeconomic variables, both national and international, was obtained from the BM, the Federal Reserve Economic Data for the US, and JP Morgan.

The first estimation consists of a probit model to determine the impact of the mentioned variables on the probability of issuing debt (endogenous variable given by the first issuing of long-term debt). To avoid endogeneity problems, we only include the first issuance of long-term debt by a given firm during the sample period, and we do not include that firm again. In addition, explanatory variables are lagged one period.

The complete list of the variables considered is presented below. The indicated sign is the one expected in this regression. For this evaluation of the possible impact of the firm characteristics, we separate variables into two groups: those affecting investors' supply of financial resources and those affecting the firms' demand for external financing—although some variables may affect both sides of the market.

The variables affecting supply of financial resources are the following:

• *Size (logarithm of assets)*. The size of the firm is one of the most important variables affecting the supply of funds for the firm, because it helps to solve the problems generated by asymmetric information that characterize most financial markets. In particular, assets can work as collateral (+).

• *Leverage (total debt/total assets)*. Leverage's effect may go either way: higher leverage captures better access to credit when this is not captured by other variables; in turn, it increases vulnerability and therefore makes the firm less attractive to investors (?).

• *Liquidity position (short-term debt/total debt)*. It captures the rollover risk associated with the accumulation of short-term liabilities (−).

• *Currency mismatch (CM = (foreign liabilities − exports)/total liabilities)*. For a certain supply of external resources, the higher the mismatch, the higher the firm's vulnerability and the less attractive it is to investors (−).

• *Maturity mismatch (MM = (current liabilities/total liabilities) − (current assets/total assets))*. A higher maturity mismatch increases the firm's fragility and makes it less attractive to investors (−).

• *Rate of return on assets (ROA = operations revenue/assets)*. It measures the firm's profitability and has a positive effect on the supply of financing resources (+).

• *Growth opportunities (sales growth as a proxy)*. In a perfect information world with complete markets, this should be the only variable affecting the supply of external resources (+).

The variables affecting the demand for financial resources are the following:

• *Liquidity*. Liquidity is defined here as: *Cash flows measured as net income after taxes + depreciation − inventory accumulation − increase of accounts receivable + increase in accounts payable − increase in interest and income taxes payable − increase in other liabilities; Cash + cash equivalents + short-term investments*. Cash flows are intended to reflect the firm's funds generated through its productive operations. These funds are available unconditionally and can be used to invest, whether the firm faces a high external financing cost or not. An alternative measure of internal funds is available liquidity. An increase in either of these two variables decreases the demand of the firm for external funds (−).

• *Investment.* It is measured as the difference in the reported total capital between periods t and $t - 1$. Reported total capital is given by the book value of machinery, equipment, and real estate minus accumulated depreciation (+).

• *Investment opportunities.* Sales growth is a proxy for investment opportunities that captures the firm's needs for external funds (+).

• *Currency mismatch (CM).* A higher currency mismatch will imply greater firm interest in issuing in pesos, but it may also reflect better access to foreign financial markets at low cost (?).

• *Maturity mismatch (MM).* Similar to the currency mismatch, it may increase the firm's interest in issuing long-term debt or simply reflect better access to foreign financial markets (?).

• *Rate of return on assets (ROA).* A more profitable firm may have lower external resource needs, but this may also indicate greater investment opportunities and resource needs (?)

• *Average cost of financing (financing cost/total liabilities).* This variable will have a negative impact to the extent that it is correlated with the current funds cost (−).

The macroeconomic environment is captured in the following variables:

• *Inflation.* This variable captures fiscal discipline and national macroeconomic performance (−).

• *Emerging Markets Bond Index (EMBI).* By assessing the risk conditions perceived by foreign investors, we consider that reductions in this variable should promote further investment (−).

• *SIEFOREs/GDP.* This ratio captures liquidity in the national market from funds managed by AFOREs (+).

• *3-month T-bill rate.* Lower rates in the United States, consistent with favorable liquidity conditions throughout the world, should reflect positively in the firm's access to international resources (−).

Finally, through a 2000 dummy variable we expect to capture the effects of the creation of CBs, the development of a long-term fixed-yield government debt market, and other financial reforms (+).

We will interpret that the financial reforms and other policy actions had an impact if any of the following applies:

• The coefficient of funds managed by AFOREs is positive and significant.

• Inflation has a negative and significant coefficient.

• The dummy variable that separates the periods before and after 2000 has a positive and significant coefficient.

• The interaction between the 2000 dummy with other variables has a significant coefficient.

Table 3.1 presents the mean and median of the major variables used in the regression analysis. By dividing these basic statistics between the two analyzed periods, changes in macroeconomic conditions and in certain firm characteristics are evident. Moreover, improvements in the bond market conditions are reflected in the increase in average maturity, the decrease in yield, and the increase in number of issues.

Because there are only a few first-time issuers in the database, it was necessary to restrict the number of exogenous variables in the analysis. Considering the relevance of finding the impact of certain variables with no variation among firms within one year, it is crucial to estimate standard errors with clusters by years in order to draw the correct inferences from them. We include interactive effects of the macro variables with firm size (measured as the log of assets) in order to allow for varying effects regarding this firm characteristic. The baseline probit regression contains all the variables listed above with the exception of the 2000 dummy. This variable is added in a second version of the regression. The third specification includes the 2000 dummy and excludes the other macroeconomic variables. The fourth and fifth specifications correspond to the periods 1994–1999 and 2000–2004, so the 2000 dummy is excluded also.

Table 3.2 shows the estimation results. Most of the firm variables proved not to be significant: leverage coefficient, cash flows, currency mismatch, maturity mismatch, sales growth, investment rates, and the average cost of financing; for this reason they are not reported. The main findings are summarized as follows:

• The log of assets coefficient is positive and declining by firm size; however, it is only significant for the second-period regression. Thus, a major factor affecting the probability of issuing debt after 2000 is the size of the firm, but its marginal effect is less important for large firms.

Table 3.1
Descriptive Statistics of Corporate Bonds

	1994–1999		2000–2004	
	Mean	Median	Mean	Median
Macro variables:				
EMBI	850	782	683	683
3-month T-bill rate	5.01	5.03	2.79	2.79
SIEFOREs/GDP	0.00	0.00	0.04	0.04
Annual inflation (%)	17.84	14.81	4.00	4.00
Firm variables (not significantly different):				
Leverage	0.45	0.44	0.45	0.43
Export/sales	0.16	0.04	0.15	0.03
Maturity mismatch	0.28	0.25	0.30	0.26
Return on assets	0.07	0.07	0.07	0.07
Firm variables (significantly different):				
Cash flow	−0.06	−0.01	0.06	1.11
$\Delta\%$ sales	−0.13	−0.14	0.57	0.04
$\Delta\%$ investment	0.07	0.01	0.73	0.01
Average cost of financing	0.13	0.10	0.06	0.06
Currency mismatch	0.17	0.23	0.13	0.21
Log assets	14.25	14.25	15.08	15.08
Issue characteristics:				
Maturity (days)	1,241	1,091	1,765	1,820
Yield (%)	21.22	20.78	12.88	11.53
Amount issued	1,748	950	1,393	730
Number of issues	16	16	71	71

Note: EMBI = Emerging Markets Bond Index.
Source: For macro variables, EMBI: JP Morgan; 3-month T-bill: Federal Reserve Economic Data; Mexican variables: Banco de México. For firm variables and issue characteristics, authors' calculations based on financial statements of firms listed at the Bolsa Mexicana de Valores and Anuarios Bursátiles.

• Return on assets coefficients are positive and significant in all experiments (except for the first-period regression); this is expected for both the demand and supply effects and considering that it could be a proxy for growth opportunities.

• The inflation rate coefficient is significant but does not have the expected negative sign.

• The 3-month T-bill rate has the expected negative sign and with a declining impact for larger firms.

• The SIEFOREs coefficient is positive and significant. The effect is larger for smaller firms.

• The dummy for 2000 is only significant when macroeconomic variables are excluded, suggesting that the expected positive effects of financial reforms on the corporate bond market have not materialized yet.

Even though this probit analysis does not show a significant improvement on the probability of issuing as a result of the 2000 reforms and certain variables did not show the expected sign, there could be a positive effect on the financing conditions. We explore if there is evidence of a change in the amount issued, maturity, or yield of the issues during the analyzed period by estimating tobit models for these three endogenous variables, hence controlling for their censoring distribution. In order to control for the size of the firm, we use as the amount issued the sum of total issues over total assets; both the maturity and yield of issues are used as averages weighted by amount issued. The specifications, the explanatory variables, and expected sign are the same as in the Probit regression (notice that the expected signs for the yield regression are the opposite of those stated above).

Table 3.3 shows the estimation outcomes. The main results are the following:

• The ROA coefficient was positive and significant in most of the exercises.

• The coefficients of the macro variables do not appear to be important, except for the trivial case of the inflation rate in the yield regression.

• The amount of assets managed by AFOREs as a proportion of GDP is significant and has the expected signs. It is positive for the amount issued and the maturity models and negative for the yield model; its effects are larger for smaller firms (as we found in the probit regression).

• Once again, the 2000 dummy is significant only when we exclude the macro variables.

The results from these different models indicate that this market has been largely influenced by macroeconomic conditions, the expansion of resources financed by AFOREs, and the expansion of international liquidity. Although Mexico's financial reforms might have had several positive effects on financial markets, these have not been fully reflected

Table 3.2
Probit Estimate: Endogenous Variable = 1 if Issuing

	1994–2004		Including dummy for period after 1999 (1994–2000)	
	Mean	dF/dx	Mean	dF/dx
Log assets $(t-1)$	14.60	0.02 (0.019)	14.60	0.019 (0.019)
Log assets squared $(t-1)$	216.48	−0.0004 (0.00051)	216.48	−0.0004 (0.0005)
Return on assets $(t-1)$	0.0676	0.0680 (0.024)***	0.0676	0.0660 (0.025)***
EMBI	777.75	0.0000883 (0.00006)	777.75	0.0000824 (0.00006)
Log assets $(t-1)$ * EMBI	11330.30	−0.0000068 (0.0000045)	11330.30	−0.0000064 (0.000004)
Inflation rate	0.13	0.395 (0.164)**	0.13	0.392 (0.162)**
Log assets $(t-1)$ * inflation	1.86	−0.0310 (0.0116)**	1.86	−0.0310 (0.000004)
3-month T-bill rate	4.17	−0.02 (0.009)**	4.17	−0.018 (0.009)**
Log assets $(t-1)$ * 3-month T-bill rate	60.24	0.001 (0.00064)***	60.24	0.001 (0.0006)***
SIEFOREs/GDP	0.02	1.645 (0.948)*	0.02	1.784 (0.966)*
Log assets $(t-1)$ * SIEFOREs/GDP	0.25	−0.089 (0.061)	0.25	−0.089 (0.059)
Dummy [2000]	—	— —	0.37	−0.004 (0.005)
Observations		1408		1408
LR chi^2		—		—
Pseudo R^2		0.157		0.158
Observed P		0.023		0.023
Predicted P (at x bar)		0.008		0.007

Note: Standard errors in parentheses. Normal density evaluated at the sample mean. A blank means the variable is not included, or is dropped because of collinearity. *, **, and *** denote significance at 10%, 5%, and 1% levels, respectively.

Including dummy for period after 1999 and excluding macro variables (1994–2000)		First period: 1994–1999		Second period: 2000–2004	
Mean	dF/dx	Mean	dF/dx	Mean	dF/dx
14.60	0.026 (0.021)	14.45	0.0001 (0.013)	14.84	0.19 (0.045)***
216.48	−0.0007 (0)	212.15	0.0000722 (0.0004)	223.80	−0.002 (0.001)
0.0676	0.0960 (0.03473)***	0.0666	0.0240 (0.029)	0.0693	0.2350 (0.04)***
—	—	840.74	−0.0000392 (0.00003)	671.16	0.0009 (0.00008)***
—	—	12186.00	0.0000023 (0.0000018)	9882.28	−0.0000649 (0.000005)***
—	—	0.18	0.103 (0.126)	0.04	1.283 (0.631)**
—	—	2.60	−0.0090 (0.0000018)	0.61	−0.0500 (0.000005)***
—	—	—	—	—	—
—	—	—	—	—	—
—	—	0.004	2.271 (1.826)	0.04	24.381 (1.581)***
—	—	0.05	−0.142 (0.111)*	0.58	−1.555 (0.111)***
0.37	0.023 (0.006)***	—	—	—	—
	1408		885		523
	—		—		—
	0.109		0.154		0.118
	0.023		0.010		0.044
	0.013		0.004		0.025

Table 3.3
Tobit Estimates

	Endogenous variable: Amount issued over assets				
	1994–2004 dF/dx	Including dummy for period after 1999 (1994–2004) dF/dx	Including dummy for period after 1999 and excluding macro variables (1994–2004) dF/dx	First period: 1994–1999 excluding interactive effects dF/dx	Second period: 2000–2004 excluding interactive effects dF/dx
Log assets $(t-1)$	0.0001 (0.0002)	0.0001 (0.0002)	0.0001 (0.0002)	−0.0000929 (0.0004)	0.0001 (0.0002)
Log assets squared $(t-1)$	−0.0000013 (0.000006)	−0.0000011 (0.000006)	−0.0000035 (0.000006)	0.0000057 (0.000013)	0.0000012 (0.000008)
Return on assets $(t-1)$	0.001 (0.0004)***	0.001 (0.0004)***	0.001 (0.0004)***	0.0009 (0.0007)	0.001 (0.0004)***
EMBI	−0.0000002 (0)*	−0.0000002 (0)*	—	−0.0000001 (0)	−0.0000003 (0)
Log assets $(t-1)$ ∗ EMBI	— —	— —	— —	— —	— —
Inflation rate	−0.001 (−1.58)	−0.001 (0.0008)	— —	−0.001 (0.0008)	0.003 (0.003)
Log assets $(t-1)$ ∗ inflation	— —	— —	— —	— —	— —
3-month T-bill rate	0.0000722 (0.000029)**	0.0000846 (0.000046)*	— —	— —	— —
Log assets $(t-1)$ ∗ 3-month T-bill rate	— —	— —	— —	— —	— —
SIEFOREs/GDP	0.041 (0.015)***	0.044 (0.017)**	— —	0.003 (0.072)	0.077 (0.034)**
Log assets $(t-1)$ ∗ SIEFOREs/GDP	−0.002 (0.0009)**	−0.002 (0.0009)**	— —	0.0002 (0.004)	−0.005 (0.002)**
Dummy [2000]	— —	−0.000068 (0.0001)	0.0002 (0.000063)***	— —	— —
Constant	−0.002 (0.001)*	−0.002 (0.001)*	−0.002 (0.001)	−0.0005 (0.003)	−0.003 (0.002)
Observations	1363	1363	1363	871	492
LR chi^2	62.27	62.4	48.66	16.99	27.52
Pseudo R^2	−0.251	−0.2516	−0.1962	−0.3391	−0.1245
Uncensored observations	38	38	38	10	28

Note: Standard errors in parentheses. Zero is taken as the lower limit. A blank means the observation is not included in the specification, or is dropped due to collinearity. *, **, and *** denote significance at 10%, 5%, and 1% levels, respectively.

Table 3.3
(continued)

	Endogenous variable: Yield of issues (weighted average)				
	1994–2004 dF/dx	Including dummy for period after 1999 (1994–2004) dF/dx	Including dummy for period after 1999 and excluding macro variables (1994–2004) dF/dx	First period: 1994–1999 excluding interactive effects dF/dx	Second period: 2000–2004 excluding interactive effects dF/dx
Log assets $(t-1)$	20.227 (14.669)	12.878 (0.98)	−6.01 (17.227)	−11.807 (3.657)**	61.926 (36.031)
Log assets squared $(t-1)$	−0.607 (0.426)	−0.35 (−0.91)	0.183 (0.544)	0.357 (0.113)*	−1.938 (1.138)
Return on assets $(t-1)$	17.729 (16.619)	25.659 (1.73)***	0.822 (18.729)	−22.737 (6.889)**	83.101 (38.262)*
EMBI	−0.071 (0.04)	−0.026 (−0.69)	—	−0.0007 (0.003)	0.041 (0.022)
Log assets $(t-1)$ * EMBI	0.003 (0.002)	0.001 (0.65)	—	—	—
Inflation rate	430.587 (379.976)	306.641 (0.92)	—	64.238 (4.157)***	229.181 (160.847)
Log assets $(t-1)$ * inflation	−24.189 (23.51)	−15.018 (−0.72)	—	—	—
3-month T bill rate	−0.675 (9.772)	−0.489 (−0.06)	—	—	—
Log assets $(t-1)$ * 3-month T-bill rate	−0.045 (0.604)	−0.201 (−0.38)	—	—	—
SIEFOREs/GDP	1751.411 (1073.28)	713.758 (0.7)	—	−1631.426 (369.139)**	1972.675 (3356.502)
Log assets $(t-1)$ * SIEFOREs/GDP	−126.927 (66.502)*	−90.087 (−1.51)	—	59.75 (22.023)*	−92.503 (185.389)
Dummy [2000]	— —	12.611 (2.62)	−7.574 (2.329)***	—	—
Constant	−136.441 (129.554)	−83.393 (−0.73)	68.492 (135.785)	114.928 (27.963)**	−549.092 (303.438)
Observations	22	22	22	10	12
LR chi²	34.71	40.68	11.1	49.42	6.71
Pseudo R²	0.2436	0.2855	0.0779	0.7761	0.102
Uncensored observations	22	22	22	10	12

Table 3.3
(continued)

	Endogenous variable: Maturity (weighted average)				
	1994–2004 dF/dx	Including dummy for period after 1999 (1994–2004) dF/dx	Including dummy for period after 1999 and excluding macro variables (1994–20004) dF/dx	First period: 1994–1999 excluding interactive effects dF/dx	Second period: 2000–2004 excluding interactive effects dF/dx
Log assets ($t-1$)	−843.435 (2970.44)	−863.915 (2986.37)	1530.618 (2263.557)	−968.188 (4130.118)	2087.689 (2923.324)
Log assets squared ($t-1$)	26.347 (78.079)	27.596 (78.173)	−31.441 (73.229)	58.689 (133.403)	28.054 (94.281)
Return on assets ($t-1$)	15025.9 (4533.939)***	14982.53 (4535.716)***	14511.34 (4492.949)***	8390.687 (7533.03)	18189.7 (5691.155)***
EMBI	−1.257 (14.478)	−1.916 (14.512)	— —	−1.178 (3.292)	−4.559 (3.448)
Log assets ($t-1$) * EMBI	−0.08 (0.936)	−0.048 (0.936)	— —	— —	— —
Inflation rate	61149.11 (76184.37)	59146.75 (82326.07)	— —	−12586.93 (8165.164)	22827.34 (38921.01)
Log assets ($t-1$) * inflation	−4786.89 (4885.919)	−4774.078 (5250.441)	— —	— —	— —
3-month T-bill rate	−4703.056 (3561.059)	−4440.014 (3633.42)	— —	— —	— —
Log assets ($t-1$) * 3-month T-bill rate	353.016 (232.294)	346.681 (234.54)	— —	— —	— —
SIEFOREs/GDP	147131.7 (349479.9)	187057.4 (364561.2)	— —	36796.84 (692817.9)	953700.3 (414871.3)**
Log assets ($t-1$) * SIEFOREs/GDP	−4075.708 (22002.77)	−4726.83 (22303.76)	— —	2435.313 (44252.24)	−62956.86 (26520.44)**
Dummy [2000]	— —	−938.999 (2033.759)	2725.883 (711.532)***	— —	— —
Constant	−3159.897 (30532.43)	−3665.791 (30857.95)	−25954.25 (17699.04)	−4780.506 (32142.31)	−43459.9 (27268.61)
Observations	1363	1363	1363	871	492
LR chi^2	69.64	69.85	52.44	18.09	29.65
Pseudo R^2	0.0703	0.0705	0.0529	0.0663	0.0428
Uncensored observations	38	38	38	10	28

in those markets' development, and it may be worthwhile to study this last finding. To this end, we next discuss the results of the survey among investors that asks them about the impact of different reforms (such as the quality of legal recourse in the event of default or the investment limits) and the relevance of various bond market characteristics (such as the quality of the credit rating and the capitalization level).

Investor Survey

For this project we surveyed investor firms among a total of 41 banks, BEHs, AFOREs, mutual funds, and insurance companies. This sample is made up mostly of large investment firms in order to have results that are representative of the industry. We applied a qualitative survey and a template for the portfolio data, either through email or by phone, to the treasurer or chief investor, trader, or manager of the financial institution. We received most answers to the perception questions by email and the remaining answers through telephone conferences.

In the analysis of the survey results, we were interested in determining the factors affecting the demand for different securities as well as in understanding how specialized portfolios are. In regards to factors affecting bond demand, the questionnaire contains inquiries referring to present market characteristics and investors' perceptions of the effectiveness of several specific reforms, including both past reforms and measures likely in the future. In addition to describing the summary statistics, we used a descriptive/exploratory technique known as correspondence analysis to further analyze questions with a perception or valuation component. This technique is designed to analyze simple two-way and multi-way contingency tables containing some measure of correspondence between the rows and columns. The results provide information that makes it possible to explore the structure of the table's categorical variables. This analysis seeks to represent the categories' interrelationships of row and column variables in a two-dimensional map.

A distance is defined as the differences between the pattern of relative frequencies for the rows across the columns, and columns across the rows, which are to be reproduced in a lower-dimensional solution. These distances, represented by the coordinates in the respective space, are not simple Euclidean distances computed from the relative row or column frequencies; instead, they are weighted distances so that the metric in the lower dimensional space is a chi-square metric.

The plot, or correspondence map, displays two of the dimensions that emerge from a principal components analysis of point distances. Points are displayed in relation to these dimensions. Let us emphasize that one cannot precisely interpret the distance between a row point and a column point under any form of standardization; instead, one must make an imprecise general statement, such as noting where particular row and column points appear in the same map quadrant. Circles around the points are drawn as a visual aid for clustering the results.

Results revealed that foreign ownership is greater than 49% in more than 41.5% of respondent firms, while 51.2% are completely Mexican. On average, each investor manages seven portfolios (7.30); the average portfolio size in 2004 was US$2,233 million.

The local corporate bond market characteristics that investors regard as most limiting for demanding corporate assets, based on the correspondence map, are the following: low liquidity of the secondary market, low market capitalization, low quality of legal recourse in the event of default, and excessive regulatory/legal constraints (figure 3.7).

Low quality of clearing and settlement systems, insufficient time for the analysis of new placements, high insolvency risk, absence of a complete benchmark yield curve, unfavorable taxation relative to other instruments, low returns, lack of timely and adequate information about issuer, insufficient clarity of the emission book, and low quality (or high cost) of the credit rating system—all of these factors are not regarded as characteristics of the market or relevant factors in the portfolio decision. The absence of a benchmark market index to track was considered by some as limiting and by others as an existing characteristic, leading us to think that information about this index is not completely available to all.

The two changes that investors regard as having the most positive impact in the demand for corporate bonds were the existence of a price vector produced by the private sector and a complete benchmark yield curve. The existence of legal recourse in the event of default was considered a matter in which the advance is insufficient by several respondents. In contrast, the possibility of establishing repurchase agreements was not regarded as important in the portfolio decision of several investors.

Because of the econometric analysis results, it is important to stress two aspects of the previous discussion. First, even though the probit and tobit estimations suggest that the financial reforms do not matter

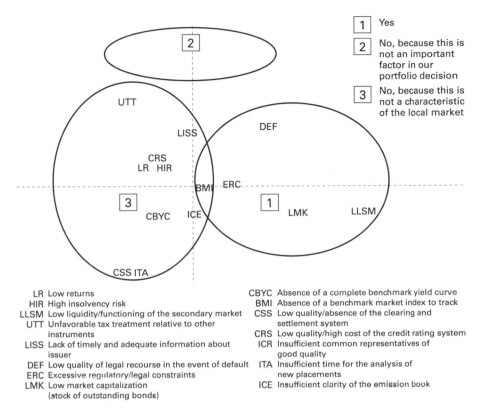

LR Low returns
HIR High insolvency risk
LLSM Low liquidity/functioning of the secondary market
UTT Unfavorable tax treatment relative to other
     instruments
LISS Lack of timely and adequate information about
     issuer
DEF Low quality of legal recourse in the event of default
ERC Excessive regulatory/legal constraints
LMK Low market capitalization
     (stock of outstanding bonds)

CBYC Absence of a complete benchmark yield curve
BMI Absence of a benchmark market index to track
CSS Low quality/absence of the clearing and
     settlement system
CRS Low quality/high cost of the credit rating system
ICR Insufficient common representatives of
     good quality
ITA Insufficient time for the analysis of
     new placements
ICE Insufficient clarity of the emission book

Figure 3.7
Investor survey: Factors limiting demand: Do you think the following characteristics of
the local corporate bond market limit your demand for this kind of asset? Rating of different restrictions by type of institutions (1: very restrictive; 5: does not restrict portfolio
decisions).

once the macroeconomic developments are included, investors regard
some market characteristics affected by financial reforms—such as the
presence of a complete benchmark yield curve—as important in their
demand decisions. Furthermore, investors also ranked as important
the existence of private price vendors and the quality of the credit rating system, two characteristics that would not have been possible to
add in a meaningful econometric estimation because of their timing.
On the other hand, the perception of the quality of recourse in the
case of default would suggest that those particular reforms have been
insufficient.

The future changes that would be regarded as most beneficial in
increasing demand for corporate bonds are the existence of credit

insurers and the presence of incentives for asset placers to become market makers. In contrast, the existence of a benchmark market index for tracking as well as the existence of consensus regarding the valuation of illiquid assets could be considered as beneficial, but the firms believe that progress in these two matters is insufficient.

The majority answered that the current regulatory framework imposes restrictions on asset allocation. Among them, insurance companies and AFOREs perceived themselves as the most restricted (all respondents answered that they were to some degree restricted), followed by mutual funds and brokerage houses. On the other hand, more than two-thirds of the banks and private pension funds answered that they were not restricted. Investment limits by type of instrument, restrictions to investment in nonfinancial private sector bonds, and high capitalization requirements for corporate bonds are ranked as the most restrictive conditions.

In the absence of restrictions, most investors would increase their portfolio allocation in derivatives, bonds issued by private companies, foreign assets, and trackers. Additional resources would be channeled to these asset types as well. In turn, most investors would decrease their portfolio allocation in government bonds. Stock holding would remain unchanged.

Private bonds indexed to the consumer price index (CPI), bonds issued by AAA institutions (World Bank, IDB, etc.) in local currency, and asset-backed securities would be the most welcomed ones by respondents if they became widely available. However, public bonds indexed to the CPI, as well as foreign bonds and stocks issued in the local stock exchange, would also have a positive reception.

Most firms agree on the following claims: the yield curve provided by public bonds is crucial for pricing corporate bonds; a large stock of public sector bonds is important for the development of the corporate bond market; and if the yield on government bonds were to increase significantly and that of private bonds remained constant, they would sell private bonds and buy government bonds. However, fewer firms agree that government and corporate bonds are substitutes for each other in the firm's portfolio. This last set of statements regarding the potential crowding out or crowding in between public and private bonds probably deserves further attention in the future. However, in light of both the previous answers about the importance of the yield curve and the strong efforts of the federal government to improve its debt composition in recent years, we are tempted to favor the conclusion that public and private funds are more complements than substitutes.

As a conclusion to this section, let us point out three aspects of the institutional framework where Mexican financial authorities have been promoting changes that the survey answers suggest as interesting lines for future analysis. The first, briefly mentioned before, involves changes in the insolvency, trust funds, and the general debt collection frameworks. The second change refers to legal investment constraints and tax arrangements that prevail for different financial institutions. The third change includes market microstructure reforms such as advances in clearing and settlement systems or the creation of a market makers program for government bonds.[32]

Final Remarks

Since 2001, Mexico has experienced a sharp increase in the size of its long-term debt market, mainly in the government segment, but the corporate market has grown as well. From the econometric analysis we can conclude that macroeconomic stability, low international interest rates, and pension fund reform are the major elements shaping the recent developments of the corporate bond market. In addition, we found that financial reforms and the lengthening of the government bonds yield curve provided no additional explanation. Regarding the investors' survey, the major conclusion was that the lack of liquidity and low capitalization are important deterrents to holding corporate bonds.

It is important to emphasize that at this stage we cannot claim that there has been a significant change in access to this market by new firms. Some tentative explanations for the limited participation of new non-financial firms to this market are:

• Real sector factors that have affected economic growth. The U.S. recession of 2001 and the entrance of China into the World Trade Organization had negative effects on the Mexican real sector, particularly manufacturing. The rigidity of labor markets and other factors have been deterrents for the entrance into new markets.

• The investment regime of the mandatory pension funds (AFOREs) implies that only securities issued by large and high-rated firms are demanded by these intermediaries.

• The lack of financing options for small and medium firms, either through private capital or from banks, limits the number of new firms that can enter the bond market.

• After the short boom of the bond market in the early 1990s, investors experienced significant capital losses with the crisis. These might have affected confidence in new or lower-rated firms.

• It takes longer to get the benefits of this emerging debt market in smaller- and lower-rated firms, so it might be that it is too soon to see any significant result in these types of firms.

Nonetheless, several positive welfare effects can be attributed to the development of this market:

• The financing cost and the available maturity have improved for firms that can access this market.

• Some firms might have the opportunity to access additional resources through financial intermediaries that can issue bonds. This has been particularly noticeable for construction firms.

• The resources obtained through the bond market have also contributed to improving access to mortgages by middle-income families.

One policy measure that may encourage corporate financing through the market is moving toward structured securities. This proposal is based on our finding that the major deterrent to investors in this market is the lack of liquidity, and on the fact that the fastest-growing segment of this market has been related to housing, where standardization was enhanced by direct government intervention. Certain actions taken in the MBS market can be used to promote similar structures beyond residential housing. First, standardized securities are crucial to guaranteeing the needed liquidity that cannot be achieved by individual issues of medium-sized firms. Second, private insurance companies are already entering the market of MBS to grant mortgage credit insurance.

Further actions to be considered include the following: the promotion of MBS for real estate other than housing, so that firms could make use of this type of collateral; the identification of a common asset between groups of firms that could potentially be used as the standard collateral to securitize (e.g., receivables); the definition of characteristics needed to standardize the credit risk of different firms' issues (e.g., financial guarantee insurance); and development banks that act as catalyzers of standardized asset types (e.g., insuring, pooling of loans).

In addition to securitization, another strategy that needs further research is the importance of providing private bonds a level playing field with respect to government securities by eliminating the withholding tax for foreign investors.

Acknowledgments

We thank Guillermo Babatz, Eduardo Borensztein, Kevin Cowan, Barry Eichengreen, Michael Hasenstab, David Margolín, Ugo Panizza, Carlos Pérez Verdía, Alfredo Thorne, and other participants in the Latin-American Research Network on the Development of Latin-American Bond Markets organized by the IDB for comments, suggestions and encouragement. The gathering of the data for this project was possible thanks to Jaime Cortina, Salvador Herrera, Gerardo Leyva, Alejandro Reynoso, Gerardo Rodríguez, Claudia Tapia and Graciela Teruel. We are grateful also for the excellent research assistance of Isaac Baley, Valeria Castellanos, Meney De La Peza, and José Luis Montiel. Lastly, the three anonymous referees for this chapter gave us several helpful recommendations to give it its final form.

The views expressed in this document do not necessarily reflect those of either Banco de México or Instituto Tecnológico Autónomo de México.

Notes

1. See chapter 1 by Borenstein, Cowan, Eichengreen, and Panizza in this volume.

2. The findings of La Porta, López de Silanes, and Shleifer (2003) suggest that securities laws matter because they facilitate private contracting rather than provide for public regulatory enforcement. They conclude that financial markets do not prosper when left to market forces alone.

3. The private sector is divided into corporate (or nonfinancial) firms and financial firms.

4. Excessive bank regulation served multiple purposes. These included financing government activities at low cost, implementing industrial policies to promote specific sectors, preserving the financial stability of these institutions, and implementing monetary policy. The list of tools employed included quantitative controls on credit, controls on both deposit and credit interest rates, and legal reserve requirements (through which monetary policy was mainly instrumented).

5. Mancera (1992) provides a thorough description of the Mexican economy's performance during the period of 1954 to 1970 known as stabilizing development (*desarrollo estabilizador*).

6. The first initial public offering was in 1977, and the first issuance of government bonds was in 1978. These were Petrobonos (oil bonds) with a 3-year maturity and quarterly coupons indexed to the price of oil.

7. In 1974 the specialized banking scheme gave way to a multiple banking system whose creation augmented institutional stability and improved economies of scale and scope, as the same institution could offer a variety of products (deposits, savings, mortgages, and trust fund management). Controls on deposit rates were lifted, and an indicator of the funding cost of banks was established.

8. For more details, see Aspe (1993).

9. In 1993, 96% of the total credit of the commercial banks was assigned to the private sector. The monetary creation process became more dependent on the activity of commercial banks.

10. See Banco de México (1994).

11. Tornell, Westermann, and Martínez (2003) analyze the relationship between financial liberalization, growth, and financial crises, finding that in countries with severe credit market imperfections (caused mainly by years of overregulation), financial liberalization may lead to growth at the cost of greater fragility.

12. Political events include the Chiapas rebellion and the assassination of the presidential candidate Colosio, among others.

13. For a more detailed explanation on the consequences of the issue of Tesobonos, see Gil-Díaz and Carstens (1996).

14. By the end of 2006, the government had issued a thirty-year fixed coupon bond.

15. In Mexico, as in many countries, states and municipalities cannot issue foreign debt. Foreign financing, mostly from development agencies, is channeled by the federal government to them through the National Bank of Public Works and Services (Banco Nacional de Obras y Servicios Públicos S.N.C., BANOBRAS).

16. See for instance, Borensztein, Cowan, Eichengreen, and Panizza, op. cit.

17. The Mandatory Pension Fund Act (Ley del Ahorro para el Retiro) distinguishes AFOREs from investment societies specialized in mandatory pension funds (*sociedades de inversión especializadas en fondos de ahorro para el retiro*, SIEFOREs), but for simplicity we will use both terms indistinctively.

18. At that time there was no formal framework for trading derivatives except for a set of dispositions given by BM to carry out "the financial operations known as derivatives" (Banco de México, Circular 2019/95).

19. While the TIIE contract has been used for hedging positions on short-term interest rates, it has also been used actively to replicate fixed to floating interest rate swaps in tenors of up to ten years (through strippable contracts). Domestic intermediaries have made active use of interest rate swaps, but foreign intermediaries appear to have played an even more important role. Offshore trading is informally reported to be significantly larger than the MXN 6 to MXN 8 billion estimated by BM to be traded daily on the domestic market.

20. Other important reforms to the Mutual Funds Law (Ley de Sociedades de Inversión, LSI), the Law of Insurance (Ley de Seguros, LS), the Bankruptcy Law (Ley de Concursos

Mercantiles, LCM), and the Guarantees' Miscellany (Miscelánea de Garantías) are explained in Martínez and Werner (2002).

21. For further details, see LMV, Article 14 bis 7.

22. CBs have largely substituted the two instruments that existed before; that is, debentures (*certificados de participación ordinaria*, CPOs) that protected investors excessively and were costly to issue, and medium-term notes (*pagarés*) that were easy to structure but provided no investor protection.

23. Participation of foreign investors in the local market may have been enhanced to a large extent by the prospect of an upgrade of the rating on Mexico's external debt to investment grade since 1998.

24. This was the result of the well-known problem of "original sin" suffered by emerging economies: in order to secure long-term financing, they had to recur to foreign financing in foreign currency.

25. In August 2006, as part of the debt management strategy of the federal government and Banco de México, BREMs will no longer be issued and instead the central bank will use other federal government bonds (Bonos de Desarrollo del Gobierno Federal, Bondes) to carry out its open market operations.

26. Although IPAB's debt enjoyed full faith and credit backing from the federal government, it used to command a premium of 30 to 60 basis points over the federal government's debt. This was partly due to the controversial nature of the bank bailout program, which prevented the federal government from taking over IPAB's debt. As a result, the agency's debt was subject to distinct congressional approval every year, creating some uncertainty over its financial status. This regime changed in 2006.

27. Mortgage-back securities (MBS) are an exception to this, as they get high gradings by adding a financial guarantee insurance to the structure, despite the lower rating of the originator.

28. According to Gamboa and Schneider (2006), the LCM reform decreased the average time spent in bankruptcy from 7.8 to 2.3 years and the frequency of APR violations decreased from 29% to 2%; it also raised the average recovery rates from 19 to 32 cents on the dollar. However, the number of yearly cases under the new law still is lower than under the old law. Castellanos (2005) explains why this last feature may be consistent with the reform being either too effective or not sufficiently effective.

29. For example, because there was strong opposition to modifying the bankruptcy law, in 1996 the Mexican Congress approved instead a reform to the General Law of Credit Operations and Titles (Ley General de Títulos y Operaciones de Crédito, LGTOC). This reform allowed commercial banks to require borrowers to use trusts, making swifter and more certain the seizure of collateral. The intent of this reform was to improve social welfare by reducing losses resulting from default, thereby reducing interest rates and encouraging lending. For more details, see Castellanos (1998).

30. FONACOT was created in 1974 to provide cheap mortgages to workers.

31. The Sociedad Hipotecaria Federal replaced the previous Fondo de Operación y Descuento Bancario a la Vivienda (FOVI), which was created in 1954 as a trust fund administered by Banco de México.

32. See, for instance, Sidaoui (2002).

References

Aspe, Pedro (1993). *Economic Transformation the Mexican Way*. Cambridge, MA: MIT Press.

Banco de México (1994). *The Mexican Economy*. México, DF: Banco de México.

Bank for International Settlements (2004). *Triennial Central Bank Survey of Foreign Exchange and Derivative Market Activity 2004*. Basel: Bank for International Settlements.

Castellanos, Sara G. (1998). "Essays on Applied Microeconomic Theory: An Analysis of Mexico's Privatization Mechanisms and Loan Market Regulation." Ph.D. diss., UCLA.

Castellanos, Sara G. (2005). Comment on Aloisio Araujo and Bruno Funchal, "Bankruptcy Law in Latin America: Past and Future." *Economía* 6(1): 202–213.

Gamboa, Mario, and Frank Schneider (2006). "Bankruptcy Reform, Litigation and Resolution of Distress." Unpublished job market paper, Harvard University.

Gil-Díaz, Francisco, and Agustín Carstens (1996). "One Year of Solitude: Some Pilgrim Tales about Mexico's 1994–1995 Crisis." *American Economic Review* 86(2): 164–169.

Jeanneau, Serge, and Carlos Pérez-Verdía (2005). "Reducing Financial Vulnerability: The Development of the Domestic Government Bond Market in Mexico." *BIS Quarterly Review* (December 2005), 95–107.

La Porta, Rafael, Florencio Lopez de Silanes, and Andrei Shleifer (2003). "What Works in Securities Laws?" NBER Working Paper No. 9882.

Luengnaruemitchai, Pipat, and Li Lian Ong (2005). "An Anatomy of Corporate Bond Markets." IMF Working Paper No. 05/152.

Lustig, Nora (2001). "Life Is Not Easy: Mexico's Quest for Stability and Growth." *Journal of Economic Perspectives* 15(1): 85–106.

Mancera, Miguel (1992). "Discurso pronunciado en el acto de recepción del Premio Rey Juan Carlos de Economía, instituido por la Fundación Celma Prieto."

Martínez, Lorenza, and Alejandro Werner (2002). "Retos y desarrollos recientes del mercado de capitales en México." In *Estabilidad Macroeconómica, Mercados Financieros y Desarrollo Económico*. México DF: Banco de México.

Sidaoui, José Julián (2002). "The Role of the Central Bank in Developing Debt Markets in Mexico." BIS Papers No. 11.

Tornell, Aaron, Frank Westermann, and Lorenza Martínez (2003). "Liberalization, Growth, and Financial Crises: Lessons from Mexico and the Developing World." *Brookings Papers on Economic Activity* 2.

Tovar, Camilo, and Serge Jeanneau (2006). "Domestic Bond Markets in Latin America: Achievements and Challenges." BIS *Quarterly Review* (June): 51–64.

4   Corporate Bond Markets in Argentina

Roque B. Fernández, Sergio
Pernice, and Jorge M. Streb

This chapter seeks to determine whether Argentine corporate bond markets are underdeveloped. There is a natural tendency to answer the question saying that the market is obviously underdeveloped. Ratios such as the size of the bond market to GDP are clearly lower for Argentina, and for Latin America in general, than for developed countries. In answering this question, our objective is to propose an alternative criterion for market development that will allow us to identify the main determinants of the current state of the bond market.

According to conventional theory, banks and bond markets serve different types of customers. Thanks to the relationships they establish with firms, banks learn over time about their characteristics and can provide loans to smaller borrowers about which there is little public information. On the other hand, for large corporations for which extensive public information is available, bond markets—where issues are subject to a substantial minimum efficient scale—are cheaper for financing substantial volumes of debt.

For Argentina, both our econometric results and our survey indicate that only large firms use bond finance. Furthermore, the number of large firms and their size in terms of firm value are much smaller in Argentina than the United States, for example. We will argue that the aggregate firm value of large firms is a useful metric for understanding bond market size; this in turn depends on fundamental factors such as institutional quality and the macroeconomic environment.

Our research suggests that seeking a ratio of bond market to GDP similar to that of high-income countries is an inappropriate objective. These ratios are misleading as a measure of bond market development, and providing incentives to reach ratios similar to those of the high-income countries would lead to inefficiencies if bond markets were the ideal financing vehicle only for large corporations.

The chapter is organized as follows. In the first section, we present landmarks in the development of Argentine bond markets. In the second section, we present theoretical fundamentals on the determinants of debt structure. In the third section we provide econometric evidence on these determinants, finding that firm size is the key determinant of corporate bond financing. The fourth section provides evidence from a survey that points in the same direction. Given that evidence, we then present some general arguments about the metric that leads to our main propositions. The last section presents the conclusions.

Evolution of Bond Finance[1]

In contrast to sovereign bonds, in Argentina the issue of corporate bonds was nil until 1989.[2] Firms had not issued bonds, regardless of firm size, due to the absence of an adequate legal framework. In 1988, Law 23.576 created the figure of corporate bonds (*obligaciones negociables* or ON). However, the market only started to take off in 1991 when Law 23.962 gave corporate bonds the same tax treatment as sovereign bonds, with tax exemptions from the value-added tax (VAT), the income tax, and taxes on the transfer of bond instruments (*títulos valores*). These tax deductions also leveled the field with bank loans. From that point on, the legal framework no longer seems to have been a limiting factor.[3]

In 1991, Argentina was also leaving behind a period of high inflation and hyperinflation through the Convertibility Plan that pegged the peso to the U.S. dollar at a one-to-one rate. Moreover, the country was normalizing its debt abroad in default after being cut off from international capital markets since the 1981–1982 debt crisis, when the government "nationalized" the foreign debt of private firms, causing a huge fiscal crisis. When completed in 1993, the Brady settlement implied that government liabilities with commercial banks abroad for US$25.5 billion were refinanced through foreign sovereign bonds, which jumped from 0.3% to 11.7% of GDP between 1992 and 1993. At that point, national government debt basically switched from bank loans concentrated in the hands of a few creditors to bonds held by many dispersed investors.

After a decade of strong growth in financial and capital markets, the stock of corporate sector was quite large by the end of 2000: the figures in Bedoya, González, Pernice, et al. (2007) show that corporate bonds outstanding at the end of 2000 reached US$24 billion (almost

9% of GDP; unfortunately, we do not have a breakdown of corporate bonds by legislation). At that time, sovereign bond debt under foreign legislation reached US$65 billion (23% of GDP) and under domestic legislation reached US$33 billion (12% of GDP).[4,5] However, since the economy had failed to recover from the recession that began in 1998, Argentina's difficulties in servicing its debt amid rising interest payments and stagnant or falling tax revenues became a salient problem. Provincial governments experienced similar problems.

After the December 2000 agreement (*blindaje*) with international financial organizations to provide cheaper funds to refinance debt amortizations of sovereign debt proved insufficient, in mid-2001 there was a mega-exchange (*megacanje*) of sovereign bonds with a face value of around US$30 billion for bonds with longer maturity. As figure 4.1 illustrates, the spread of global government bonds (subject to foreign law) over US Treasuries started to skyrocket after that. The spread between government bonds issued under domestic and foreign legislation, on bonds of similar duration, also widened in late 2001, after having hovered around 200 basis points in previous years.

From the point of view of the fiscal intertemporal budget constraint, the fiscal crisis perhaps had more to do with the failed handling of a sudden stop than with the problem of debt overhang. In terms of net present value (NPV), debt did not rise with the mega-exchange because the NPV of the old bonds was equal to the new bonds; however,

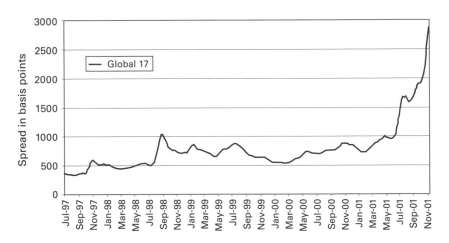

Figure 4.1
Spread of foreign law government bonds over US Treasuries of similar duration, 20 days moving average.

debt increased significantly in nominal terms and as a percentage of GDP without any actual financing of public sector expenditure. The problem was that short-term debt was being exchanged for long-term debt at a moment when the interest rates faced by Argentina shot up to annual rates in dollars around 15%.[6] Discounted at those interest rates, the NPV of government tax collection (which closely follows the evolution of GDP) suffered a severe collapse, and default was inevitable. In the section "Bond Market Size Metric," we further discuss the issue that the relevant collateral for debt outstanding is the present value of the debtor's income.

A new exchange was launched in November whereby large domestic bondholders—basically banks and pension funds—exchanged at par value US$41.7 billion in sovereign bonds for a guaranteed loan (*préstamos garantizados*) at an interest rate lower than the original ones, which lead to a reduction in the NPV of debt. The crisis finally exploded in the financial system at the beginning of December 2001 when capital flight accelerated and the government imposed restrictions on withdrawing funds from banks, an action that became known as the *corralito*. On December 24, 2001, the Argentine government declared default on the great majority of public debt—basically that part comprising sovereign bonds.

In February 2002, after abandoning convertibility and devaluing the peso, the government decreed the pesification of domestic debt. By that decree, all bonds issued under domestic legislation and all guaranteed loans were converted to pesos at a parity of 1.4 pesos per dollar. Pesified debt was indexed by CER (*coeficiente de estabilización de referencia*, an index that reflected lagged CPI inflation) and paid a spread that varied by instrument.[7] What was peculiar about the default period was that—unlike previous episodes of fiscal crises and very high devaluations—the economy did not return to a regime of high inflation, in part because of quantitative restrictions on bank withdrawals (*corralito, corralón*). The public sector also managed to keep its fiscal accounts in order, thanks to the relief provided by default, the important tax increases instituted in 2001 and 2002 on checks and on agricultural exports, and the fact that pension payments were not indexed to inflation, which meant that they eroded in real terms.

In the January 2005 restructuring of Argentine debt under foreign legislation, sovereign bonds eligible for exchange represented US$81.8 billion. Despite some holdouts, the exchange had an acceptance rate of 76%. New bonds were issued for US$35.2 billion, with a deep reduction in the face value of debt. Additionally, coupons indexed to the GDP were handed over to creditors. The spreads on government bonds over US Treasuries fell once the country was able to step out of default in March 2005.

For the corporate sector, the 2002 devaluation was different from past experiences in the 1970s and 1980s, when a devaluation melted down debt denominated in domestic currency, leaving companies in a better financial situation. Though bank debt in dollars was pesified at a rate of 1 to 1, loans to the private sector had been continuously falling since 1998 while the ease of access to external credit and the good international financial conditions stimulated the growth of foreign debt. Hence, the 2002 devaluation provoked a financial suffocation of many companies. However, all debt in foreign currency not related to the financial system was converted by Decree 214 of 2002, Article 8, to pesos at a ratio of one dollar equal to one peso, and the resulting amount was indexed by CER (Article 4). This decree applied only to corporate bonds under domestic legislation, however, and not to those under foreign legislation.

In early 2002, the risk-rating agencies placed almost all firms in selective default in regard to liabilities in foreign currency. However, some companies were much less exposed than others to these risks. The greatest probability of default was for firms serving the domestic market that had suffered the pesification and freezing of their rates, such as distributors of gas and electricity and the telephone companies. These firms were all heavily indebted abroad in foreign currency.

Due to widespread corporate default, after the 2001 debt crisis the corporate bond market came to a standstill. As figure 4.2 shows, about two-thirds of corporate issuers rated by Standard & Poor's went into default in 2002, and the process of renegotiation proved quite lengthy. However, by the end of 2005, most firms had renegotiated their debt.

In 1995, Law 24.522 reformed bankruptcy proceedings and introduced cram-down rules that made it possible for a bidder to take over an indebted firm with the agreement of a majority of the creditors. The modernization of the law made the procedures more agile, though some observers have doubts about the reliability of the domestic judiciary system, and there have been complaints of corruption in the administration of bankruptcies and in the selection of bankruptcy trustees. In early 2002, after the sovereign default, Congress amended the bankruptcy law to protect private debtors, but the amendments were partially vetoed by the president, and most of the earlier

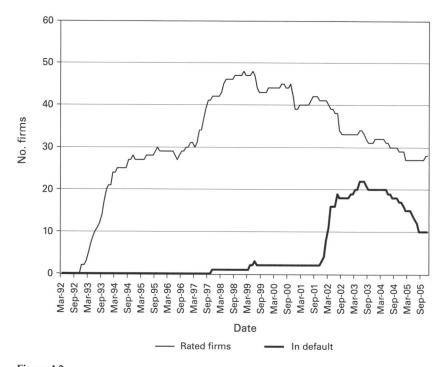

Figure 4.2
Corporate bond issuers in Argentina, rated by Standard & Poors and by number of firms in default.

protections for creditors were restored. In June 2003 a special law was approved to limit foreign ownership of cultural goods, including media and Internet companies; media companies were exempted from cram-down rules in restructuring and bankruptcy.

Determinants of Debt Structure

The natural conceptual framework to investigate the debt structure of firms is the Modigliani-Miller "irrelevance" proposition, which states that financing policy should not be expected to affect firm market value under the following conditions:

• There are no corporate or personal taxes.
• There are no contracting costs.
• Corporate investment policy is fixed.
• There are no information costs.

Empirically, the value of the firm is not independent of its financing policy, so the conditions for the Modigliani-Miller theorem are not satisfied. As Barclay, Smith, and Watts (1999) argue, using the theorem in the logically equivalent way $(A \Rightarrow B) \Leftrightarrow (\sim B \Rightarrow \sim A)$, the financial structure of firms:

1. must affect taxes paid by issuers or investors, or

2. must affect contracting costs (this may include costs of issuing debt, as well as the probability and costs associated to getting into financial difficulty or bankruptcy), or

3. must affect management's incentives to follow the value-maximizing rule of investing in all positive NPV projects, so investment and operational decisions are influenced by financing decisions, or

4. must provide a signal to investors of management's confidence about the firm's future earnings in a context of information costs and asymmetric information.

In the United States, the third reason—incentive problems—is by far the most important determinant of leverage level (Barclay, Smith, and Watts 1999). The particular debt instrument chosen, which in turn affects the maturity of the debt, is also affected strongly by the second reason—cost of issuing debt (Barclay and Smith 1999). The first reason—taxes—is of course important, but taxes do not change very often in the United States.

We conjecture that these same reasons drive the financing decisions in Argentina and all of Latin America. These mechanisms will help us motivate the econometric models and interpret our results in the following sections.

As to the first reason, taxes, the previous section showed that once corporate bonds received a more favorable tax treatment in comparison to other sources of funding, this led in 1991 to the emergence of a significant corporate bond market for Argentine firms.

How can financial decisions generate incentives for managers to change investment decisions—the third reason? Suppose a firm is largely debt-financed, and that, due to a crisis, the firm is not able to pay its debt. If new investment opportunities with positive NPV emerge, the stockholders will probably not invest unless they negotiate a debt reduction because a large part (or all) of their investment would become a transfer of money to bondholders. The financing decisions of the past may thus generate incentives to deviate from the strategy to "invest in all positive NPV projects." On the other hand, if the firm had been all equity-financed, the stockholders would inject more cash in NPV > 0 investments because that would increase their wealth.

From the point of view of an Argentine firm that does business in a region prone to crises, it is not a value-maximizing strategy to have mostly debt financing. The reason is that when calculating the present value of their cash flows (i.e., the firm's value), one would have to allow for the probability of crises in which managers will have incentives to pass up positive NPV projects, or the company will default on its debt. Anticipating this, creditors would only provide financing at a very high cost.

The best alternative is to have a debt structure less sensitive to crises. For example, it is not a value-maximizing strategy to have long-term debt. The reason is that the lender will not be willing to lend long-term if the probability of a crisis (that would imply a default) is high, unless the interest is extraordinarily high; the borrower, facing such a steep term structure, would prefer to use debt of shorter maturity. This implies that the typical maturity should be shorter—given the volatile macroeconomic environment described in the previous section—in Argentina than in the United States.

Debt structure is a multidimensional concept. We not only have the leverage ratio and maturity but also covenant restrictions, convertibility, call provisions, and security—not to mention whether the debt is privately placed or held by widely dispersed public investors. Very important as well are the expected costs of renegotiation (even if the "renegotiation option" is not explicitly written in the contract).

Focusing on the leverage ratio and maturity, the arguments above suggest that firms whose managers have greater discretion in changing investment strategies would tend to have smaller leverage ratios and shorter maturities on their debt. A proxy for these companies is the market-to-book ratio. The difference between market value and book value of a firm reflects the value of investment opportunities (or growth options) requiring managers' discretion to properly exploit them. If a company has a large market-to-book ratio, such a difference is large. On the other side of the spectrum, companies with a low market-to-book ratio are companies whose value comes primarily from assets in place that could serve as good collateral and should be expected to have higher leverage ratio and larger maturities.[8]

An alternative and related proxy is "tangibility," the proportion of "fixed" assets over firm value. Note that the inverse of the market-to-book ratio is assets over firm value, so the two variables are related. However, we want to distinguish between the two in order to separate out the effect of those assets ("fixed") that represent the best collateral.

According to conventional theory, different forms of debt have different natural clienteles, and bond finance is typical of large firms. The size of firms is a relevant variable for understanding debt structure as a result of contracting costs and economies of scale—the second reason. Banks can economically provide finance for smaller borrowers, while bond markets—where issues are subject to a substantial minimum efficient scale—can do so at lower cost for large corporations with substantial funding needs. Indeed, according to a widely cited study by Blackwell and Kidwell (1988), although the interest rate is lower, the fixed issue costs of public debt issues are generally much higher than the fixed costs of a bank loan or private placement, so only larger firms tend to issue public debt.

Barclay and Smith (1999) also find firm size is statistically significant and economically important in determining the debt maturity for US firms: moving from the 10th to the 90th percentile for firm size reduces the fraction of short-term debt by 70%. They attribute this effect of size on maturity to the fact that banks for regulatory reasons cannot issue long-term loans. In contrast to small firms, which borrow mainly from banks because of issuing costs, large firms borrow a much larger proportion of their debt issuing bonds that tend to be of larger maturity. On the other hand, though there is a statistically significant positive effect of firm size on the leverage ratio for US firms, Barclay and Smith (1999) find the economic impact is very small. For example, the largest firms had leverage ratios that were only about 1 percentage point higher than the average of 21%.

Evidence from the Stock Exchange

We apply the theoretical framework presented above to the econometric analysis of the debt structure of nonfinancial firms quoted on the Bolsa de Comercio de Buenos Aires (BCBA). Our source is the Economática database.

We first model the leverage ratio. However, our focus is on the behavior of the maturity structure of debt and the issue of corporate bonds. Hence, the dependent variable $y_{i,t}$ is first leverage, then the term structure of debt and finally a measure of bond finance, where i stands for firm and t for time:

$$y_{i,t} = \alpha + \beta_1 size_{i,t-2} + \beta_2 tangibility_{i,t-2} + \beta_3 q_{i,t-2} + \beta_4 roa_{i,t-2}$$

$$+ \beta_5 year_{t-2} + u_{it}.$$

Our main explanatory variables are linked to reason two—contracting costs and economies of scale, with firm size as a proxy—and reason three—incentive problems, with market-to-book ratio and tangibility as proxies. Though we do not expect size to affect leverage, our conjecture is that it is an important determinant of the use of bond finance.

We use the log of total assets (book value of total assets, in thousands of US dollars) to measure *size*. For *tangibility*, we use the ratio of the book values of fixed and total assets, and the market-to-book ratio q is the ratio of firm value to total assets. Firm value is the book value of liabilities plus market value of equity. Following Rajan and Zingales (1995), we control for *roa*, the ratio of net income to total assets. Because we use a panel and not a cross section, we also add a year dummy to control for time effects.

For leverage, we use two measures. In accordance with the standard practice in the finance literature of focusing on market leverage, *leverage1 = liabilities/firm value* is the ratio of total liabilities to firm value. We also report book leverage, measured as the ratio of total liabilities to the book value of assets, *leverage2 = liabilities/assets*. These are broad definitions of leverage, because total liabilities are larger than total debt, which basically consists of bank debt plus bonds.

Since leverage will be either market or book leverage and varies mostly in the 0–1 interval, with left-censored observations at 0, we estimate a random-effects tobit regression. This is the same specification as in Rajan and Zingales (1995). Because we lag the explanatory variables by two years to avoid endogeneity problems, the estimates use biennial data that cover the 1992–2004 period.

Rajan and Zingales (1995) measure *size*, the size of firms, with the log of sales, finding it has a significantly positive relation to leverage in four of the Group of 7 (G-7) countries they study (however, in Germany it is significantly negative). Consistent with our theoretical framework, Rajan and Zingales find that *tangibility*, the share of fixed assets over total assets, has a positive effect on both market and book leverage in all G-7 countries, and q, the market to book ratio, has a negative effect.

Rajan and Zingales (1995) also control for *roa*, the return on assets, which almost always has a negative effect (only two of fourteen coefficients are positive, but these are not statistically significant). The result that return on assets has a negative effect on leverage seems natural to us, if higher returns indicate higher risk. However, it is unexpected if higher returns are an indication of quality, for example because of better corporate governance, as Bebczuk (2005) shows for firms in Argentina.

Something implicit in the empirical literature on the subject is that more market leverage and debt outstanding represent more availability of credit. However, there is an ambiguity that we explore here: instead of measuring credit availability, high leverage might indicate financially distressed firms—something especially relevant for Argentina after the 2001 default. To explore this, we modify the basic setup by introducing *dumleverage*, a dummy that takes value 1 for firms extremely indebted in the past (that is, for which *leverage* two years before was larger than 0.9—we are excluding financial firms from our sample) and interact it with return on assets.

In table 4.1, columns (1) and (2) show the random-effects tobit regressions for market and book leverage. In column (1) for market leverage, the variable *size* is insignificant as is usual in many studies for U.S. firms. However, neither *tangibility* nor q is significant; slow and uncertain legal proceedings in Argentina might make collateral less effective than in the United States, which perhaps explains why *tangibility* is not relevant to having more access to credit. The dummy *dumleverage* has a significantly positive effect, which suggests that for some firms, current market leverage is driven by past overindebtedness.[9]

In column (2) for book leverage, the most statistically significant variable is return on assets. To a great extent, what drives the result on the negative relationship between profitability and leverage are firms that were highly indebted in the past, perhaps because financially distressed firms with higher returns are forced to cancel debt.[10] We explore this further in the term structure of debt, because short-term credit has less inertia than long-term credit, which is driven by decisions taken far in the past.

As for the maturity structure of debt, measured by the share of short-term debt in total bank and bond debt, columns (3) and (4) of table 4.1 show the random-effects tobit regressions. The variable *size*

Table 4.1
Leverage and Maturity of Argentine Firms' Capital Structure: Random-Effects Tobit Regressions, 1992–2004

Explanatory variables	leverage1 = liabilities/ firm value (1)	leverage2 = liabilities/ assets (2)	short-term debt/total debt	
			using leverage1 (3)	using leverage2 (4)
size(-2)	−.1095	.0191	−11.9021	−12.0147
	(.1260)	(.0369)	(4.3671)***	(4.3378)***
tangibility(-2)	−.0934	.0082	−5.4731	−6.0600
	(.0976)	(.0201)	(2.4575)**	(2.4176)**
q(-2)	−.0223	.0729	−7.1912	−4.9986
	(.1933)	(.0412)*	(5.0152)	(4.7504)
roa(-2)	−.0062	−.0018	.4230	.2163
	(.0064)	(.0009)*	(.1515)***	(.1240)*
dumleverage	.9830	−.1704	−4.3135	−17.9528
	(.2247)***	(.2083)	(5.8300)	(23.9058)
dumleverage * roa(-2)	.0071	−.0112	−.5887	−.3880
	(.0090)	(.0047)***	(.2617)**	(.6537)
cons	1.0782	.2118	123.84	123.21
	(.7061)	(.2030)	(24.75)***	(24.31)***
year dummies	yes	yes	yes	yes
Wald chi^2	39.88***	37.99***	23.74**	19.19*
Number of observations	236	259	243	243
Left-censored observations	2	0	1	1
Number of firms	63	68	66	66

Note: Standard errors of coefficients in parentheses. ***, **, and * denote significance at 1%, 5%, and 10% levels, respectively. In columns (1) and (3), dumleverage = 1 when liabilites/firm value(-2) > 0.9; in columns (2) and (4), dumleverage = 1 when liabilites/ assets(-2) > 0.9.
Source: Economática, unconsolidated balance-sheet data.

has a strongly significant and negative effect on the share of short-term debt, which is consistent with a story based on contracting costs and economies of scale. The variable tangibility is significant at the 5% level and has the expected sign while the market-to-book ratio q is not significant.

We find that, except for highly indebted firms, firms with higher returns have more short-term debt.[11] Under the interpretation that high roa represents high risk, it is natural for higher-risk firms to have less long-term credit. However, this does not explain why highly indebted firms with high returns have more long-term credit, pointing instead to the problem of debt overhang mentioned before.

If leverage is indeed distorted by financially distressed firms, this will be reflected in the maturity structure. Once creditors refuse new credit to the firm, short-term debt should drop: it has maturity of less than one year, so in contrast to long-term debt, it represents only recent decisions. Hence, measures of debt that include long-term debt have to be interpreted with some caution. Short-term debt is less affected by past decisions that have nothing to do with the present willingness of creditors to provide loans (as the 2001 crisis of Argentina attests), so it may reflect availability of credit in the margin better than total liabilities.[12]

The fact that *size* has a negative effect on the share of short-term debt is related, by our discussion on the theoretical framework, to the use of bonds as a financing vehicle by larger firms. For the question of whether a firm issues bonds, we estimate in table 4.2 a random-effects probit model, where the dependent value *bonds* takes a value of 1 if there is bond financing and zero otherwise. In column (1), our random-effects panel estimates show that *size* is a very significant determinant of the use of bond finance, which is consistent with the cost of issuing and economies of scale hypothesis (refer to the second reason from the Modigliani-Miller theorem).

The same happens in the tobit regressions in columns (2) and (3) with the amount of bonds issued, because *size* has a strong positive effect on the ratios of *bond debt/firm value* and *bond debt/assets*. The other variables do not have any clear and systematic relationship to the decision to issue bonds. Although leverage measured using total liabilities does not increase with *size*, both bank and bond debt do. Hence, we also look at the ratio of *bond debt/(bond + bank debt)* in column (4), which shows that the share of bonds in debt strongly increases with *size*. So, although bigger firms use both more bank loans and bonds, bond finance becomes increasingly important with *size*. This is consistent with the cost of issuing and economies of scale hypothesis.

As table 4.2 shows, *size* is—from an economic viewpoint—extremely significant: firms two standard deviations above the mean have 43 percentage points (p.p.) more *bond debt/firm value*, 32 p.p. more *bond debt/ firm value*, and 68 p.p. more *bond debt/(bond + bank debt)*. The fact that size is an important determinant of the use of bond finance, and of the amount used, will be linked in the sixth section with the hypothesis that bond markets are not highly developed in Argentina because most firms are relatively small in size.[13]

Table 4.2
Issuance of Corporate Bonds and Debt Ratios of Argentine Firms: Random-Effects Regressions, 1992–2004

Explanatory variables	bonds = 1, no bonds = 0 (1)	bond debt/ firm value (2)	bond debt/ assets (3)	bond debt/ (bond + bank debt) (4)
size(-2)	1.6623	.3102	.2250	.4827
	(.3752)***	(.0539)***	(.0532)***	(.1151)***
tangibility(-2)	.0879	.0273	.0096	.0425
	(.1947)	(.0289)	(.0278)	(.0541)
q(-2)	.6241	−.0057	.0251	.1599
	(.4066)	(.0713)	(.0522)	(.0959)*
roa(-2)	−.0009	−.0007	.0002	−.0003
	(.0091)	(.0016)	(.0011)	(.0022)
cons	−10.062	−1.9441	−1.4132	−2.9067
	(2.083)***	(.3254)***	(.3135)***	(.7894)***
year dummies	yes	yes	yes	yes
Method	Probit	Tobit	Tobit	Tobit
Wald chi^2	23.52***	43.87***	23.26***	25.21***
Number of observations	259	236	258	243
Left-censored observations	—	148	165	150
Number of firms	68	63	67	66
Economic significance of size:				
Mean × coefficient	—	1.6924	1.2218	2.6351
(Mean + 2sd) × coefficient	—	2.1259	1.5366	3.3106
Effect of treatment (%)	—	43.4	31.5	67.5

Note: Standard errors of coefficients in parenthesis. ***, **, and * denote significance at 1, 5, and 10% levels, respectively.
Source: Económatica, unconsolidated balance-sheet data.

Survey[14]

We present the results of our survey that provides further support for the idea that firm size is the variable driving corporate bond financing.

Survey of Firms (Sell Side)

To construct the sample of firms to survey, we selected firms with more than 200 employees. We also added firms with less (or an unknown) number of employees that had over 150 million Argentine pesos (US$50 million, given the exchange rate of 3 pesos per dollar) in annual revenue. From the base sample of 769 firms, we randomly selected 250 companies stratified by principal activity (mining; manufacturing, subdivided in four groups; electricity, gas, and water; communications; and others) to closely match the sector composition in the National Survey of Large Firms by INDEC (the National Institute of Statistics and Census). The final result was 56 answers, which closely matched the distribution of the original sample in terms of principal activity.[15] Of the 56 firms in survey, 61% had over 50% foreign ownership, in 3% foreign ownership was below 49%, and 36% had no foreign owners. The firms responding the survey tended to be very large, with an average of 1,964 employees and 1,745 million pesos in annual revenue.

In addition to analyzing the answers in general, we also look carefully at the impact of size on the responses in the analysis that follows. For the purpose of this analysis, we will call large those firms that have assets larger than 600 million pesos (about US$200 million); the rest are small firms. Four firms did not respond in regard to asset size, which leaves 18 large firms and 34 small firms.

Overall, 25% of firms reported recent experience with corporate bonds (i.e., they had corporate bonds outstanding or had issued bonds in recent years) or were planning to issue them or were at least uncertain about it for the near future. The remaining 75% were completely out of the corporate bonds market.

Of the nine companies with recent experience in the bond market (16% of the sample), only one small firm had recent experience issuing bonds, and it was foreign. Firms with experience were significantly larger than those without such experience—both in terms of number of employees and in terms of annual revenue (both t-tests are significant, $p < 0.05$). All but one of the firms that had issued bonds had more than 1,500 employees. In contrast, among the 47 firms without recent experience issuing corporate bonds, 79% had less than 1,500 employees.

When asked about factors that might be a problem for financing operations using local corporate bonds (question 5 in the survey), 19 firms (34%) declined to answer and marked the issue as not relevant for their business. These nonrespondents corresponded to only 17% of the large firms and 41% of the small firms. Of the 37 firms that did provide answers, only seven had recent experience with bonds while 11 planned to issue bonds in 2005–2006, of which five had no recent experience with bonds. Respondents identified the problems listed in column "All" of table 4.3.

Table 4.3
Problems for Domestic Bond Financing

	All	Large	Small
Underwriters' fees	29	13	40
Credit rating agencies' fees	23	7	35
Disclosure requirements	46	33	55
Minimum issue requirements	23	0	40
Other regulatory requirements	23	13	30
Very small market	49	73	30
No junk bond market	26	13	35
Other	14	13	15

Note: Numbers are percent of firms responding that the specified factor is a problem for them in seeking financing.

As we can see in the other two columns in table 4.3, perceptions regarding factors that represent problems for issuing domestic bonds were very different among large and small firms. The two most important overall problems for issuing bonds were "The market is very small" (49% of firms) and "Disclosure requirements" (46%). But while 73% of large firms complained about small market size, only 30% of small firms did so. As to disclosure requirements, 33% of large firms and 55% of small firms find them to be a problem. Even more extreme, the 23% of firms that considered "Minimum issue requirement" to be a problem were all small.

Question 6 of the survey asks firms the same questions for domestic bank financing and domestic bond financing (To what extent are the following factors a problem for financing their operations?). A priori these alternatives might be the actual financing alternatives for many of the firms (foreign financing are not actual alternatives for small firms). Table 4.4 summarizes the answers.

For the questions regarding domestic banks, there are only 6% of nonrespondents (NR), a percentage that does not differ across large and small firms. On the contrary, of the 54% of nonrespondents for domestic bonds, the difference between large and small firms is noteworthy: 22% and 71%, respectively. By not responding, small firms are sending the message that bond financing is irrelevant for them.

Of the firms that did answer, the answers in table 4.4 suggest that small firms face very different problems from large firms, which make bond financing useless for small firms. For example, the minimum amount required was not a serious problem for bank loans. However, 25% of firms found it to be a problem for bonds; when conditioned by

Table 4.4
Problems for Domestic Bank and Bond Financing

Factor	Y overall	Y large	Y small	NR overall	NR large	NR small	Y+NR overall	Y+NR large	Y+NR small
Domestic banks:									
Speed	24	6	34	6	6	6	29	11	38
Maturity	57	76	47	6	6	6	60	78	50
Interest rate	55	65	50	6	6	6	58	67	53
Minimum required	12	6	16	6	6	6	17	11	21
Collateral	27	12	34	6	6	6	31	17	38
Information	18	6	25	6	6	6	23	11	29
Other	6	12	3	6	6	6	12	17	9
Domestic bonds:									
Speed	58	43	80	54	22	71	81	56	94
Maturity	50	57	40	54	22	71	77	67	82
Interest rate	46	57	30	54	22	71	75	67	79
Minimum required	25	7	50	54	22	71	65	28	85
Collateral	38	29	50	54	22	71	71	44	85
Information	38	21	60	54	22	71	71	39	88
Other	8	14	0	54	22	71	58	33	71

Note: Y = percent of firms (large or small) responding that the specified factor is a problem for them in seeking financing; NR = percent of firms (large or small) not responding to this question on the survey.

size, only 7% of large firms said so, compared to 50% of small firms that answered the question (in addition, 71% of small firms did not respond). In general, this question shows that small firms basically do not use bonds as a form of financing.

In question 7, firms were asked to order, for each of a series of attributes, the relative advantages of different forms of credit (1 is best, 5 is worst). The forms of credit are domestic bank loans, domestic bonds, foreign bank loans, foreign bonds, and credit from suppliers. The attributes are interest rates, availability of credit in local currency, availability of alternatives of indexation, availability of long-term credit, costs unrelated to interest rates, taxes, possibility of renegotiation, costs associated with information requirements, and size of potential market. Table 4.5 shows domestic bonds ranked fourth in the general order, beating only foreign bonds as a form of financing. For large firms domestic bonds also ranked fourth; for small firms domestic bonds ranked third, above both foreign bonds and foreign bank loans (small firms basically do not have access to foreign financing in the wake of the 2001 Argentine default).

The answers are clearly discriminating. For example, for small firms credit from suppliers is the alternative of choice or the second for almost all the attributes. However, small firms rank it as the worst form of financing from the point of view of long-term credit, which reflects the fact that credit from suppliers has a very short maturity.

The fact that Argentina (like Latin America in general) has a crisis-prone economy has major effects on the debt structure of firms, making "possibility of renegotiation" an important factor when deciding on the debt instrument used. For the total as well as for small firms, credit from suppliers is ranked as the best form of credit for this attribute, and large firms ranked supplier credit as second best after domestic bank loans. Domestic bonds, on the other hand, were ranked fourth by all firms, small and large, beating only foreign bonds.

The survey results clearly show that firm size is a strong determinant of the debt instrument chosen, which supports the hypothesis that bonds are only used by very large firms.

Survey of Investors (Buy Side)

For the survey of investors, we collected 41 answers representative of the four main groups of institutions on the buy side: pension groups (AFJPs), banks, general insurance companies, and mutual funds.[16]

Table 4.5
Advantages of Credit Instruments by Attribute

Instrument	Order	Interest rates	Credit local currency	Indexation	Long-term credit	Non-interest costs	Taxes	Renegotiation	Costs of information	Size of market
Total firms:										
Domestic bank loans	2	4	1	3	4	2	2	2	2	3
Domestic bonds	4	5	2	1	3	4	3	4	4	5
Foreign bank loans	3	2	4	4	2	3	5	3	3	2
Foreign bonds	5	3	5	5	1	5	4	5	5	1
Credit from suppliers	1	1	3	2	5	1	1	1	1	4
Large firms:										
Domestic bank loans	3	5	1	5	4	1	4	1	1	5
Domestic bonds	4	4	2	1	3	4	2	4	4	4
Foreign bank loans	1	1	4	3	2	3	5	3	3	2
Foreign bonds	5	3	5	4	1	5	1	5	5	1
Credit from suppliers	2	2	3	2	5	2	3	2	2	3
Small firms:										
Domestic bank loans	2	4	1	1	4	2	2	2	2	1
Domestic bonds	3	5	3	3	1	4	3	4	4	4
Foreign bank loans	4	3	4	4	2	3	4	3	3	2
Foreign bonds	5	2	5	5	3	5	5	5	5	5
Credit from suppliers	1	1	2	2	5	1	1	1	1	3

Note: 1 represents best form of credit, 5 represents worst.

Regarding foreign ownership, 19 firms had over 50% of ownership in the hand of foreigners. An additional 18 firms did not have foreign owners, and the remaining four firms had foreign ownership below 49%. The average number of portfolios under management was 11, and the average amount of each portfolio was 1,558 million pesos.

Responses to question 4 of the survey showed that, in the opinion of the buy side, low liquidity of the secondary market (80%), low quality of legal recourse in case of default (61%), low market capitalization (56%), high risk of insolvency (59%), and absence of a benchmark curve (59%) represent the main factors that limit the demand for corporate bonds in Argentina. Note that low liquidity of the secondary market and low market capitalization are direct consequences of the fact that there are very few large companies. Responses to question 9 showed that Argentine investors do not perceive government and corporate bonds as substitute of each other (no crowding-out effect).

The survey presented in this section, like the econometric results in the previous section, indicates that firm size is the most important determinant of the use of bonds.

Bond Market Size Metric

In the 1990s, many economists and policy makers in Argentina and elsewhere were quite confident that the country's financial reforms would result in dramatic growth in capital markets, particularly corporate bond markets. Today, confronted with data such as in column (1) in table 4.6—which show that the Latin American average of private domestic bonds as a share of GDP is 7% while for the high-income countries such an average is 40%—common sense seems to indicate that those expectations were too optimistic.

One of the questions that motivated this study ("Are Latin American bond markets underdeveloped?") seems to have a trivial "yes" as an answer. A recent study concludes that Latin American capital markets have grown less than expected (De la Torre and Schmukler 2004). That study, along with many others, uses market capitalization over GDP as the variable to measure the level of development of capital markets. Market capitalization over GDP seems to be the generally accepted ratio for analyzing the level of development of capital markets.

When confronted with the second question motivating this study ("What are the main determinants of the current situation?"), the

Table 4.6
Bond Markets in Different Regions of the World

Country	Share of GDP (1)	Share of total private debt (2)	Share of financial system (3)
Argentina	4.8	19	5
Brazil	9.6	26	13
Chile	22.8	27	14
Colombia	0.2	1	1
Mexico	2.5	15	7
Peru	4.3	15	9
Latin American average	7.0	17	8
East Asia average	32.0	22	13
United States	109.0	72	38
High-income average	40.0	27	18

Note: Private domestic debt is the sum of private domestic bonds and domestic bank credit to the private sector. The total financial system is equal to total private domestic credit plus stock market capitalization. All averages are computed as simple averages.
Source: Bank for International Settlements, International Financial Statistics. The data is taken from table 1 of the "IADB Call for Research Proposals on the Development of Latin-American Bond Markets," March 24, 2005.

answers tend to be less clear (De la Torre and Schmukler 2004). In our study we have found that one variable consistently displays the greatest explanatory power: firm size. This is entirely consistent with standard theory: as a result of economies of scale, small firms tend to prefer bank financing, and large firms prefer bond financing. So it seemed only natural to think that the answer to the second question is the following: "The size of the corporate bond markets is what it is simply because in Argentina (and in Latin America, and in fact in all the developing world) there are very few big companies." Anecdotal evidence seems to confirm such an intuition.

If this is so, it is easy to check with a "back of the envelope" calculation.[17] As column (1) of table 4.6 shows, private domestic bonds in Argentina amount to 4.8% of its GDP while for the United States the share is 109%. Let us consider the size of the respective GDPs as of year 2001 (the argument, qualitatively, does not change if we choose a different year for comparison). In 2001 the Argentine GDP was US$484 billion, while the US GDP was US$11,750 billion. The ratio of GDPs is then 24:1. The percentages above then imply that the size of the Argentine corporate bond market was approximately US$23 billion, while the size of the US corporate bond market was approximately US$12,807 billion. The ratio of the size of the US corporate bond market to the size of Argentina's is then 552:1.

Since we know that both in Argentina and in the United States only large firms tend to use the bond markets, are there about 552 times more large firms in the United States than in Argentina? If this estimation is correct, it would explain the difference in size of the corporate bond markets.

The 1997 US census tells us that the number of firms with more than 500 employees was 16,079. In Argentina we know that there were approximately 300 firms of such size or larger.[18] The ratio between the two is 54:1. So the ratio of the number of US large firms to Argentine large firms is indeed larger than the ratio of their GDPs, but this is not nearly enough to explain the ratio of size of their corporate bond markets.

Axtell (2001) shows that the size distribution of firms will not change much if different criteria for company size are used, such as number of employees, revenue or assets, or if the cutoff (say, in terms of number of employees) is varied. Our calculations on the distribution of the size of firms in Argentina and the United States are based on number of employees with a cutoff at 500, but Axtell's results would suggest that the ratio between the number of large companies in the United States and Argentina would not change much if we used a different criteria for size. The ratio will have an order of magnitude around 50:1. Unfortunately, we have to explain a ratio of about 500:1.

The conclusion is that while firm size is the relevant variable that drives the use of bonds in Argentina, as discussed above, the number of large firms in Argentina is not small enough to explain the fact that the market is so small. So we have to pause and think.

Bond market capitalization as a share of GDP is the metric used in all the studies related to the subject at hand. It is also the metric that suggests that our capital markets (and the bond market in particular) are underdeveloped. But GDP is the value of goods and services that a country produces in a given year, while "bonds outstanding" is an intertemporal concept. Because of the usual market practice of issuing bonds at par, bonds outstanding (i.e., the sum of the principal of the bonds outstanding) is a reasonably good measure of the present value of the cash flows that these bonds represent. To take the ratio of bonds outstanding to GDP is like calculating, for firms, the ratio of firm value over revenues, in the sense that both are ratios of present values over flow measures. Different industries naturally have different ratios of firm value over revenues, due to the nature of their business. No market analyst would ever conclude from this that one industry is in better shape (or more developed) than the other. For the same reason, bonds outstanding to GDP is simply not the right variable to look at if we want to measure the level of corporate bond market development.

The relevant variable to gauge whether the present value of bond liabilities is small or large is to compare it with the present value of the cash flows that the firms will generate, and which they will use in part to pay these bonds. Such present value is precisely firm value (i.e., the market value of equity plus the market value of debt).

This line of reasoning leads us to suspect that maybe the reason the bond market is small is that firm value is small for Argentine firms (and for emerging market firms in general): if the present value of the cash flows generated by the firm is small, the bonds outstanding (which, as we said, is a proxy of the present value of the cash flows associated to these bonds) should be correspondingly small.[19] This would still be consistent with the fact that firm size is the most powerful explanatory variable for understanding the use of bonds. Firm size is relevant to understand the size of the bond market not so much because there are very few large firms, but because large firms in Argentina are very small when measured by firm value.

The problem in testing this is that we know firm value only for firms that trade publicly. Not only are there many more firms that trade publicly in the United States than in Argentina, but also not all the firms that issue bonds trade shares publicly (this last point may not be so important quantitatively because a large proportion of the bonds outstanding come from firms that trade publicly). Therefore, if we want to compare the firm value of US and Argentine firms we have to try to avoid the bias caused by the greater proportion of US firms that trade publicly. This is why "total market capitalization" is not ideal for comparing firm value in both countries.

To partially avoid this bias, we can calculate the ratio of the sum of the firm values of the 500 largest public US firms to the sum of the firm value of the 10 largest public Argentine firms (source: Económatica database, 2004). Since $500/10 = 50$ is approximately the ratio of large firms in the United States and Argentina, if this ratio is greater than 50:1, this would imply that the largest US firms tend to be greater than the largest Argentine firms as measured by firm value, which is precisely what we want to check. Performing the calculation, one obtains a ratio of 322:1, far greater than 50 and on the order of 500 (the ratio of the size of the bond markets). If we do the same with the 1,000 largest US firms and the 20 largest Argentine firms, the ratio is about 317:1, that is, almost unchanged.[20] In other words, when we calculate ratios of firm value we obtain a result much closer to the ratios of bonds outstanding.

This simple comparison between Argentine and US firms by firm value suggests that the reason that the bond market is small in Argentina is that the value of their firms is small: the ratio of bonds outstanding is similar to the ratio of firm values.

Is this fact valid for other countries as well? In column (3) of table 4.6, we have for all the countries in the table the ratios of total private domestic bonds to total financial system (total financial system is total private domestic credit plus stock market capitalization; that is, a proxy for the sum of the firm values of the firms that trade publicly). As we mentioned above, the fact that we have "total" market capitalization distorts the ratios because in some countries (especially high income countries), a larger proportion of firms trade publicly than in others. However, the differences between countries are much smaller in column (3) that in column (1). For example, the average for Latin America is now 8%, while for high income countries it is 18% (to be compared with 7% and 40% in column 1).

In other words, we were focusing on column (1) of table 4.6, which seems to shout that bond markets are underdeveloped in Latin America. But column (3) of the same table suggests a different view: bond markets in emerging countries (and Latin American countries, in particular) are so small because the firm value in these regions is very small as well. And of course, conceptually one cannot have a small firm value and large bonds outstanding—the cash flows simply cannot match.

Our approach also has implication for sovereign bonds. In particular, it would suggest that the ratio of government debt to the present value of government receipts is the relevant metric for estimating optimal debt. This can help explain the phenomenon of debt intolerance described by Reinhart, Rogoff, Savastano (2003). Emerging countries face much higher and more volatile interest rates than developed economies, so this channel implies that the level of government debt for developing countries should be much lower in terms of GDP than in developed economies.

Conclusions

This project was motivated by the challenge of determining whether the corporate bond market in Argentina was underdeveloped. In trying to answer that question, we studied the main determinants of the current state of corporate bond market development. Our analysis seems to point toward the following answers.

As to the main determinants of the current state of the corporate bond market, we have a very simple answer: the firm value of Argentine firms is very small. The present value of debt can never be greater than firm value; ergo the present value of debt should be very small. Bonds outstanding is a proxy of the present value of bond debt, which is a subset of total debt. If firm value is very small, bonds outstanding should likewise be very small.

Regarding the level of development of corporate bond markets, we certainly are unable to conclude that they are underdeveloped just by looking at the ratio of bond market over GDP. Our study suggests that the reasons underlying small corporate bond market size are probably the same as those underlying low firm values. These may include, in particular, a higher cost of capital for firms, low institutional quality, and macroeconomic instability. All these reasons are structural to the Argentine and Latin American economies and not particular to corporate bond markets.

Turning to policy measures, we would urge caution in regard to the desire to promote corporate bond markets. We saw that during the late 1980s and early 1990s the relevant legislation and tax treatment for the development of corporate bond markets were enacted, and liberalization of capital markets facilitated the access of firms to credit at home and abroad. We believe that the present state of the market reflects fundamentals of the economy, so providing additional incentives to reach ratios of bond market to GDP similar to those of the high income countries by ad hoc measures may lead to inefficiencies. Bond markets are the ideal financing vehicle only for large corporations, and the firm value of Argentine firms is very small. Our study leaves an open question: Why are firm values in Latin America so small?

Acknowledgments

This research was supported by a grant from the IDB Research Network as part of a project on the development of Latin American bond markets. The team that directed this general study was composed by Eduardo Borensztein (IDB), Kevin Cowan (Banco Central de Chile), Barry Eichengreen (University of California, Berkeley), and Ugo Panizza (IDB). María Alegre, Alejandro Bedoya, and Celeste González coauthored background papers for this chapter. We appreciate the able research assistance of Eugenia Cobanera, Alejo Czerwonko, Leandro Díaz Santillán, and Belén Sbrancia, as well as the econometric advice from Daniel Lema. We thank Standard & Poor's for providing data on bond ratings and Banco de Valores, Bolsa de Comercio de Buenos Aires, Economática, Mercado Abierto Electrónico, and Reuters for helping us with financial data.

Notes

1. This section is based on Fernández, González, Pernice, and Streb (2007).

2. Sovereign bonds had a low participation in government debt, amounting to only US$3 billion in 1988 (Melconian and Santángelo 1996). The stock of domestic sovereign bonds increased substantially when US$4.5 billion of Bonex 89, ten-year government bonds in dollars, were issued (about 8% of GDP at the time) in exchange for government debt, part of which was compulsory exchanged for time deposits by a government decree at the end of 1989. In the following years the government made sizable issues of domestic bonds to consolidate previous liabilities with pensioneers—the Bocones (Bonos de Consolidación) Previsionales—and with state suppliers—the Bocones Proveedores.

3. By Decree 1.087 of 1993, a simplified regime allowed small and medium enterprises (SMEs) to issue up to 5 million pesos in bonds, after registering them at the Comisión Nacional de Valores, the local securities and exchanges commission. Despite this regime, bond finance overwhelmingly corresponded to large firms.

4. The budget deficit, though low in comparison to previous decades, was positive in part because of the reform of the pension system by which Argentina partially switched in 1994 from a pay-as-you go pension system to a capitalization system. The reduction of the "implicit bond" in the pay-as-you go pension system, which services debt with taxes just like explicit government debt, was equivalent to an increase in the fiscal surplus. However, the reduction of future government liabilities was not registered either in the cash or accrued budget deficits, both of which are measured on the basis of explicit flows.

5. In the official statistics of the Ministerio de Economía, debt is registered the moment that the bond is issued and given to the creditor. López Isnardi and Dal Din (1998) show how a great deal of the growth of debt in the early 1990s can be explained by the recognition of debt generated in previous periods. This debt was originally not registered in the flow versions of the budget deficit (neither in the cash version nor in the accrual version).

6. In the late 1990s, some voluntary exchanges of debt had increased duration, with the aim of improving the profile of debt services. This also increased nominal debt without any actual financing of government expenditure. However, the interest rates the government faced were much lower then.

7. Though the government was in default, almost US\$24 billion in Boden were issued to compensate the financial system and the depositors for the income transfers from the pesification of deposits and loans, to retire provincial monies from circulation, and to compensate the 13% reduction in government salaries and pensions carried out in 2001. New series of Bocones were issued to consolidate debts with pensioners and state suppliers. The national government also took over a great deal of bank loans to provinces and provincial bonds through the Bogar.

8. In the United States, companies with ample investment opportunities (growth-option companies) issue less debt and have shorter maturities. This not only protects lenders against the greater uncertainty associated with growth firms but also serves to preserve their own financing flexibility and future ability to invest. Growth companies are also likely to choose private over public sources of debt because renegotiating a troubled loan with a banker (or a handful of private lenders) will generally be much easier than getting hundreds of widely dispersed bondholders to restructure the terms of a public bond issue (Barclay, Smith, and Watts 1999; Barclay and Smith 1999).

9. Results for a panel regression with 1,473 observations that includes Brazil, Chile, Colombia, and Peru are similar, though q almost has a significantly negative effect on market leverage at the 10% level.

10. In a panel regression with 1,715 observations that includes Brazil, Chile, Colombia, and Peru, the main difference is that q has a significantly negative effect on book leverage.

11. In a panel regression with 1,490 observations that includes Brazil, Chile, Colombia, and Peru, the results are quite similar, except for *tangibility* that has a significantly positive effect on the share of short-term debt. Controlling for country effects, firms from Chile have a significantly smaller share of short-term debt.

12. A better measure of credit availability would be unused credit lines. Streb et al. (2003) explore this idea, based on the fact that most bank credit is based on loan commitment contracts (Melnick and Plaut 1986). Another possibility might be to jointly consider both debt ratios and the spreads on debt.

13. Probit estimates that include Chile and Colombia (1,385 observations), though similar, have significantly positive dummies for Chile and Colombia, so all else equal firms in those countries are more likely to issue bonds. In tobit estimates for the ratios of *bond debt/firm value*, *bond debt/assets*, and *bond debt/(bond + bank debt)*, with respectively 1,190, 1,385, and 1,188 observations, except for *roa* that has a significantly negative effect, other coefficients are similar. The dummies for Chile and Colombia are again significantly positive, so controlling for other variables firms in Chile and Colombia have larger amounts of bonds outstanding. However, the interpretation of these dummies is not clear to us. The unconditional sample means for firms in Argentina are larger than for firms in Chile and Colombia: for *bond debt/firm value*, means are 9%, 4%, and 2%; for *bond debt/asset*, 7%, 3%, and 2%; and for *bond debt/(bond + bank debt)*, 21%, 19%, and 11%.

14. This section is based on Alegre, Pernice, and Streb (2007).

15. From September 2005 until June 2006, 230 CFOs were personally contacted three or more times. Of the companies that refused to participate, the most frequent reasons were that it was against company policy to answer surveys (25%), lack of interest (24%), unwillingness to disclose confidential information (24%), and that questionnaire was too long (17%).

16. Of the 41 companies surveyed, the respondent was the portfolio manager for 17 of the companies, the CFO for 9, and "other" for 15, including the president of the company in one case.

17. The following arguments use a comparison between Argentina and the United States for pedagogical purposes only, but the conclusions we will obtain seem to have general validity.

18. The source is *Guía Senior* from 2004, a commercial guide produced by the company of the same name, which includes information regarding 17,000 Argentine companies and is updated three times a year (see http://www.guiasenior.com).

19. Regarding causality (whether the corporate bond market is small because firm values are small, or firm values are small because the corporate bond market is small), our view is that there is an interaction between both variables that is the result of structural reasons such as low institutional quality, macroeconomic instability, and so forth, which are not specific to corporate bond markets. After financial liberalization in the 1990s, we do not believe that companies do not get enough access to financing because of obstacles directly related to bond market structure.

20. If we were to calculate the ratio of the sum of the firm values of the 960 largest public US firms to the sum of the firm value of the 40 largest public Argentine firms, where $960/40 = 24$ is the ratio of GDPs, one obtains a ratio of approximately 302:1, which is very similar to magnitudes in text.

References

Alegre, María, Sergio Pernice, and Jorge M. Streb (2007). "Determinants of the Development of Corporate Bond Markets in Argentina: Survey to Firms and Investors." Documento de Trabajo 345, Universidad del CEMA.

Axtell, Robert L. (2001). "Zipf Distribution of U.S. Firm Sizes." *Science* 293 (7 September): 1818–1820.

Barclay, Michael J., and Clifford W. Smith (1999). "On Financial Architecture: Leverage, Maturity and Priority." In D. H. Chew, Jr., ed., *The New Corporate Finance: Where Theory Meets Practice.* Boston: Irwin/McGraw-Hill.

Barclay, Michael J., Clifford W. Smith, and Ross L. Watts (1999). "The Determinants of Corporate Leverage and Dividend Policy." In D. H. Chew, Jr., ed., *The New Corporate Finance: Where Theory Meets Practice.* Boston: Irwin/McGraw-Hill.

Bebczuk, Ricardo (2005). "Corporate Governance and Ownership: Measurement and Impact on Corporate Performance and Dividend Policies in Argentina." Research Network Working Paper No. 516, Inter-American Development Bank.

Bedoya, Alejandro, Celeste González, Sergio Pernice, Jorge M. Streb, Alejo Czerwonko, and Leandro Díaz Santillán (2007). "Database of Corporate Bonds from Argentina." Documento de Trabajo 344, Universidad del CEMA.

Blackwell, David W., and David Kidwell (1988). "An Investigation of Cost Differences between Public Sales and Private Placements of Debt." *Journal of Financial Economics* 22(2): 253–278.

De la Torre, Augusto, and Sergio Schmukler (2004). *Whither Latin-American Capital Markets?* Washington, D.C.: World Bank.

Fernández, Roque B., Celeste González, Sergio Pernice, and Jorge M. Streb (2007). "Loan and Bond Finance in Argentina, 1985–2005." Documento de Trabajo 343, Universidad del CEMA.

López Isnardi, Norberto, and Claudio Dal Din (1998). "La deuda pública argentina 1990–1997." Documento de Trabajo 56, Buenos Aires, Fiel.

Melconian, Carlos, and Rodolfo Santángelo (1996). "El endeudamiento del sector público argentino en el período 1989–1995." Proyecto ARG/91/R03, United Nations Development Programme.

Melnik, Arie, and Steven Plaut (1986). "Loan Commitment Contracts, Terms of Lending, and Credit Allocation." *Journal of Finance* 41: 425–435.

Rajan, Raghuram G., and Luigi Zingales (1995). "What Do We Know about Capital Structure? Some Evidence form International Data." *Journal of Finance* 50: 1421–1460.

Reinhart, Carmen, M., Kenneth S. Rogoff, and Miguel A. Savastano (2003). "Debt Intolerance." *Brookings Papers on Economic Activity* 1: 63–70.

Streb, Jorge M., et al. (2003). "The Effect of Bank Relationships on Credit for Firms in Argentina." In Arturo Galindo and Fabio Schiantarelli, eds., *Credit Constraints and Investment in Latin America*. Washington, D.C.: Inter-American Development Bank.

5 Development of Colombian Bond Markets

Camila Aguilar, Mauricio
Cárdenas, Marcela Meléndez,
and Natalia Salazar

In spite of recent progress, the Colombian financial sector remains small and shallow, and largely dominated by the banking sector. In the debt market, Colombia is nonetheless a medium-size player, both in terms of domestic public debt and of the corporate bond market.

This chapter deals specifically with the determinants and the consequences of the development of the corporate bond market. This is an interesting issue, considering the recent growth of this segment of the capital markets (in 2004 the real value of outstanding corporate bonds was four times higher than in 1997). In spite of its recent growth, there are a relatively small number of issues and issuers (on average only 39 issuers per year between 1997 and 2004). The issuing firms, mostly in manufacturing and services, tend to be large and profitable. For example, bond issuers were on average 42 times larger in asset terms than nonissuers in 2004. More importantly, issuing firms have grown much faster than nonissuers.

We use a large firm-level data set for the period 1997–2004 and find some interesting results. First, the larger the firm, the higher the probability that it will issue bonds. Second, more profitable and more leveraged firms are more likely to issue bonds. Third, cost per peso issued has, as expected, a negative impact on the number of firms that issue corporate bonds, suggesting that only larger firms are able to issue bonds because they spread the entry costs over larger issues.

We also explore the interplay between the public debt and the corporate bond market, which is a complex and relevant issue. At least for the case of Colombia, the evidence suggests that crowding-out effects dominate: the larger the treasury bond market, the lower the probability that a firm will decide to look for financing in the market. This conclusion is at odds with the alternative view of these two markets as complements.

On the demand side, we use detailed information from institutional investors (all pension funds, both mandatory and voluntary, and severance pay funds are investors in corporate bonds). The main results indicate that investors with larger portfolios have a higher probability of holding corporate bonds. Interestingly, a large portfolio share invested in public debt tends to decrease the investor's probability of holding corporate bonds. This is an important result because it indicates that the crowding-out effects of a large stock of treasury bonds negatively affect not only the supply of but also the demand for corporate bonds. In addition, from the viewpoint of investors, average bond issue size is a critical variable. Only large issues are sufficiently liquid to stimulate the appetite of potential investors.

The chapter concludes with a discussion on the consequences of the development of the corporate bond market. Using a third database, we examine loan performance in different economic sectors. The sectors with more corporate bonds (as a percentage of total liabilities) have greater loan quality. In other words, these sectors have a much lower share of nonperforming loans. More importantly, this result is stronger during periods of banking crises. The normative implication is that the bond market plays a countercyclical role during periods of financial stress. Thus, policies aimed at improving the workings of this market have a potentially large dividend.

The chapter is structured in the following way. After a brief literature review, we present an overview of the Colombian financial sector (which can be omitted by the reader familiar with its history and evolution). We subsequently describe Colombian bond markets and introduce the databases that were constructed for this chapter, then use those data to estimate models that explain the probability that a firm issues bonds (supply) as well as the probability that an institutional investor holds them (demand). The next section provides some empirical evidence to support the idea that having a larger bond market is desirable. The chapter ends with a brief section of conclusions and policy recommendations.

Literature Review

The relatively scarce literature addressing the issue of bond market development has focused on the factors that explain the market's development in a multicountry regression setting. For example, Eichengreen and Luengnaruemitchai (2004) study the causes for the slow development of the Asian bond market, using a cross section of developing and developed economies. They find that larger country size, stronger institutions, less volatile exchange rates, and more competitive banking sectors are positively associated with bond market capitalization. Asian countries' strong fiscal balances have not resulted in growth of the government bond markets. Their results suggest that the region's structural characteristics and macroeconomic and financial policies fully account for differences in bond market development between Asia and the rest of the world.

Zervos (2004) documents the costs of debt and equity issuance, both in the domestic and the international markets, for firms in Brazil, Chile, and Mexico, collecting data on investment banking and legal fees, regulatory and exchange listing costs, taxes, rating agency fees, and expenditures for marketing and publishing. The paper suggests that Brazilian firms face similar costs in local markets and abroad when issuing debt, but they face significantly higher costs in local markets when issuing equity. Chilean firms can issue debt more cheaply in the international markets, and while issuing equity in their local market is less expensive, transaction costs have resulted in a preference for bonds over equity as a source of financing. Finally, Mexican firms face the lowest costs when issuing debt, but the highest in issuing equity. In addition, the paper underscores the role played by the investor base in influencing the ability of firms to access domestic capital markets.

Beck and Levine (2002) study whether market-based or bank-based financial systems are better at financing the expansion of industries that depend heavily on external finance, at facilitating the birth of new establishments, and at improving the efficiency of capital allocation across industries. They do not find evidence for either the market-based or the bank-based hypothesis. While the efficiency of the legal system and the overall degree of financial development boost industry growth, having a bank-based or market-based system does not per se seem to matter for the formation of new establishments or for an efficient capital allocation. Levine (2002) also explores the relative merits of bank-based and market-based financial systems. Using a broad cross-country database, his results indicate that although overall financial development is robustly linked with economic growth, there is no support for either the bank-based or the market-based view.

Faulkender and Petersen (2003) examine whether, rather than being constrained in their access to incremental capital by the risk of their cash flows and by their characteristics, firms may in fact be rationed by lenders. They find that firms with access to public bond markets have significantly different leverage ratios. Even after controlling for the firm characteristics previously found to determine observed capital structure and the possible endogeneity of having a bond rating, they find that firms which are able to raise debt from public markets have 40% more debt.

More recently, Burger and Warnock (2006a) analyze the development of 49 local bond markets. They show that countries with stable inflation rates and strong creditor rights have more developed local bond markets and rely less on foreign currency-denominated bonds. Their results suggest that emerging economies are not inherently dependent upon foreign-currency debt and that by improving policy performance and strengthening institutions they may develop local currency bond markets, lower their currency mismatch, and decrease the likelihood of future crises. In a follow-up paper, Burger and Warnock (2006b) analyze foreign participation in the bond markets of over 40 countries. They find bond markets in less developed countries have returns characterized by high variance and negative skewness, and that these factors largely explain the lack of participation of US investors. While results based on a three-moment capital asset pricing market (CAPM) indicate that what US investors avoid is diversifiable idiosyncratic risk, their analysis suggests that by reducing macroeconomic instability countries can improve foreign participation.

For the case of Colombia, the literature has focused on capital markets in general, but not specifically on the bond market. Fedesarrollo (1996) led an umbrella project to examine the obstacles to the development of capital markets from different angles, including a revision of the institutional and regulatory restrictions, of the potential suppliers and market participants, and of the structural macroeconomic variables that affect that development. The result of this study, known as the Mission of the Capital Markets, is a set of policy recommendations that led the way for the development of a government bond market and proposed several regulatory and institutional reforms regarding the supply and demand of corporate debt.

More recently, Anif and Fedesarrollo (2004) studied the determinants of firms' capital structure in an effort to understand their reluctance to issuing debt and equity. Using the input from interviews, workshops, and a survey, this study found that only large firms participate, and that the market is still heavily concentrated in short-term debt. The diagnosis from the point of view of both firms and institutional investors was not far from that provided by the Mission of the Capital Markets a decade before.

Overview of the Financial Sector

In spite of having experienced significant growth over the last 15 years, the Colombian financial sector is still small and shallow. Both the Colombian banking and nonbanking financial sectors are relatively small compared to those of the developed countries and to the Asian emerging economies, in particular with regard to the banking sector and the stock market (see table 5.1). Within Latin America, the banking sectors in Colombia, Mexico, and Peru are of similar size, but much smaller than those of Brazil and Chile. The picture is slightly different for the debt markets, in which Colombia appears as a medium-sized player, both in terms of the domestic public debt and the corporate bond market. In 2004, only Chile and Argentina had larger corporate bond markets (relative to GDP).

Table 5.1
Bank Credit, Stock Market Capitalization, and Outstanding Domestic Debt as Percent of GDP, 2004

	Bank credit	Stock market capitalization	Domestic debt		
			Government	Financial	Corporate
Mature markets:					
Japan	94.4	78.5	141.0	25.6	16.3
United States	45.8	129.0	47.1	94.4	22.0
Euro area	103.9	54.6	53.6	29.8	10.0
Emerging markets:					
Asia	103.6	74.1	22.3	13.4	6.9
Europe	24.3	34.1	26.9	0.5	1.0
Latin America	20.9	40.2	28.9	5.3	2.6
Argentina	10.4	30.7	5.8	3.4	6.4
Brazil	25.2	50.0	44.7	10.8	0.6
Chile	56.8	114.8	19.6	10.2	11.3
Peru	17.6	28.3	5.6	1.3	3.1
Mexico	14.3	25.4	22.6	0.8	2.7
Colombia	18.0	24.3	22.8	4.3	3.9

Source: IMF (2005). Data for Colombia: Banco de la República de Colombia, Superintendencia Financiera.

The Colombian bank-based financial system is much larger than the market-based segment. Thus, the banking sector remains the main source of funding of all productive activities. The stock market, which has been active since the 1960s, and the more recent private bond market are both still concentrated in a small number of issuers and issues and are relatively illiquid.[1] The performance of the public debt market has been, by contrast, very dynamic since the early 1990s.

In the remainder of this section we describe the main developments of both the banking and nonbanking sectors since the 1990s.

The Banking Sector

Prior to the 1990s, the Colombian banking sector operated under a model of specialized institutions. Commercial banks had a monopoly on checking accounts and held about 60% of the sector's total assets. The remaining 40% was divided among three types of intermediaries: investment banks, mortgage banks, and consumer loan companies. Investment banks appeared in the late 1950s with the purpose of facilitating long-term financing to the real sector through the issue of stocks and bonds. Their role, which has remained largely unfulfilled, was to aid the development of the capital markets. Mortgage banks were the result of a housing finance system reform in the early 1970s that gave these intermediaries a monopoly on the use of the constant purchasing power unit (UPAC in Spanish) an indexation mechanism applying both to saving deposits and mortgages.

Financial repression was pervasive between the mid-1960s and the 1980s; in the context of import substitution, industrialization credit was directed toward certain sectors while interest rates were heavily controlled and regulated. In addition, reserve deposits—monetary policy's main instrument at the time—and forced investments represented between 35% and 40% of total deposits. Foreign ownership of banks was heavily restricted, foreign exchange controls prevented the development of a foreign exchange market, and direct central bank lending to the government made the development of a public debt market unnecessary. All of these factors contributed to the financial sector's slow development.

In addition, during the early 1980s the Colombian financial sector was under severe stress as a result of the Latin American debt crisis. The lack of adequate prudential regulation and supervision led to the takeover and nationalization of several intermediaries at an estimated net cost of 3% of GDP.[2]

As a result of the crisis, financial regulation and supervision were strengthened in line with the Basel standards,[3] and a deposit insurance scheme was created. Simultaneously, the predominant instrument of monetary policy shifted from reserve deposits to open market operations (purchases and sales of central bank securities).

An intense process of financial reform took place in the early 1990s. Law 45 of 1990, Law 9 of 1991, and Law 35 of 1993 substantially changed the structure and operation of the financial sector. Reserve deposits were lowered, most forced investments were eliminated, and subsidized direct central bank lending to the government was made unconstitutional. Although interest rate controls had been lifted before, reforms restricted their use even more by limiting their potential application to 90 days only. In addition, restrictions on the foreign ownership of banks were dismantled while intermediaries were authorized to engage in a wider range of activities. At the same time, exchange rate controls were removed, allowing intermediaries to participate in a growing foreign exchange market.

As a result of the reforms, as well as of large capital inflows, financial intermediation grew rapidly. M3/GDP rose to 43.2% of GDP in 1997, up from 28% in 1990. The number of financial intermediaries increased, several public banks were privatized, and foreign ownership in the banking sector went from 10.2% in 1992 to 29% in 1998.

Given the unsustainable rates of growth in public and private expenditures, the current account deficit reached 5.4% of GDP in 1997 and the central government deficit increased up to 5% of GDP in 1998, making the economy vulnerable to the effects of the Asian and Russian crises. In response to the attacks on the currency resulting from the sudden stop in capital inflows, the central bank raised interest rates at the beginning of 1998. The economic consequences of the reversal in capital flows, the increase in interest rates, and the reduction in expenditures, as well as the balance sheet effects of the depreciation of the currency, resulted in a severe contraction of the economy in 1999 (−4.2% of GDP).

This crisis had far-reaching repercussions for the financial sector. The share of nonperforming loans over total loans rose to 16% in 1999, up from 6% in 1997. Progress in terms of size and depth of the financial intermediation suffered a major reversal as well. The stock of loans, which had risen from 28% to 40% of GDP between 1990 and 1997, fell to 25% in 2001. While commercial credit and consumer loans started recovering in 2002, the stock of mortgage loans fell to 4% of GDP in 2005, down from over 13% before the crisis (1997).

As a result of the crisis, financial regulation and supervision were elevated to new levels—where risk is more adequately evaluated and provisions are stricter—and this is apparently proving fruitful. In addition, the financial crisis triggered a reform of the bankruptcy law (Law 550 of 1999) given the large number of firms that were under severe stress. Existing legislation (Law 222 of 1995) was considered inadequate, and its application would have resulted in the liquidation of a large percentage of firms during the crisis.

The new law was conceived as a transitory mechanism, initially for five years but later extended until the end of 2006. Although the law provided incentives for creditors and debtors to negotiate "restructuring agreements," 28% of the firms under restructuring ended in liquidation, suggesting that in a large number of the cases, the law delayed the execution of creditor rights.

Under the law, voting rights allowed for coalitions between shareholders and small creditors (euphemistically called *internal creditors*), which were in most cases detrimental to creditors in the financial sector. In addition, tax authorities had privileges over other creditors. The law, although partially useful under a period of severe financial strain, had an anti-creditor bias.

Given these problems, a new bankruptcy law was approved at the end of 2006 (Law 1116 of 2006). The new law follows international standards, providing better protection of creditor rights.

The Nonbanking Sector

Several important developments have taken place in this market since the early 1990s. In particular, the liberalization of foreign portfolio investment, the appearance of new institutional investors, the development of mortgage securitization, and the progress made toward an improved market infrastructure (credit ratings, the unification of stock exchange markets, and the modernization of transactional systems, among others) imply more progress in recent years than in the preceding decades.

In Colombia, firms' preference for bank loans over market-based instruments is to a large extent the result of policy choices. In 1951, for instance, the central bank became a development bank by providing subsidized loans to specific sectors, creating a bias against bonds or equity financing. Tax measures were also a determining factor in this direction. Perhaps the most important was the 1953 reform that introduced a system that taxed simultaneously corporate profits and shareholders' dividends. This measure, which proved detrimental for the development of the stock market, was eliminated in 1986. During the inflation acceleration of the 1970s the stock market growth was also negatively affected by the tax deducibility of the inflationary component of interest payments.

Later measures were designed to correct these and other policies to facilitate the development of capital markets. Decree 1321 of 1989, for example, eliminated taxes on capital gains in the stock market. Law 49 of 1990 established that profits from the transfer of shares through the stock market would not constitute income or capital gains, and that investment funds and mutual funds that administrated trusts would be exempt from income taxes.

Only in the 1990s would significant progress be observed in the non-banking sector. Law 9 of 1991 allowed inflows of portfolio foreign investment, which in 1997 reached US$1.5 billion dollars. After drastically falling as a result of the Asian and Russian crises, these flows have recovered in recent years. However, these funds continue to be relatively small (0.4% of GDP).

Labor and pension reforms in the 1990s (Law 50 of 1990 and Law 100 of 1993, respectively) created new institutional investors that have played a key role in the development of Colombia's capital markets. The first of these reforms obliged employers to make a contribution equivalent to one month's salary per year. These contributions are deposited in the employees' individual accounts administered by severance pay funds (employees are allowed to withdraw money in case of unemployment or, under certain circumstances, for education and housing). The assets of these funds represented about 1.3% of GDP in 2005.

The pension reform created the private mandatory pension funds to administer the defined-contribution pension regime.[4] As in the case of severance pay funds, pension contributions deposited in individual accounts are invested in the capital markets. Since their creation in 1993, the pension funds have grown to become the most important player in the market, with a portfolio growing from 0.04% of GDP in 1994 to almost 12% of GDP in 2005. Law 100 also created voluntary pension funds. Although they are not large (only 0.2% of GDP in 2005), they have grown dynamically in the recent years because of a tax benefit that applies to the contribution of high salary individuals. The pension reform also created new business opportunities for life insurance companies (pension fund insurance and life annuities), providing them with additional resources to invest in capital markets.

Several other elements have also been key for the capital markets' recent development: (1) the creation of custody service entities in the early 1990s to reduce operating risks and add safety to financial transactions; (2) the development of mortgage securitization as an alternative long-term investment opportunity, introduced by Law 35 of 1993 and extended by Law 546 of 1999, to provide mortgage banks with longer-term financing (by the end of 2005, mortgage securitizations amounted to 1.5% of GDP); (3) the merger of three local stock exchanges (Bogotá, Medellín, and Occidente) into one national stock exchange in 2001 to avoid the inefficiencies resulting from market segmentation; and (4) the development in the 1990s of a unified electronic transaction systems, providing real-time information on trades and speeding transactions.[5]

In 2005, the supervision of banks and securities was merged into one agency with the goal of eliminating the "regulatory arbitrage" between the two segments of the market. Also in 2005, legal changes improved corporate governance, requiring independent board members in entities that issue securities, with the purpose of protecting small investors. While these developments are still too recent to show any results, they are steps in the right direction.

Bond Markets

Figure 5.1 shows the evolution of the Colombian private and public bond market. In 2004, the total outstanding debt in the Colombian bond market was close to US$33 billion. About 70% was public debt while the remaining 30% was equally split between corporate bonds and bonds issued by financial institutions.

The market size doubled between 1997 and 2004. The public debt component more than tripled over the same period, while the corporate debt market, although much smaller, also increased significantly. Debt issued by the financial sector appears to have lost market share. In fact, the share of treasury bonds rose to 23% of GDP in 2004, up from 8% in 1997. During the same period, debt issued by the financial

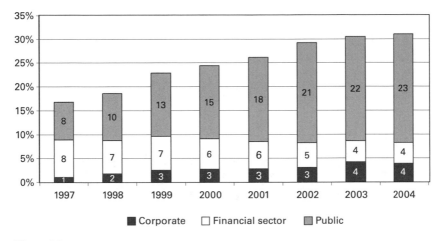

Figure 5.1
Bonds by type as percent of GDP, 1997–2004. Source: Superintendencia de Sociedades, Superintendencia Financiera, and Ministry of Finance of Colombia.

sector fell from a similar starting point (7.8%) to about half (4.3%) as percent of GDP. Corporate bonds, on the other hand, rose to 3.9% of GDP in 2004 from close to 1% in 1997. This is a significant increase that we discuss in greater detail below.

These numbers suggest that, while overall debt market evolution has been driven by a large and increasing public debt component, its performance has not hindered that of corporate debt in an evident way. On the contrary, the growth dynamics of the public debt market in Colombia may have facilitated the incipient development of the corporate bond market that remains small by international standards but shows significant growth in size in recent years. The low growth of bank loans over the period 1997–2004 could explain the decline in the share of debt issued by financial institutions.

The Public Bond Market

The Constitution of 1991 set the way for a new model of government financing by restricting the use of primary financing (which requires the unanimous approval of the independent central bank's board of directors). Treasury bonds (TES) rose to 35.7% of the total public debt in 2004, compared to 13% in 1995 (see figure 5.2). This rapid increase reflects the critical role played by bonds in financing the central government's deficit.

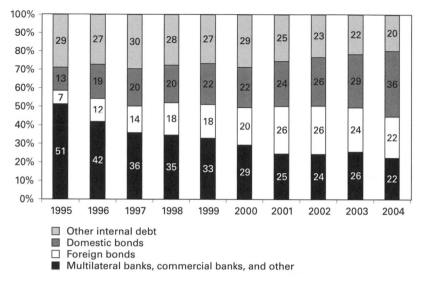

Figure 5.2
Public debt by source (percent of total). Source: Banco de la República de Colombia, Boletín de Deuda Pública, September 2005.

Not all treasury bonds are allocated through market mechanisms. A-type treasury bonds are issued with the exclusive purpose of covering the government's liability with the central bank and do not reach the market. These are a minority of the total treasury bonds outstanding. B-type TES treasury bonds are used to raise funds in the market through three alternative mechanisms: auctions; agreed operations with decentralized public sector entities (at market interest rates); and mandatory TES investments, which capture the excess liquidity of publicly owned companies or public entities. As a share of the total public debt, B-type TES grew from 3.4% in 1994 to 35.6% ten years later, mostly allocated through auctions and agreed operations.

The government's foreign debt composition also shows an increasing reliance on market-based instruments. Foreign debt bonds increased from 7.3% in 1995 to 22.3% in 2004 as a share of total debt, reflecting the lower dependence on loans from agencies, governments, multilateral organizations, and commercial banks (see figure 5.2). The resulting recomposition of external financing lowers the degree of conditionality on certain policy reforms, common in multilateral lending.

Without a doubt, the dynamism of the public debt market, both domestic and external, has reflected the emergence of large fiscal imbalances; public debt increased from 15% of GDP in 1999 to nearly 50% of GDP in the recent years. Also, the internal public debt market has allowed the government to substitute domestic debt for foreign debt: while in the early 1990s more than 80% of public debt was external, since 1996 this share has fluctuated around 50%, subject to the conditions of both internal and external markets.

The growth of internal public debt market is also explained by demand factors. The growing supply of treasury bonds has found sufficient demand in the market, mostly from new institutional investors. In addition, credit stagnation during the financial crisis of 1998–2000 contributed toward boosting this demand, and credit risk considerations led financial intermediaries to substitute loans for investments in treasury bonds during that period. In recent years, particularly since mid-2002, demand for treasuries has continued to thrive in response to an expansive monetary policy in a context of reduced alternative investments. The financing needs of the government, in addition, have resulted in attractive returns on treasury bonds relative to returns on alternative investments.

The public debt market has not only grown in size but has also progressed both toward alternative denominations and longer average maturities. In addition to the peso denomination (68.4% of the total outstanding in 2004), B-type TES are also denominated in indexed units (36.4% of the total outstanding in 2004) and in US dollars (6.7% of the total outstanding in 2004). With respect to maturities, the share of B-type TES with maturities of less than 5 years has dropped significantly (bonds with maturities less than one year are now nonexistent) while the share of B-type TES with maturities between 6 to 10 years has grown from nil to 52.7% over the same time period. These numbers demonstrate considerable success in replacing short-term debt with longer-term debt, which has been a goal of the government. Undoubtedly, the development of a more complete yield curve has contributed to the deepening of the debt market. The behavior of the share of B-type TES of maturities longer than 10 years is more random, however, and reflects the difficulties faced by the government in issuing long-term bonds in the local market.

On the demand side, financial institutions have been the largest buyers of government securities (their share in the outstanding central government bonds increased from 35.5% in 1995 to nearly 53% in 2004). Other private sector investors have also increased their holdings of government debt (from 11% in 1995 to near 19% in 2004), while other public sector entities now hold less debt issued by the central government (29.6% of the total, from a starting point of 53.5%).

The Corporate Bond Market

Only a small share of Colombian firms finances their activity through the bond market.[6] Between 1997 and 2004 there were on average only 39 issuers per year, defined as firms reporting bonds outstanding in their balance sheets (in contrast, on average there were on average 7,243 nonissuing firms per year). Using the same definition, the median numbers of issuers and nonissuers were 46 and 7,092, respectively.[7] Bond issues have tended to be concentrated in the manufacturing and services sectors (14 and 16 issuer firms on average per year in each of these sectors, respectively). Issuing firms in other sectors are very scarce.

There are some marked differences between firms that have access to the bond market and firms that do not, which are apparent when considering their accounting statements for 2004. The first and most obvious difference is size. Bond issuers in 2004 were on average 42 times larger than nonissuers, as measured by their assets. When measured by the median, the difference in size appears even larger, by about 91 times. There is also less dispersion in size among issuers. These differences are statistically significant.

Additionally significant are the differences between issuers and nonissuers with respect to the composition of their liabilities. The share of debt with the banking sector is on average 12.7% for the former as opposed to 23.7% for the latter. The median issuing firm reports no debt at all with the banking sector, for the median nonissuing firm bank loans represent 15% of total debt. However, not all bond issuers have completely substituted bank debt. Interestingly, accounts payable are also on average a much lower share of total liabilities in the case of issuers (13.1% compared to 27.8% for nonissuers), and the difference among median firms is also substantial (9.1% compared to 17.4% for nonissuers). In 2004, outstanding bonds represented 25% of the total liabilities in issuing firms (22.9% in the case of the median issuer firm). This share was only 12.1% in 1997.

Finally, issuing and nonissuing firms also differ in terms of their profitability. Issuers are not only more profitable—on average their operating profit as a share of assets is 5.4% as opposed to 3.7% for nonissuers—but also they show much less dispersion in profitability (compare a standard deviation of 1.25 to one of 17). This difference is statistically significant as well. There is no evidence, however, of significant differences between issuers and nonissuers with respect to their leverage.

A more careful review of issuers and issue characteristics between 1997 and 2004 shows at least two interesting facts (see table 5.2). First, issuing firms, defined this time as those reported by Superintendencia Financiera as having issued bonds each year, are much larger (in asset terms) in 2004 than they were 7 years before. The largest issuing firm is 9.6 times larger, the median firm is 13.2 larger, and the smallest issuing firm is 11.7 times larger in 2004 than in 1997. Second, total amounts issued each year have considerably increased over time (the market size in 2004 was four times larger than in 1997). Considering that the total number of issues per year has not increased over time, the average issue size has shown a remarkable increase (compare the average issue size of US$202.3 million in 2004 to that of US$16.1 million in 1997, or the evolution of the median and the minimum issue sizes over the same period).

Thus, the size of the Colombian corporate bond market is explained by a small number of large issues placed by very large firms. The evidence points toward a pattern of bond market development that is increasingly supported by fewer and larger issues: a market growing in size but apparently not getting deeper.

In other words, regardless of the small number of firms participating in the bond market, the large size of participating firms means that the overall share of market-based financing has increased over time, in part replacing bank credit as a source of funding (see figure 5.3).

To complete the picture of the corporate bond market, we take a look at the role corporate bonds play in the portfolios of the institutional investors. Table 5.3 summarizes the findings for 2004. Mandatory pension funds are the largest institutional investors in Colombia as measured by their portfolio size, which amounted to about 50% of the total investment portfolio in 2004. They are distantly followed by banks and investment banks.

Out of a total of 153 potential institutional investors in 2004, 56 do not report any participation in the corporate bond market in their financial statements. Nonparticipants represent a majority of the consumer loan companies, investment banks, trust companies, and banks, and, to a lesser extent, insurance companies. All pension funds, both mandatory and voluntary, and severance pay funds are investors in

Table 5.2
Issuer and Issue Characteristics, 1997–2004

	1997	1998	1999	2000	2001	2002	2003	2004
Firms:								
Real assets in 2004 (million US$)								
maximum	479,036	90,067	2,750,759	515,367	494,927	3,838,823	4,297,296	4,622,397
minimum	100,062	90,067	97,317	2,894	44,330	33,240	124,396	1,165,800
median	113,784	90,067	283,188	167,685	280,742	215,507	420,410	1,497,680
Average corporate debt as share of total liabilities	12.1%	2.9%	28.0%	17.7%	17.9%	26.4%	35.2%	22.3%
Number of issuers	4	1	7	5	5	9	6	3
Number of issues	9	1	11	6	5	11	6	3
Total amount issued in 2004 (million US$)	145.24	6.43	397.13	158.10	213.77	935.53	856.44	606.76
Average issue size in 2004 (million US$)								
mean	16.14	6.43	36.10	26.35	42.75	85.05	142.74	202.25
median	22.52	6.43	23.55	16.78	30.18	18.80	50.77	125.54
minimum	0.94	6.43	6.25	10.83	22.63	11.75	13.24	62.77
Total including holdings:								
Number of issues	13	3	13	10	11	14	8	9
Total amount issued in 2004 (million US$)	182.77	7.15	582.11	255.55	405.40	1,050.71	856.31	1,258.90
Average issue size in 2004 (million US$)	14.06	2.38	44.78	25.56	36.85	75.05	107.04	139.88

Source: Superintendencia Financiera.

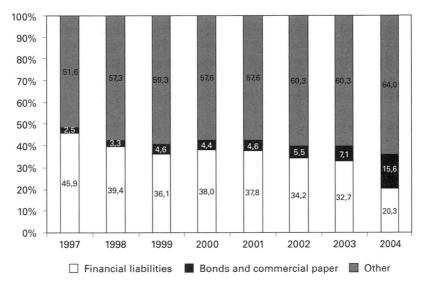

Figure 5.3
Liabilities by type, 1997–2004 (percent of total). Source: Superintendencia Financiera.

corporate bonds. On average, however, the share of their portfolios invested in corporate bonds is near 11%, far below the ceiling of 30% permitted for both mandatory pension funds and severance pay funds. Nonetheless, in 2004, mandatory pension funds held 76% of outstanding corporate debt. Severance pay funds and voluntary pension funds followed at a distance, with 9% and 7%, respectively.

The contrast is striking when we look at the shares of the various portfolios invested in treasury bonds (31.7% for the median institutional investor). Both mandatory pension funds and life insurance companies invest in treasury bonds at levels close to the respective ceilings of 50% and 60% dictated for them by the regulation, and the shares of the median severance pay fund and the median bank portfolios invested in public debt in 2004 are 70% and 65%, respectively.

The public component of the Colombian bond market is evidently absorbing a large share of market liquidity. However, it is unclear whether there is indeed a liquidity restriction affecting the development of the corporate bond market or whether there are other types of restrictions that are more binding. Before we explore this issue further in the following section, it is important to mention the results of an investors' survey that we conducted for the purposes of this project.[8] According to answers provided by investors, low appetite for this type

Table 5.3
Institutional Investors by Type, 2004

	Banks	Consumer loan companies	Trust funds	Invest-ment banks	General insurance companies	Life insurance companies	Mandatory pension funds	Severance pay funds	Voluntary pension funds
Number of investors with corporate bonds outstanding in their portfolio	13	1	7	4	16	17	7	6	7
As share of total	28.3%	1.6%	12.7%	11%	39.0%	68.0%	100%	100%	100%
Portfolio size in 2004 million dollars:									
Mean	493,357	3,899	6	391,707	52	87	1,550,366	210,614	209,392
Standard deviation	539,482	3,062	7	288,946	50	100	1,089,213	119,593	189,196
Median	290,259	3,124	3	362,023	32	41	1,689,383	218,739	122,594
Portfolio share in corporate bonds:									
Mean	2.4%	0.0%	2.9%	2.1%	4.2%	8.3%	11.5%	10.7%	11.0%
Standard deviation	5.8%	0.2%	9.2%	1.5%	5.4%	8.3%	4.5%	6.9%	4.9%
Median	0.0%	0.0%	0.0%	2.0%	2.5%	7.2%	12.9%	9.3%	13.1%
Ceiling imposed by the regulation					30.0%		30%	30%	
Portfolio share in treasury bonds:									
Mean	63.7%	63.6%	54.9%	29.0%	52.4%	64.8%	47.9%	68.2%	47.6%
Standard deviation	22.3%	28.9%	37.0%	13.7%	21.4%	20.3%	14.1%	10.0%	17.3%
Median	64.6%	74.7%	53.3%	31.7%	56.2%	67.1%	53.1%	69.9%	43.1%
Ceiling imposed by the regulation					60.0%		50%		

Source: Superintendencia Financiera.

of securities is the result of the absence of a complete reference index (which restricts adequate pricing) and the lack of a yield curve (apart from the low size and liquidity of the market, which are almost always present in the responses). Institutional issues attract attention as well: 53% of the surveyed investors mentioned excessive regulation as an obstacle, while 45.2% mentioned the weakness of creditor rights. A very large share of the institutional investors believed that prudential regulation imposed unnecessary restrictions on portfolio allocation.

The fact that the bond market, with respect to both its public and private components, is in the hands of a few large players subject to substantial regulation is an issue to revisit in gauging the long-term health of the market.

The Market Participation Choice

This section explores firms' decisions to issue bonds and investors' decisions to acquire them. We use econometric techniques with the available firm-level data. The results of these exercises are summarized in table 5.4.

The Firm's Decision to Issue Bonds

We were able to construct a firm-level data set for the period 1997–2004 that provides firm characteristics and information about the firm's activity in the corporate bond market, which allows us to estimate a model explaining a firm's probability of issuing bonds. Both firm characteristics and market characteristics were considered as explanatory variables.

Firm characteristics include size (measured by the log of the firm's assets), leverage (total liabilities/total assets), and profitability (measured by the ratio of operating utility to total assets). The coefficient on the size variable is expected to have a positive sign since the evidence in Colombia points toward large size as a key determinant of a firm's decision to seek financing through the bond market. The signs on the other two firm-level variables are uncertain, however, because there is no clear-cut difference between the leverage of issuers and that of nonissuers. While profitability tends to be slightly higher at the mean and median for issuers relative to nonissuers, this evidence does not necessarily guarantee a positive sign.

Table 5.4
Probit Regressions to Explain Decisions to Participate in the Bond Market

Dependent variable	Coefficient	dF/dx
Dummy $= 1$ if firm issued bonds at time t:		
Constant	-135.27	
	(35608)***	
Size $(t-1)$	0.47	$2.55e^{-10}$
	(0.062)***	
Leverage $(t-1)$	0.44	$2.40e^{-10}$
	(0.158)***	
Profitability $(t-1)$	0.45	$2.48e^{-10}$
	(0.230)***	
Dummy $= 1$ if firm issued bonds in $(t-1)^2$	0.57	$2.87e^{-09}$
	(0.213)***	
Dummy $= 1$ if firm issued stocks before $(t)^2$	0.63	$4.02e^{-09}$
	(0.306)**	
Corporate debt market entry cost	-11.45	$-6.26e^{-09}$
	(3.413)***	
Stock market size	-6.67	$-3.65e^{-09}$
	(1.947)***	
Financial intermediaries market size	4.20	$2.30e^{-09}$
	(1.185)***	
Public debt market size	-0.51	$-2.79e^{-10}$
	(0.175)***	
Relative size stock vs. financial intermediaries markets	2.94	$1.61e^{-09}$
	(0.871)***	
Number of observations	$46{,}813$	
Loglikelihood	-107.59	
Dummy $= 1$ if investor has corporate bonds outstanding in its portfolio at time t:		
Constant	-14.16	
	(1.934)***	
Investor size $(t-1)$	0.34	0.006
	(0.032)***	
Share of investor's portfolio in treasury bonds $(t-1)$	-0.29	-0.005
	(0.128)**	
Average issue size	0.82	0.014
	(0.155)***	
Number of observations	$1{,}864$	
Loglikelihood	-264.30628	

Note: Standard errors in parentheses. *** denotes significance at 1%. ** denotes significance at 5%. Standard errors are robust standard errors that correct for the clustered nature of the yearly data. dF/dx is for discrete change of dummy variable from 0 to 1. Time dummies and investor-type dummies were included in the investor's decision estimation.

A firm's participation in the market as a bond issuer in the previous period is controlled for by the inclusion of a dummy variable equal to 1 if the firm issued bonds at time $t - 1$. A firm's activity in the capital markets is also controlled with a dummy variable $= 1$ if at any previous time, before time t, the firm issued stocks. Both variables are expected to have a positive coefficient, since they capture the fact that previous market activity facilitates subsequent participation.

The explicit inclusion of variables identifying whether the firm was listed at the local or foreign stock exchanges, or whether it was under the supervision of Superintendencia Financiera at the time of issue, is not possible because of the lack of variation of the dependent variable within these categories. This is also true of the inclusion of fixed effects by sector of activity. Because participation in the bond market occurs only in a few sectors, the inclusion of three-digit ISIC sector dummy variables results in lack of variation of the dependent variable within groups, rendering estimation impossible.[9]

Market characteristics included as explanatory variables are meant to capture particularities of the Colombian markets that are common to all firms and should affect their choices with regard to financing. We have chosen to focus on the role played by financial markets' characteristics.[10]

The first variables considered is a proxy of the cost per peso issued, constructed as the annual average cost per peso across all issues recorded by the Superintendencia de Valores. Costs considered in this calculation include (1) the cost of registration at the Bonds and Stocks Registry (Registro de Valores) required for each issue, and (2) the cost of obtaining the issue authorization from Superintendencia Financiera. Both of these costs are calculated as a percentage of the amount issued with rates that vary with the issue size.[11] The expected coefficient on this variable is negative, since a large cost of entering the market should reduce the probability of participating.

Measures of the size of the stock market (value of domestic equities over GDP, also known as stock market capitalization), the depth of financial intermediaries (M3 over GDP), and the public debt market (treasury bonds outstanding over GDP) are included in the regression in order to capture the degrees of complementarity or substitutability across markets. Stocks should be a close substitute to corporate bonds, so the expected coefficient on the first of these variables is negative. With regard to the depth of financial intermediation, the expected coefficient has a positive sign. Finally, the sign on the public debt market size measure is uncertain. A negative sign will indicate a crowding-out effect, while a positive sign will signal that the development of the public debt market has aided the activity of the private side of the bond market.

The last explanatory variable considered is the size of the capital market relative to the financial intermediaries market. The proxy used as a measure in this case is the ratio of the value of domestic equities over M3. A larger capital market, in relative terms, should facilitate the development of the corporate bond market, so the coefficient expected on this variable is positive. Note that this relative size measure may increase due to growth of the capital market either in volume or in prices. The expected impact on the decision to issue bonds is positive regardless of which of these prevails.

The estimation shows that all proposed explanatory variables are significant at the 5% level.[12] Although the resulting marginal effects of these variables are small, the estimation serves well the purpose of explaining a firm's decision to issue bonds[13] (see table 5.4).

The model estimated underscores the importance of scale economies in a firm's decision to use market-based financial instruments. In line with large firms' participation in the market over the years, the positive sign on the one-period lag of the firm size proxy indicates that the larger the firm, the higher the probability that it will issue bonds to finance its activity. There thus appears to be a threshold firm size below which the cost of obtaining financing through the corporate bond market is higher than that of obtaining banking credit.

The leverage and profitability variables both display positive coefficients as well. The positive sign on the former indicates that more leveraged firms have a higher probability of financing through bond issues. This suggests that the probability of financing through bonds is higher for firms with a history of active participation in the financial sector. The positive sign on the profitability proxy indicates that, after controlling for size, more profitable firms are more likely to search for financing through the bond market.

The coefficients on the dummy variables controlling for state dependence and previous activity in capital markets are both positive, as expected. While potential biases from the inclusion of the lagged dependent variable in the right hand side of the regression are not explicitly controlled for, the results obtained are robust to the exclusion of this variable.

The coefficient on the corporate debt market entry cost variable is negative. This result is evidence that the cost per peso issued is a deterrent for firms to finance their activities through the market. In combination with the coefficient obtained on firm size, it may be pointing toward the fact that larger firms are able to issue bonds because they spread the entry costs over larger issues; recall that entry costs are calculated by issue value on the basis of percentage rates that vary with the issue size.

The financial markets' size variables also yield interesting results. The estimated coefficients have the expected signs for both the stock market and the financial intermediaries market. The coefficient on the stock market size is negative, signalling that indeed stocks and bonds behave as substitutes. Growth of the equity market does not per se motivate bond issuance, and on its own may be detrimental for the development of the corporate bond market. For its part, the positive coefficient on the financial intermediaries size proxy confirms that the larger the financial intermediaries sector (the more liquid the market), the higher the probability that a firm will choose to issue bonds. Perhaps the most interesting of these results is the negative sign of the coefficient obtained on the public debt market size measure, which provides evidence that there may be a crowding-out effect: the larger the treasury bond market, the lower the probability that a firm will decide to look for financing in the market. This may be due to the difficulty of competing with treasury bonds in terms of both risk and return, the latter having been high relative to other investment opportunities.

Finally, the size of capital markets relative to financial intermediaries shows a positive coefficient. This result is in line with the idea that firms will be more likely to participate in a more developed capital market. It also says that the market's relative size matters. It is not only a large capital market that is desirable from the corporate bond market development perspective, but also a capital market that is large relative to the financial intermediaries sector.

The Institutional Investor's Decision to Buy Corporate Bonds

We use the firm-level data available for the period 1995–2004, which include the accounting statements of each institutional investor and detailed information about the composition of its investment portfolio, in order to estimate a model explaining the investor's decision to hold corporate bonds.

Investor characteristics used as explanatory variables include a measure of firm size (the log of the investor's investment portfolio); the share of the investors' portfolio invested in public debt (the ratio of treasury bonds holdings to total portfolio investments); the average issue size at time t, a dummy variable that controls for investor type and a time dummy that controls for macroeconomic effects.[14] Firm-level variables enter the regressions lagged in order to control for potential endogeneity problems.

The probability of holding corporate bonds is expected to increase with portfolio size, as larger investment portfolios ought to be more diversified, so the coefficient on the size variable should be positive. With respect to the share of the portfolio invested in public debt, while the extent to which the firm is invested in treasury bonds can influence the investor's decision to hold corporate bonds, it is impossible to know ex ante what sign to expect on this variable's coefficient. It may be that investors holding more public debt in their portfolios tend to acquire fewer corporate bonds, in which case there would be evidence of a crowding-out effect (a negative effect). Alternatively, it may be that portfolios more strongly invested in public debt, with investments in treasury bonds at the ceiling imposed by the regulation, tend to be also more invested in corporate bonds (a positive effect).

The dummy variables by investor type are intended to control for characteristics specific to each investor type. In particular, there are regulatory restrictions that may affect the possibility of investing in corporate bonds. These regulations have limited variance over time and differ only across investor types, so the inclusion of investor-type dummies should capture their impact.

The average issue size at time t (value of total bonds issued over number of issues) is included in the regression to capture the role of the corporate bond supply in inducing investors to buy corporate bonds. Because investors are concerned about the liquidity of their investments, it is reasonable to expect that their decision to buy corporate bonds will depend to some extent on the size of the bond supply available. On the one hand, if they buy a small issue of corporate bonds, their market movements may alter prices and expose them to the risk of not achieving the mandatory minimum profitability required by law. On the other hand, the larger the issue, the larger the number of buyers; thus more participants may be interested in buying bonds when the investor needs to sell its bond holdings. The bond supply average size is measured as the log of the total amount issued divided by number of issues at time t. This market-level variable is constructed using the firm-level bond issue data from Superintendencia Financiera introduced above.

The coefficient on the investor size variable is positive and significant at the 1% level, indicating that investors with larger portfolios have a higher probability of holding corporate bonds. This result may also indicate that larger portfolios tend to be more diversified. The coefficient on the portfolio share invested in public debt is negative and significant at the 5% level. Apparently a large portfolio share invested in public debt tends to decrease the investor's probability of holding corporate bonds. This result, in line with that obtained while exploring the firms' choice to issue corporate bonds, signals once again that the market for public debt may be hindering the development of the corporate bond market in Colombia.

Perhaps the most interesting result of this exercise is the finding that the average bond issue size is a critical variable. The coefficient on this variable is positive and significant at 1%, indicating that the probability of investment is strongly dependent on the availability of a large bond supply in the market. Regardless of the number of firms in the market or the frequency of their issues, investors are apparently willing to buy these bonds. This result tells us that investment bankers have a key role to play in designing coordination schemes to make bond issuance an alternative for smaller players.

Role of the Corporate Bond Market

Up to this point we have explored what drives Colombian firms to use the market as a source of financing (or what limits them in their financing choices), and we have revised the demand-side elements that seem to play a role in determining the development of the corporate bond market. We have so far obtained three main findings. First, the evidence suggests that bonds are not a cost-efficient financing alternative for smaller firms. Second, the public debt market does not appear to have facilitated private bond market development in recent years. Third, the probability of stimulating demand for corporate bonds depends strongly on the size of the issue, a factor that excludes firms with smaller financing needs.

Do these findings, however, justify government involvement in the development of the bond market? Further evidence must be gathered in order to answer this question. In particular, it remains to be seen whether any of these issues has an impact on economic growth and development. This section attempts to answer that question by analyzing the impact of the existence of a corporate bond market on the performance of the banking sector in an empirical setting.

Firms that are able to obtain financing through bonds should display better bank loan performance during periods of crisis. In theory, this should be the case: such firms are low-risk because they enjoy access to long-term financing through the market and thus face lower cash constraints during periods of crisis. If this is true, then the existence of a large corporate bond market aids the performance of the banking sector during periods of crisis, and its existence is desirable for purposes of macroeconomic stability.

We use loan performance data available at the ISIC three-digit sector level from the Superintendencia Financiera for the period 1998–2004, in combination with accounting information from the firm-level databases mentioned above, to determine whether the sectors that issue bonds perform better in their interaction with the banking sector during periods of financial stress.

The dependent variable in the regression is the ratio at time t of sector i's loans rated C, D, or E (i.e., low-quality loans) to sector i's total loans—a measure of the sector's loan performance at time t. A measure of the size of the corporate bond debt outstanding per sector, a banking crises dummy variable, and their interaction are included as explanatory variables to capture the impact of the bond market on the bank credit market during crisis periods.

The size of corporate bond debt outstanding for each sector i at time t is measured as the ratio of bonds outstanding to total liabilities reported by the firms in their financial statements aggregated to the ISIC three-digit sector level. The coefficient on this variable should be negative if lower dependence on banking credit improves loan performance.

The banking crises dummy variable was constructed to equal 1 during the years in which Fogafin (Fondo de Garantías de Instituciones Financieras), the public entity in charge of deposit insurance, made large rescue payments to the banking sector. By construction, the coefficient expected on this variable is positive.

The interaction term captures whether sectors active in the bond market during crisis periods display better loan performance. A negative coefficient on this variable would indicate that it is desirable, from a macroeconomic stability perspective, to have a large and well-developed corporate bond market.

The regression also includes among the explanatory variables a measure of each sector's profitability constructed as the ratio of the sector's operating profits to its total assets, the sector's leverage (total liabilities to total assets), and sector-level dummies to control for other unobserved sector-specific characteristics. The expected coefficient on the profitability variable is negative, because better operating performance should translate into better loan performance. In contrast, the coefficient on leverage should be positive, because more leveraged firms tend to default more on their obligations than less leveraged firms.

Contemporaneous and lagged real GDP growth rates are included as macroeconomic controls. The expected signs on these variables are both negative, reflecting the impact of recessions on loan quality; estimation results are presented in table 5.5. All coefficients in the regression have the expected signs and are significant at the 10% level at least.

The coefficients on current and lagged real GDP growth are both negative, confirming that economic growth also contributes to better credit market performance. Good average performance at the sector level likewise contributes to better loan performance (see the negative coefficient on the sector average profitability and the positive coefficient on the average leverage level). The coefficient on the sector's average liabilities share represented by corporate bonds has a negative sign, indicating that the alternative of financing through the corporate bond market does contribute to better loan performance. The coefficient on the banking crises dummy is indeed positive, and, most relevant to the question posed in this section, its interaction with the share of bond finance (in total corporate finance) yields a negative coefficient, suggesting that during periods of banking crises the existence of this alternative source of financing plays a countercyclical role, contributing to a better performance of banking loans.

The findings of this section lead to the conclusion that a well-functioning corporate debt market is key for macroeconomic stability, and thus it is desirable to design policies oriented to facilitating and promoting that market's development.

Table 5.5
Impact of the Corporate Bond Market on the Banking Sector

Dependent variable: Loan performance	
Constant	9.84***
	(2.28)
Bonds outstanding/total liabilities (BO)	−0.42**
	(0.13)
Financial crisis dummy (FC)	2.81**
	(0.94)
FC × BO	−0.68***
	(0.13)
Profitability (operating utility/assets)	−0.46***
	(0.08)
Leverage (total liabilities/total assets)	0.10*
	(0.05)
GDP growth	−0.42***
	(0.09)
Lagged GDP growth	−0.67***
	(0.09)
Number of observations	367
Adjusted R-squared	0.17

Note: Standard errors in parentheses. Standard errors are robust standard errors that correct for the clustered nature of the yearly data. The equation includes sectoral control dummies. *, **, and *** denote significance at the 10%, 5%, and 1% levels, respectively.

Concluding Remarks and Policy Recommendations

Despite having experienced significant growth over the last 15 years, the Colombian financial sector is still small and shallow. Both the Colombian banking and nonbanking financial sectors are small compared to those of the developed countries and the Asian emerging economies.

The development of Colombia's capital markets is recent and directly connected to a set of reforms introduced in the early 1990s that included the liberalization of foreign portfolio investment, the appearance of new institutional investors, the development of mortgage securitization, and significant progress toward an improved market infrastructure. Prior to these reforms, economic policy induced firms to depend on bank loans for financing.

The Colombian bond market doubled in size between 1997 and 2004, largely because of the dynamics of the public debt component. Corporate debt, although much smaller in size, also increased over time, contributing to the development of the nonbank segment of financial markets.

Using new firm-level data, this chapter confirms the findings of the previous literature that the corporate bond market in Colombia has been to date a source of financing available only to larger firms. Our empirical approach allows us to go one step further to derive policy implications. We show that having the market as a source of financing alternative to banking loans plays a critical stabilizing role during periods of banking crisis, and the economy as a whole holds up better when the firms in the productive sectors are not exclusively dependent on banking credit. If nothing else, this evidence should underscore the value of having a well-developed corporate bond market and the importance of pursuing the appropriate policies to facilitate its growth.

Regarding market participation decisions of both firms and investors, the findings in this chapter indicate that issue size is a key driver of this market's activity. Firm size matters, but only to the extent that larger firms have so far been the only ones able to place large issues on the market. This is in line with a market preference for more liquid investments and for investments in which the market price is not exposed to fluctuations induced by the movement of individual players.

Investment banks evidently have a key role to play as market developers if they understand the relevance of devising schemes to package the financing needs of smaller firms and coordinating those schemes in order to reach the market with placements of appropriate size. In doing so, investment bankers must overcome their reticence to work for smaller players. Likewise, regulatory authorities must work to facilitate these coordination schemes. Efforts needed may include a revision of the credit rating standards behind the institutional investors' portfolio choices—some of which are imposed by regulation regarding the portfolio management of institutional investors. For instance, asymmetries in the minimum profitability requirement currently affecting the mandatory pension funds ought to be revised since the regulation does not reward above-average portfolio performances, which encourages investments only in top-rated investments. Also, it is in the hands of the regulatory authorities to make investment-banking services accessible in terms of price to the smaller players.

We further find that the entry cost to the bond market discourages firm participation; this also explains why only large firms are issuers. While packaging the financing needs of the smaller players, as suggested in the previous paragraph, will surely aid in spreading these fixed costs, the government should also consider directly lowering them. In addition, priority should be given to reducing the amount of time required to obtain the required permissions and licenses from the Superintendencia Financiera in order to increase efficiency. In addition to lowering its own entry costs, the Stock Exchange of Colombia could assist in the selection of candidate firms to "package" (reducing structuring costs) and in disseminating information on the benefits of bond financing.

Finally, we find evidence that the competition of the public-debt component for the market liquidity has limited the growth potential of the corporate bond market. The fact that public debt has been placed at relatively high interest rates (because of the size of the fiscal deficits that need to be financed) raises questions regarding the long-term consequences of Colombia's fiscal policy. While it is not the aim of this paper to determine the ways in which the fiscal policy of Colombia should be adjusted, much progress needs to be made in this area.

Acknowledgments

We are grateful to Ugo Panizza, Kevin Cowan, Eduardo Borensztein, Barry Eichengreen, Franco Fornasari, and the participants at the seminars of the IDB Research Network "The Development of Latin American Bond Markets" for useful comments. Camila Casas provided excellent research assistance and Fabián García helped in the editing of the paper.

Notes

1. Only around 100 companies are listed.

2. See Echeverry and Salazar (1999) and Caballero and Urrutia (2006).

3. Dictated by the Basel Committee on Banking Supervision, created in 1974 and formed by the central banks' governors of the G-10 member countries. The goal of the standards is to improve the supervision guidelines that central banks or similar institutions impose on wholesale and retail banks.

4. The pay-as-you-go regime continues to be administered by a public entity, the Instituto de Seguro Social (ISS).

5. Before having a single stock exchange, each of the three stock exchanges had developed its own electronic transaction systems for fixed income operations and variable income operations. These systems were integrated with the creation of the Stock Exchange of Colombia.

6. Information about the workings of the Colombian corporate bond market during the period 1997–2004 is not available from a single source. Firm-level data are available from the Superintendencia de Sociedades (SS) and at the Superintendencia Financiera (SF). The SS database contains the annual financial statements of 7,317 medium- and large-size firms, obliged to report to this agency. The SF also includes accounting data, but only for the firms that issue equity or bonds. It contains information about the amounts issued by each of these firms at each point in time. Both databases were merged for the purposes of this research. Finally, detailed accounting statements are available at the firm level for all institutional investors for the period 1995–2004 from Superintendencia Financiera. This section and the sections that follow are based on these sources.

7. In the database, 350 firms on average per year do not have a sector identifier.

8. Investors' perceptions about the corporate bond market in Colombia were captured with a survey.

9. Firms' characteristics that enter as explanatory variables are lagged to control for potential endogeneity.

10. Time-dummies were included as explanatory variables in an alternative model firm's financing decisions. The coefficients on the firm-level variables were robust to the specification to control for elements of the macroeconomic environment that may affect the inclusion of these controls, but the significance of the market variables was swept away by it. We consider the alternative model specification—without time dummies—much more interesting.

11. The calculated cost per peso issued does not include the costs paid to investment bankers and other costs that may be incurred during the issue process, so they underestimate the real costs.

12. Standard errors are robust standard errors that correct for the clustered nature of the market-level variables.

13. A version of the same model was estimated, restricting the sample to include only the firms that report bonds outstanding in their balance sheets in each period. We found that the variables driving the decision of a firm to issue bonds are robust to whether the firm is a new or an experienced bond issuer. The results of this exercise are available from the authors.

14. A measure of firm performance—the firm's return on equity (ROE)—was included in alternative model specifications and discarded due to lack of significance. Results are available from the authors.

References

Anif and Fedesarrollo (2004). "Colombia: Diagnóstico de la estructura de financiamiento del sector real e identificación de obstáculos que han impedido que estas empresas acudan al mercado de valores." Mimeo.

Beck, T., and R. Levine (2002). "Industry Growth and Capital Allocation: Does Having a Market or Bank-Based System Matter?" NBER Working Paper No. 8982.

Burger, J. D., and F. E. Warnock (2006a). "Local Currency Bond Markets." NBER Working Paper No. 12552.

Burger, J. D., and F. E. Warnock (2006b). "Foreign Participation in Local Currency Bond Markets." NBER Working Paper No. 12548.

Caballero, Carlos, and Miguel Urrutia (2006). *El impacto del sector financiero en el crecimiento*. Bogotá: Editorial Norma.

Echeverry, J. C., and N. Salazar (1999). "¿Hay un estancamiento en la oferta de crédito?" Archivos de Macroeconomía, No. 118.

Eichengreen, B., and P. Luengnaruemitchai (2004). "Why Doesn't Asia Have Bigger Bond Markets?" NBER Working Paper No. 10576.

Faulkender, M., and M. A. Petersen (2003). "Does the Source of Capital Affect Capital Structure?" NBER Working Paper No. 9930.

Fedesarrollo (1996). *Misión de estudios del mercado de capitales—Informe final*. Bogotá: Fedesarrollo.

International Monetary Fund (2005). "Development of Corporate Bond Markets in Emerging Countries." Financial Stability Report.

Levine, R. (2002). "Bank-Based or Market-Based Financial Systems: Which Is Better?" NBER Working Paper No. 9138.

Zervos, S. (2004). "The Transactions Costs of Primary Market Issuance: The Case of Brazil, Chile, and Mexico." World Bank, Policy Research Working Paper No. 3424.

6 Development of the Chilean Corporate Bond Market

Matías Braun and Ignacio Briones

Since the 1980s, following five decades of financial repression, Chile has experienced an impressive record of financial development resulting from the implementation of a series of marked-oriented reforms. The total amount of financial liabilities grew from 10% of GDP in 1970 to nearly 200% of GDP today, a value well beyond that of any other Latin American country, similar to Korea and Australia, and half that of Japan or the US.

This chapter deals with a specific component of this evolution, namely the development of the fixed-income securities market in general, and the corporate bond market in particular.

The Chilean bond market as a whole represents nearly 30% of total financial assets, as compared to 20% for banking credit and 50% for equity (figure 6.1). These figures make the Chilean fixed-income market the largest in Latin America.[1] The stock of public and private bonds was 25% of GDP in the average Latin American country during the last 10 years, barely half the figure for Chile (48% of GDP). This stock is, however, much smaller than that of the typical developed economy (85% of GDP), and is not significantly high when compared to other countries of similar income level (Braun and Briones 2006).

Where Chile does indeed stand out is in the size of its corporate debt segment, which reached an average of 7% of GDP in the last 10 years. When compared to 8% of GDP in the typical industrial country, where the fixed-income market is heavily biased toward the public and financial segment, the figure is certainly impressive.

Not only is the corporate segment large, but the 16-year average maturity of the corporate issues in Chile is much longer than almost anywhere else, including the developed world (around 7 years). Finally, the share of issues denominated in local currency is also quite high in Chile when compared to other countries in the region or economies of

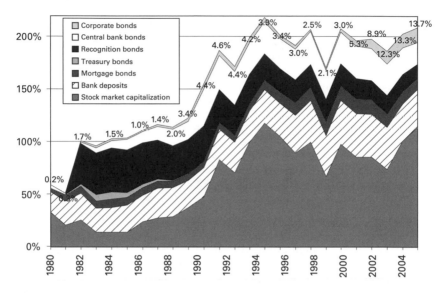

Figure 6.1
Chilean financial market size (percent of GDP). Source: Central Bank of Chile, SVS, and
Budget Department of the Chilean government (DIPRES).

similar degree of development. Interestingly, while the Chilean capital
market as a whole began its expansion in the mid-1980s, the development of the corporate bond market dates only from the very end of the
1990s. The expansion has been impressive. The stock of corporate
bonds increased from 3% of GDP in the late 1990s to 15% of GDP
today. Understanding this process of development is critical.

The rest of the paper is organized as follows. The next section briefly
provides the necessary institutional background to understand the recent evolution of the Chilean capital markets. We later analyze the
development of the corporate bond market since 1990. We first document the corporate bond market expansion and identify the main characteristics of the bonds issued. Based on 3,000 different firm-year
observations coming from the balance sheets of all the bond-issuing
companies and for all the publicly listed, nonissuing companies, we
identify the variables affecting the firms' access in bond financing. The
information is complemented with a survey of more than 70 companies and institutional investors. We then ask whether the recent and
impressive development of the corporate bond market responds to a
structural change or to transitory elements. The last section concludes
and provides some policy lessons.

The Institutional Development of the Chilean Financial System (1973–2005)

First Round of Market Reforms: Deregulation (1973–1981)

Starting in the 1930s, a number of restrictive regulations, including controlled interest rates, quantitative restrictions on credit, and explicit interventionism in its allowance to priority sectors, were progressively set. Financial repression reached a peak during President Salvador Allende's Unidad Popular government (1971–1973), when the state controlled nearly 90% of the domestic bank credit[2] and accounted for nearly 93% of all financial assets of the economy.[3]

Between 1973 and 1974, after the military coup, the government aimed at normalizing the financial system. It eliminated a tax on interest rates and decreed a progressive liberalization of the interest rate structure. Starting in 1975, the state-owned banks were privatized using high-leverage financing schemes,[4] and the government relaxed several entry restrictions into the banking industry. Deregulation also focused on introducing more flexibility regarding the remaining segments of the financial system such as the bond, insurance, and stock markets. The government enacted a new law concerning the superintendence of banks (1975) and mutual funds (1976), and allowed banks and financial institutions to perform brokerage operations. In 1976 a securities registry was created, and public disclosure of information became mandatory for listed firms. At the same time, the government extended the inflation indexation scheme to all financial instruments with maturity longer than 90 days.

The beginning of the 1980s was associated with a consolidation of the existing financial institutions and the standardization of their general regulation. During the decade, the government authorized banks to offer indexed savings accounts (1979) and enacted a new organic law for the state-owned bank. A new company law was introduced in 1981, and a Superintendence of Securities and Insurance (SVS) was created. The SVS became the main regulatory body of the domestic financial market, supervising all activities and entities participating in the Chilean securities and insurance markets. A private system of pensions (AFPs) based on individual capitalization accounts was created in 1980 and set up in 1982. As we will document later, the AFPs soon became the largest institutional investors in the domestic financial market and, according to Corbo and Schmidt-Hebbel (2003), important players in the financial and economic development experienced afterward.

In contrast to the aforementioned regulatory framework, the banking industry lacked prudential regulation. Lending to related entities within economic conglomerates owning banks was not precluded. A combination of implicit state guarantees for deposits and highly leveraged banks resulting from the privatization process deteriorated the quality of banks' portfolios. This, in combination with a major external shock that significantly impacted Chile's terms of trade, resulted in a severe banking and economic crisis starting in 1982.

The Banking Crisis and the Second Generation of Reforms during the 1980s

The state responded to the crisis by intervening in the banking system. It provided liquidity to banks that, in turn, assumed a subordinated debt in favor of the central bank. This debt had to be repaid in a maximum of 50 years. After the intervention, banks were reprivatized following a system called "popular capitalism." One relevant legacy of the banking crisis was the large amount of outstanding government bonds (mostly issued by the central bank).

The post-crisis period came along with a second wave of regulation of the financial market, and an increase in the power vested on the Superintendence of Banks and Financial Institutions (SBIF). A new banking law enacted in 1986 gave priority to prudential aspects, including (a) the establishment of reserve requirements as well as limits on the banks' leverage ratio; (b) the setting of incentives for private monitoring through mandatory disclosure requirements and partial state guarantees on deposits; and (c) the separation of the banking business form the one of subsidiaries related to a common economic conglomerate.

In 1982 a new bankruptcy law was enacted clarifying owner responsibilities in cases of failure. At the same time, the state disengaged from most of its public utility companies (communication and energy), and an ambitious plan of privatization was launched. In 1984 a tax reform eliminated the privileged treatment of firms' debt over their equity, and in 1985 the restrictions of pension funds on acquiring public equity were partially removed. All these factors contributed later to a huge development of the stock market. In 1987 the Insurance Law and the Securities Market Law were amended to require all instruments eligible for investment by the private pension funds to have a risk rated by an official entity. Finally, in 1989 the Central Bank of Chile became independent. The deregulation of international capital flows followed during the 1990s.

Third Phase: External Financial Deregulation during the 1990s

During the 1990s, many of the reforms carried out before were strengthened. Several constraints affecting the capital account of the balance of payments were removed. In 1997, a law regulating the participation of retail banks in other nontraditional banking industries such as investment banking, insurance, and factoring was approved by the Congress. For instance, firms with outstanding risk ratings were allowed to raise capital abroad (typically through the ADR mechanism) or to issue foreign bonds. The external constraints preventing institutional investors, such as pension funds and insurance companies, from holding international assets were removed up to a certain amount of their portfolios. International capital controls setting minimum permanence requirements for direct investment were progressively relaxed. Capital controls intended to lower the volatility of international short-term portfolio investments were de facto removed in 1998. In turn, in October 1999, the country switched from a managed exchange rate to a fully floating system. In 1999 the proportion of the assets that pension funds could invest abroad was raised from a range of 6–12% of the total (depending on the kind of fund) to a range of 10–20%. In March 2004 it was further increased to 20–30%. As a result, the share of foreign assets has jumped from 5.7% in 1998 to more than 27% in 2004.

Although it is not required by law, since 2000 the fiscal policy has been guided by a budget structural surplus rule calling for a budget surplus of 1% of GDP adjusted for the effects of the business cycle and fluctuations in the price of copper. As a result, the central government debt, which is marginal nowadays, is expected to disappear.

Fourth Phase: MKI and MKII Reforms

In 2001 the government launched a new major set of reforms known as the MKI (Capital Markets I) reforms. The framework had three main pillars: taxation, institutional reforms, and pension funds. The reforms were intended to increase the level of domestic savings, improve the liquidity and depth of financial markets, and raise competition between banks, insurance companies, and pension funds. The tax reforms eliminated the capital gains tax (15%) on the sale of stocks with high trading volume, the sale of stocks for three years after an initial public offering, and the short selling of stocks and bonds. The institutional reforms included the deregulation of the insurance industry by relaxing the limits on its investment portfolios. Insurance companies could invest up to 25% of their portfolios in corporate bonds rated above BBB and up to 5% in bonds that do not comply with these risk criteria. They can also invest overseas up to 20% in bonds, stocks, and mutual funds, including 5% of bonds rated below BBB. The latter resulted in an increase in the share of corporate bonds in the insurance companies' portfolios from less than 10% during the 1990s to 33% in 2004.

Mutual funds management companies benefited from modifications that simplified the trading of stocks, allowed the managers to develop complementary activities, and standardized the capital requirements. Finally, MKI authorized the creation of new entities called "general fund administrators" that could manage simultaneously multiple funds such as mutual funds, investment funds, and mortgage portfolios. In March 2002, the limits on voluntary contributions to pension funds (APVs) were raised and such contributions were granted a series of tax incentives.[5] In August 2002 pension funds were allowed to manage five different risk profile funds instead of the existing two. Ranging from A to E, the level of risk is determined by the proportion of the fund that can be invested in stock market–related securities. The workers can directly choose their funds. Since then the share of stocks in the total assets of the pension funds has grown from 9% to 15% in 2004.

A second round of reforms was presented in 2003 by the government through the MKII project. Its major goals are: (a) to stimulate the venture capital industry by means of proposing temporary tax exemption on capital gains in the stock market; (b) to facilitate the creation of limited liability corporations (which seem to be more flexible for venture projects); and (c) to set up a national registry of assets aimed at widening access to credit by using assets as collateral.

MKII is also intended to improve the supervision and enforcement powers of local regulatory institutions (SVS and SBIF) by raising the levels of transparency in the securities market, encouraging electronic issuance and trading of securities, setting new minimal capital requirements for financial intermediaries, and promoting the self-regulation of stock exchanges. In the same line, MKII also proposes to broaden the criteria to obtain a license to operate banks, life insurance companies, and pension funds.

As has been largely documented in the recent literature (La Porta et al. 2000, 2001, 2003; Hart 1999, among others), the existence of sound corporate governance, a regulatory framework ensuring investor protection, and bankruptcy codes clearly defining investors' rights and enforcement procedures appear to be key pieces in the development of financial markets in general and of corporate bonds in particular (IMF 2005a, 2005b). For instance, in Braun and Briones (2006), we find that creditor rights appear to be the most important institutional variable for the development of the corporate bond market, a result that is consistent with the findings of De la Torre and Schmukler (2004) for Latin American countries.

Chile performs relatively well in terms of investor protection. According to the World Bank Doing Business Database (2006), Chile ranks 18th out of 174 countries, largely above the Asian economies and similar to the average OCDE standard. The existence of accounting standards that are not in compliance with the International Financial Reporting Standards criteria is still a problem, but full convergence is expected by 2009.

Regarding creditor rights and insolvency procedures some important shortcomings prevail. According to the IMF-World Bank Report on Observance of Standards and Codes (2004), the judiciary framework for commercial enforcement and insolvency proceedings is independent, but the related proceedings are lengthy and complicated as confirmed by the Doing Business Database. Chile ranks 73rd in terms of the efficiency of its enforcement process and 107th regarding the weaknesses of its bankruptcy law and procedures. The average time for closing a business is 5.6 years, more than twice as long as in the average Latin American country, and four times the OCDE standard. The situation has not improved since the creation of the index in 2003.

The treatment of contractual obligations in insolvency is not well developed in the Insolvency Law, which also lacks clear provisions on subordination of debt agreements and financial contracts when bankruptcy occurs. In addition, there are no courts specializing in commercial or insolvency issues in Chile. Financial institutions rely too heavily on real estate as collateral. Pledges are not developed enough because the legislation on movable assets is fragmented and the registration mechanism for pledges is not sufficiently reliable.

Aside from some amendments introduced in 2002 and 2005 that created an independent Superintendence of Bankruptcies, no major reforms have occurred since the enactment of the Insolvency Law of 1982. MKII considers some important new amendments to this law and corrects part of the aforementioned problems by means of: (1) introducing provisions on subordination of credits; (2) expanding the concept of related obligations to include those arising from swaps or financial derivatives as well as the introduction of compensation procedures in the case of bankruptcy; and (3) introducing new regulations on pledges without conveyance and the creation of a unified registry of pledges. MKII is expected to be approved by the Parliament during 2007.

The Importance of Institutional Investors: Pension Funds and Insurance Companies

A key Chilean institutional feature is the tremendous importance of the two major institutional investors—pension funds and insurance companies. In 2004, together they held nearly 60% of the stock of central bank bonds, and 80% of the mortgage and corporate bonds. Proportional to GDP, the share of their combined financial assets is almost ten times higher than the average for Argentina, Brazil, and Mexico. In 2004, the assets of the five existing private pension funds and the insurance industry accounted for US$59 billion (60% of GDP) and US$19 billion (20% of GDP), respectively. This is almost half the total stock of financial liabilities of the Chilean economy.

During the 1990s, pension funds held more than 50% of the total amount outstanding of corporate, mortgage, and central bank bonds. In the most recent years these shares have been declining as a result of the regulatory changes allowing pension funds to increase their investments overseas. In turn, insurance companies have become the largest holder of corporate bonds, increasing from nearly 30% of the total amount outstanding during the 1990s to 49% in 2004. This pattern is consistent with the MKI reforms previously discussed.

Interestingly, the increase in the share of corporate bonds held by the insurance companies almost exactly compensates the decrease observed in the pension funds (this is also true for the mortgage bonds). The latter highlights a critical aspect of the corporate bond market in Chile: the stability of the combined demand of the two major institutional investors. Indeed, between 1990 and 2004, corporate bonds held by the pension funds and the insurance companies combined have ranged from 80% to 90% of the total amount outstanding of corporate bonds. This information will provide important insights for the analysis we present in the last section.

Although in principle there are no legal rating provisions for issuing bonds, the tremendous importance that institutional investors have in Chile determines that risk rating is a key aspect of the issuing process. Both insurance companies and pension funds are precluded from buying bonds ranked below BBB. In practice, this determines that all eligible bonds (both private and public) are relatively close substitutes in terms of their risk profile.[6] The most important risk agency in Chile is the semipublic Risk Classification Commission (CCR), which is officially in charge of approving the instruments eligible for AFP investment. There are also four private rating agencies operating in the country: Fitch, Humphreys, Feller Rate, and Duff & Phelps.

The Corporate Bond Market

Five families of securities comprise the Chilean bond market. From the public sector, there are (1) the bonds issued by the central bank, (2) treasury bonds, and (3) pension bonds, both issued by the central government. On the private side, the main instruments are (4) mortgage bonds issued by banks and financial institutions, and (5) corporate bonds. The basic characteristics and relative importance of these instruments are presented in box 6.1.

At the corporate level, the development, though recent, has been impressive. The amount outstanding of corporate bonds surged from US$2 billion (3% of GDP) in 1999 to US$14.5 billion (12.6% of GDP) in 2005 (see table 6.1). Almost 90% of the amount issued during the last 15 years was issued after 1999. In the last 15 years, the size of a typical corporate bond has increased threefold, the number of bonds outstanding has increased fivefold, and the number of issuers has almost tripled (tables 6.1 and 6.2). On the international side, 14 companies have placed 32 different bonds abroad since 1993, with a cumulative amount issued of US$11.4 billion.

In this section we document the evolution of the corporate segment. We analyze the main characteristics of the corporate bond issuers, and the kinds of the bonds they issue. By comparing the issuing and nonissuing companies along several financial indicators, we identify the variables affecting the firms' access to bond finance. The information is

Box 6.1
Other Fixed-Income Securities of the Chilean Market

Mortgage bonds are long-term instruments used basically for real estate financing. After a long period of relative repression, the market experienced a phase of strong development during the 1990s. The amount of mortgage bonds outstanding rose from US$2 billion (6.5% of GDP) in 1990 to US$10 billion (10.5% of GDP) in 2004.

Central bank bonds are the main component of the fixed-income securities market. They are used as a mechanism to regulate the monetary base through open market operations, and to determine the benchmark yield curve for the economy. Most (90%) of these instruments are long-term bonds, with an average maturity of 13 years in the 2000–2004 period. Until 2000, these bonds were almost exclusively CPI-indexed, though during the last three years the situation has changed. In 2004, foreign-currency-denominated and non-CPI-indexed bonds grew to 30% and 15% of long-term bonds, respectively. Since 2001 the amount outstanding of central bank bonds has significantly declined, from 31% of GDP in that year to 21% of GDP in 2004. We will argue that this pattern is related to the increase observed in the corporate segment.

Treasury bonds from the central government are almost nonexistent in Chile, and this situation is expected to remain unaltered in the near future as a consequence of Chile's structural budget surplus rule (1% of GDP) introduced in 2000. The amount outstanding of sovereign bonds is relatively small as well. Lacking a sovereign benchmark to facilitate private bond placement in international markets, since 1999 the government has placed six sovereign bonds, with a total amount outstanding representing 3.8% of GDP in 2004.

Recognition bonds (*bonos de reconocimiento*) originated from the transition from the pay-as-you-go pension system to the private pension funds scheme implemented in the early 1980s. Workers who chose to join the new system were granted a *bono de reconocimiento* to account for the contribution they had made into the old system. In practice these are "virtual" bonds rather than real bonds in circulation. Only if the worker decides to anticipate his retirement is the bond really issued and traded in the market. Otherwise, the worker holds this virtual obligation until maturity and the state proceeds to pay the worker's pension. Until 2004, recognition bonds effectively placed into the market accounted for nearly US$4.8 billion (5.2% of GDP), representing 37% of the total "virtual" amount outstanding. These bonds are held by the private pension funds (56%) and life insurance companies (44%) until maturity. As a consequence, they have extremely low liquidity in the secondary market.

Table 6.1
Amount Outstanding of Corporate Bonds Issued Domestically

	No. of indebted companies	No. of bonds	Debt outstanding (% GDP)	Debt outstanding (million USD)	Mean debt per instrument (million USD)
1990	28	47	4.4%	1386	29
1991	35	65	4.6%	1688	26
1992	37	71	4.4%	1942	27
1993	39	70	4.2%	2000	29
1994	43	82	3.9%	2148	26
1995	46	87	3.4%	2415	28
1996	42	81	3.0%	2308	28
1997	35	75	2.5%	2047	27
1998	35	125	2.1%	1699	14
1999	35	133	3.0%	2156	16
2000	36	151	5.3%	3974	26
2001	67	215	8.9%	6076	28
2002	82	235	12.3%	8293	35
2003	65	260	13.3%	9790	38
2004	74	254	13.7%	12931	51
2005	73	241	12.6%	14574	60

Note: Numbers exclude securitized bonds.
Source: Authors' database.

complemented with a survey of more than 70 companies and institutional investors.

Investment Banks and the Cost of Issuing Bonds

Corporate bonds are normally placed by one of the existing investment banks. The domestic level of competition among investment banks appears to be relatively important. Since 2000, 26 investment banks have been actively involved in placing corporate bonds. Indeed the investment banking fees for a standard-size (US$100 million) plain vanilla bond are extremely low in Chile, just 0.1% of the face value.[7] The figure is well below the one reported by Zervos (2004) for countries like Brazil (2.4%) or Mexico (1%). While the remaining costs involved in the issuance process (legal and regulatory fees, rating agency, road show, and stock exchange registration) are negligible,[8] the total cost of issuance in Chile is around 1.8% of the face value. This is explained by the existence of a stamp tax of 1.608% affecting every credit operation, including bonds.[9]

Economic Classification of the Issuers

Table 6.2 presents the economic classification of corporate bond issuers (SIC classification, 2 digits) in the domestic market. Since 1990, the public utilities and transportation sector has been the largest issuer, accounting for nearly half of the number of bonds and more than 40% of the average amounts issued. Until 1998, companies from these two sectors were almost the only issuers of domestic bonds. The sector has also been the largest issuer of international bonds, accounting for roughly half of the amounts placed abroad.

From the late 1990s, construction, manufacturing, and retail have become relevant players in the domestic segment as well. Construction, mainly driven by the private concession scheme used in the financing of public infrastructure, has accounted for 22% of the total amount issued since 1998. Manufacturing and retail had shares of 13% and 10%, respectively. Construction and retail had the highest proportion of issuers in relation to the total number of companies included in each of these categories (11% and 10%, respectively, as compared to 8% for transportation and public utilities and 4% for the manufacturing sectors).

Characteristics of the Bonds Issued

• *Currency and size.* The principal of a typical corporate bond issued domestically has increased from US$25 million between 1990 and 1997 to nearly US$75 million afterward (table 6.2). However, this value is nearly five times lower than the value a typical bond issued overseas (table 6.3). For the firms that have issued both domestically and abroad, the average size of the latter was three times higher than the former (US$115 million). This suggests that one important reason why companies decide to issue abroad is the relatively small size of the domestic capital market.

Table 6.2 also reveals that the vast majority of corporate bonds issued between 1990 and September 2005 have been indexed to the consumer price index. On average, CPI-indexed bonds accounted for 94% of the cases and 93% of the total amount issued. In turn, bonds indexed to the US dollar represented 5% of the number of instruments

Table 6.2
Corporate Bonds Issued Domestically

	Agriculture, forestry, and fishing	Mining	Construction	Manufacturing	Public utilities and transportation	Retail	Finance, insurance, and real estate	Services	Total	Average amount per bond issued	CPI-indexed (%)	US$-indexed (%)
1990	—	—	—	60	94	—	—	—	154	17	100%	0%
1991	—	28	—	251	216	—	—	—	495	31	100%	0%
1992	—	—	40	16	24	—	—	—	81	12	100%	0%
1993	—	10	—	—	223	—	—	—	234	58	9%	91%
1994	—	—	26	92	282	—	—	—	400	27	97%	3%
1995	—	—	—	—	26	—	13	—	39	10	100%	0%
1996	—	—	—	—	41	—	—	—	41	41	100%	0%
1997	—	—	—	—	54	—	—	—	54	18	100%	0%
1998	—	—	151	—	628	—	—	—	779	111	48%	52%
1999	—	219	79	92	183	74	40	—	688	53	45%	55%
2000	—	—	209	234	486	136	362	—	1427	68	97%	3%
2001	—	—	197	473	1341	349	13	9	2382	61	100%	0%
2002	13	244	417	146	501	48	—	—	1369	72	99%	1%
2003	171	—	698	91	357	342	81	26	1766	74	95%	2%
2004	—	—	831	118	678	380	240	—	2247	118	100%	0%
2005	226	223	184	300	689	52	88	104	1867	89	98%	0%
Total	411	725	2833	1874	5825	1380	836	139	14023	63	93%	7%
Share	3%	5%	20%	13%	42%	10%	6%	1%	100%			

Note: Figures are in million US dollars. Financial sector excludes leasing, factoring, and securitized operations.
Source: Authors' database.

Table 6.3
Corporate Bonds Issued Abroad

	1993	1994	1995	1996	1997	1998	1999	2000	2001	2002	2003	2004	2005	Total
No. of bonds issued	3	0	1	4	3	2	5	1	2	2	5	4	2	34
Amount issued (million USD)	321.9	0	300	1370	1400	650	1260	300	865	725	2050	1300	900	11442
Share of total bonds issued (1990–2005)	58%	0%	89%	97%	96%	45%	65%	17%	27%	35%	54%	37%	33%	45%

Note: Financial sector excludes leasing, factoring, and securitized operations.
Source: Authors' database.

and almost 7% of the amounts placed. With the sole exception of 1994, this composition has been quite stable in time. The strong preference for CPI-indexed instruments should not be surprising, since almost every public bond (basically the central bank instruments) defining the Chilean benchmark yield curve has also been CPI-indexed (at least until the beginning of the nominalization process in the early 2000s).

• *Maturity structure.* A second striking feature of corporate bonds is their very long maturities. Between 1991 and 2005, the typical maturity of a Chilean corporate bond was 16 years. This is almost three times longer than the average maturity of corporate bonds in other developing countries.[10] Moreover, as table 6.4 shows, this long maturity has tended to increase during the last five years.

This very long maturity was not the consequence of a possible bias introduced by a large economic sector having a natural preference for long-term issuances. As expected, bonds issued by the construction and transportation and utilities sectors (which are the largest issuing industries) had longer maturities than the average (21 and 17 years, respectively). However, maturities also remain significantly high in other sectors.

As long as the inflation risk is eliminated, issuing long-term bonds becomes more attractive. In this sense, one could think that the Chilean strong preferences for CPI-indexed bonds and long-term maturities are possibly related. Several arguments partially contradict this view. On the one hand, inflation is not a real concern in Chile, at least since 2000. However, as previously mentioned, we observe that maturities have increased since then. Besides, it is hard to explain the Chilean long maturities in relation to developed countries where inflation risk is not a real concern (see Braun and Briones 2006), or in relation to corporate bonds denominated in foreign currency in less developed countries.

One could also argue that maturity has much to do with the quality of the issuer. Indeed, while any company would prefer to issue long-term bonds, high-quality issuers are expected to have more chances to issue this type of bonds than weak issuers. Nevertheless, we find that since 1991 there has been no significant difference between the maturity of bonds issued by large (supposedly less risky) and small companies (two last columns of table 6.4).

Together, these counterarguments are indicative that long maturities are peculiar to the Chilean economy. A more plausible explanation for such a pattern is related to the demand structure of the corporate bond

Table 6.4
Maturity of Corporate Bonds Issued (Years from Issuance)

	Economic sector									All companies		
	Con-struction	Finance	Manu-facturing	Primary	Retail	Services	Telecom	Transport	Utilities	All	With sales below the median	With sales above the median
1990			7.6				11.4	8.0	16.8	10.2		
1991	12.0	21.0	13.2	12.0			16.9		10.6	13.2	12.3	15.2
1992			10.3						13.4	12.4	13.0	10.3
1993								18.0	14.0	17.3	15.5	10 (*)
1994	15.6		17.5			9.0	14.9	25.0	12.5	15.5	8.8	17.5 (*)
1995		12.0	13.0				15.6		14.0	13.2	13.0	12.0
1996								30.0		30.0	30.0	
1997						2.0	16.5	30.0		19.8	30.0	12.0
1998	9.0						19.3	30.0	21.0	15.4	25.5	15.5
1999	18.0	25.0			16.5			30.0	22.0	21.1	21.0	27.5
2000	20.0	9.6	11.5		10.1		16.3	30.0	15.2	13.7	13.5	12.2
2001	20.0	6.0	12.1		12.8	6.2	10.5	24.6	13.7	14.6	14.7	14.3
2002	19.4		11.1	10.0	7.0		9.7	25.8	13.9	15.0	21.5	10.4 (*)
2003	21.5	20.1	10.1	9.0	12.9			26.7	13.6	17.0	15.8	18.9
2004	23.9	12.0	13.9		11.2			23.2	16.4	18.6	21.4	11 (*)

Note: Financial sector excludes leasing, factoring, and securitized operations. *denotes significance at the 5% level.
Source: Authors' database.

market, which is dominated by pension funds and insurance companies (80% of the total amount outstanding of corporate bonds). Because of their business, these institutional investors are more likely to be long-term investors, thus inducing companies willing to issue bonds to place long-term securities that comply with the needs of the main buyers. Eventually, the high rating requirements (BBB or above) of eligible bonds for pension funds and insurance companies can be part of the explanation as well. We find that companies that have issued bonds hold more financial liabilities (in relation to assets) and have a higher proportion of long-term financial liabilities than companies that have not issued bonds.

A second factor inducing firms to issue long-term bonds is the existence of a stamp tax dating from 1980 and affecting any credit operation, including bonds. As previously seen, the tax represents the lion's share of the total cost of issuing a bond. Because it must be paid again if a company issues a new bond in order to roll over a previous one, the tax heavily increases the relative price of issuing short-term bonds. Besides, bank bonds are exempted from the tax, thus putting corporate bond financing in an unfavorable position vis-à-vis bank financing.

• *Risk.* Relying on the risk classification of the corporate bonds issued since January 2000,[11] we find that one of the main characteristics of the recent development of the corporate bond market is the increasing share of bonds rated AAA and AA. Together these bonds accounted for nearly 75% of the amount outstanding of corporate bonds in 2004; since 2000, almost every new issuance has been rated in one of these categories (see data set). Part of the reason for this pattern is the increasing share of bonds issued by the private construction industry participating in the private public works concession scheme developed in the 1990s. Because their cash flows have state guarantee, most of the bonds issued by these companies were rated AAA. Triple-A issuances from building companies represented nearly 70% of the total amount of AAA bonds issued since 2000. The remaining 30% was accounted for by issuances from state-owned companies (CODELCO, Metro, and EFE).[12]

In practice, non-investment-grade bonds are almost nonexistent in Chile: corporate bonds rated below A represent only 2% of the total as compared to 40% in Japan or 10% in the United States or the European Union (IMF 2005a, 119). Once again, this Chilean pattern has much to do with portfolio restrictions affecting institutional investors.

• *Purpose of issuance: use of funds.* The issuance prospectuses of the
bonds placed domestically between 1991 and 2005 allow us to compute the main declared use of the funds obtained by the companies.
We find that the main reasons for issuing bonds were related to refinancing long-term liabilities and to financing new investments.[13]
Bonds issued exclusively for one of these two purposes explain more
than 60% of the total number of bonds issued. Also, a quarter of all the
bonds served exclusively to refinance long-term liabilities, while the
proportion of bonds in which at least part of the funds served this purpose was above 45%. Investment financing, as a unique use of funds, is
associated with 21% of the bonds, while the proportion of cases in
which at least part of these funds were used for this goal is close to
50%.

From a dynamic perspective, some additional interesting results
emerge. First, although on average refinancing long-term liabilities
appears to be an important reason to issue bonds, until 1999 it was not
a relevant motivation. Indeed, from 1990 to 1998 no company declared
it would use the funds obtained for the sole purpose of refinancing
long-term liabilities. Instead, the main reasons for issuing bonds during that period were to refinance short-term liabilities and to finance
new investments. This pattern in the use of external funds is not surprising. As shown in figure 6.2, what basically happened after 1998
was that the yield curve shifted downward, thus inducing firms to refinance their previous—more costly—long-term financial liabilities.
However, as we will discuss in the next section, the latter did not
mean that the fall in the interest rate was a pushing factor to prefer
bonds over other sources of external financing.

Determinants of Corporate Bonds Issuance

A critical point for understanding the market is comparing the characteristics of the issuing and the nonissuing companies. This would allow
us to detect the main common features of the issuers and thus to suggest some determinants of corporate bond issuance at the firm level.
Based on yearly balance sheet information for all of the bond-issuing
companies and for all the nonissuing companies registered at the SVS,
we compared these two categories on some key financial indicators
just before the issuance. All in all, from 1991 to 2004, we have nearly
3,000 different firm-year observations.

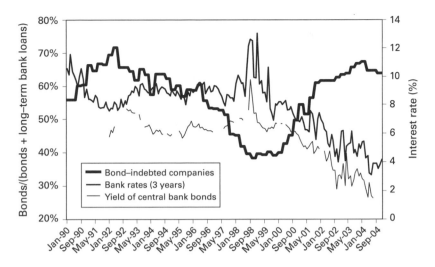

Figure 6.2
Interest rates and the structure of corporate financial liabilities. Source: Central Bank of Chile and author's database.

Table 6.5 depicts a first set of average indicators emerging from the time series analysis. Several interesting observations are in order. First, size appears to matter: the average size in terms of assets of corporate issuers is twice as high for issuers as for companies that do not issue bonds. Issuers have higher sales as well. Second, corporate issuers have higher leverage ratios than nonissuing companies. Between 1991 and 2004, the average value for the former was 22%, compared to 16% for the latter. Interestingly, the relative distance between issuers and nonissuers in terms of leverage has tended to increase after 1998. Third, issuers appear to have a higher fraction of tangible assets. These three results are significant at the usual confidence levels, and are in line with the preliminary findings of previous research (Gallego and Loayza 2000). In turn, we cannot reject the hypothesis that issuers and nonissuers are similar in terms of their profitability, thus indicating that this is not a critical variable when issuing bonds.

In general, these results are confirmed when looking within sectors. With the exception of companies from the primary sectors (agriculture, forestry, and fishing), bond issuers have higher assets and sales than companies in their economic sector that do not issue bonds. In all the cases, bond issuers have higher leverage ratios than nonissuing firms. The results are mixed regarding asset tangibility. Issuers have higher

Table 6.5
Characteristics of the Domestic Issuers and Nonissuers during the Period Preceding the Issuance (Average Values per Company)

	Assets (thousand USD)		Leverage		Tangibility		Log sales (thousand USD)		Profitability		Sample	
	Issuers	Non-issuers	Issuers	Non-issuers	Issuers	Non-issuers	Issuers	Non-issuers	Issuers	Non-issuers	Issuers	Non-issuers
1991	518287	102903	0.22	0.14	0.65	0.48	11.32	8.70	0.07	0.06	13	137
1992	110663	149930	0.15	0.14	0.58	0.48	10.19	9.09	0.07	0.07	5	150
1993	1150023	147324	0.19	0.15	0.82	0.45	11.33	9.25	0.03	0.07	3	174
1994	411978	153722	0.22	0.14	0.56	0.44	10.91	9.24	0.08	0.06	10	176
1995	94182	212677	0.30	0.14	0.71	0.43	10.49	9.58	0.10	0.05	3	188
1996	607714	227446	0.21	0.14	0.77	0.42	10.90	9.58	−0.04	−0.48	1	206
1997	402754	260359	0.37	0.14	0.76	0.40	10.74	9.67	0.03	−0.02	2	218
1998	1708579	264534	0.22	0.15	0.42	0.39	12.24	9.49	0.02	0.04	5	227
1999	444500	305269	0.17	0.17	0.34	0.39	10.94	9.48	0.03	0.03	7	227
2000	801027	307492	0.23	0.17	0.40	0.37	11.58	9.37	0.02	0.03	13	231
2001	1043511	273182	0.28	0.17	0.33	0.39	10.90	9.37	0.02	0.02	21	230
2002	515259	323698	0.25	0.17	0.55	0.37	11.00	9.44	0.04	0.02	12	238
2003	454028	342944	0.26	0.17	0.38	0.37	10.65	9.53	0.01	0.02	14	230
2004	691518	388949	0.35	0.17	0.42	0.36	11.52	9.38	0.01	0.02	14	237
Average	672836	259386	0.25	0.16	0.47	0.40	11.09	9.40	0.03	0.00	9	205

Source: Authors' database.

tangibility ratios in the case of the public utilities and transportation sector. However, the relation is less clear in the construction and retail sectors, whereas it appears to go in the opposite direction in services, manufacturing, and the primary sector.

Table 6.6 presents the results of probit and tobit regressions that explore the firm-level determinants of bond issuance in a multivariate setting over panel data. Firm-level determinants include size (as measured by sales in US dollars), leverage (financial debt over total book assets), profitability (operating income over assets), and whether the firm is publicly listed or not. All these variables are lagged one year in order to address potential endogeneity problems; errors are clustered at the firm level to take into account the nature of the data.

The first three columns examine the determinants of the decision to issue bonds at a given point in time. Size enters with a strong, significant coefficient. The effect is very significant in economic terms: a 10% increase in sales is associated with a 3.9% increase in the probability of issuing bonds. Leverage enters positively, which suggests that firms already involved with the financial system are more likely to issue bonds. Although the economic effect appears to be large, the coefficient is not significant in statistical terms. Profitability has a significant negative effect, consistent with the pecking order theory and previous results regarding leverage in general. Other things being equal, firms that are publicly listed are less likely to issue bonds. This suggests that stock and bond financing are indeed substitutes from the standpoint of the issuer. Column (2) seems to confirm this intuition. The probability of issuing bonds decreases when firms are able to obtain equity financing on favorable terms (though the coefficient for the stock market price-earnings ratio is not significant at conventional levels). Column (3) shows that prices are also important for the decision between issuing bonds and obtaining bank loans: an increase of 100 basis points in the spread between bank loans and bond rates (one standard deviation) is associated with a 36% increase in the probability of issuing bonds.

Whether a firm has bonds outstanding or not depends on very much the same factors mentioned above (column 4). In this case, however, the effect of leverage is statistically significant while that of profitability is not. These results speak more directly to the structural determinants of bond issuance as opposed to the cyclical ones above.

In columns (5) and (6) we explore the determinants of the amount of bond financing. In order to control for the clustered nature of the data

Table 6.6
The Decision to Issue Bonds

Dependent variable	Dummy = 1 if firm issued bonds in t			Dummy = 1 if firm has bonds	Bond/long-term debt	Bond debt/assets
	(1)	(2)	(3)	(4)	(5)	(6)
Ln(sales)$_{i,t-1}$	0.389	0.389	0.390	0.271	0.071	0.022
	0.106***	0.106***	0.106***	0.046***	0.021***	0.005***
Leverage$_{i,t-1}$	0.842	0.842	0.842	1.972	0.699	0.551
	0.642	0.642	0.642	0.373***	0.330**	0.086***
Profitability$_{i,t-1}$	−1.471	−1.471	−1.471	−0.935	0.036	0.001
	0.388***	0.388***	0.388***	0.667	0.114	0.031
Publicly listed$_{i,t-1}$	−0.692	−0.692	−0.692		−0.549	−0.170
	0.411*	0.411*	0.411*		0.122***	0.032***
Stock market p/e ratio$_t$		−0.028				
		0.074				
Long-term bank rate − bond rate$_t$			0.358			
			0.119***			
No. of observations	1821	1821	1821	2400	202	242
Loglikelihood	−90.62	−90.62	−90.62	−1081	−128.7	−9.13
Pseudo R-squared	0.29	0.29	0.29	0.20	0.18	0.88

Note: (1)–(4) Probit regressions. (5)–(6) Tobit regressions with left-censored observations at 0 over firm data averaged over the years. (1)–(3) Robust errors clustered at the firm level. (5)–(6) Standard errors. *, **, and *** denote significance at the 10%, 5%, and 1% levels, respectively. Constant and time-fixed effects included but not reported.

in the tobit regressions, we first average the firm-level data across the years. Again, size and the level of leverage enter positive and significantly. Interestingly, profitability ceases to be significantly negative. Conditional on having issued bonds, stronger, more profitable firms seem to be able to issue more. Once again, having the option to raise equity finance also limits the amount firms are willing to raise in the form of bonds.

Finally, the size effect that we find when issuing domestically is even more relevant when deciding to issue bonds abroad, a result that is in line with previous findings by Benavente, Johnson, and Morandé (2003) (not reported). The "typical" Chilean firm that had placed bonds in the international market since 1993 had assets twelve times larger than the firms that had not done so, and had nearly five times more assets than companies that issued bonds in the local market only. In short, if size matters when issuing bonds domestically, it matters even more when issuing bonds abroad.

Survey Data

We carried out a survey including 40 listed companies (issuers and nonissuers of bonds) and 32 investors. The basic results we obtained complement some of our previous findings.

Among the firms with some experience in issuing bonds, the main perceived problem is the small size of the domestic market. High fees from credit rating agencies also appear to matter domestically, but particularly when firms decide to issue abroad. Underwriter fees do not count much when issuing locally but they are relevant when issuing foreign bonds. Minimum size requirements are an additional limitation to issue abroad. Regarding the firms without experience in issuing bonds, the main obstacle has to do with disclosure requirements.

Domestic bank loans are perceived as having a relative advantage in terms of the availability of lending in local currency and the probability of renegotiation, while bonds issued domestically lead in terms of the availability of long-term lending and indexation alternatives. Bonds issued abroad have a relative advantage in terms of the size of the potential market.

Among investors, low liquidity in the secondary market is the main factor limiting the demand for corporate bonds. Indeed, while Chile ranks first in terms of its amount outstanding of corporate bonds in Latin America, it exhibits one of the lowest turnover ratios (see chapter

1 of this volume, table 1.2). The existence of a 35% tax on capital gains is likely to be behind the observed low liquidity. On the one hand it increases the incentives for a buy-and-hold strategy (the tax does not have to be paid if bonds are held until maturity). On the other hand, it limits the entry of foreign investors, thus reinforcing the tremendous importance of local institutional investors in the domestic market. Because of the nature of their business, pension funds and insurance companies tend to hold bonds to maturity. Insolvency risk and the quality of legal recourse in case of default do not appear to matter much for investors. Once again, this result has much to do with the characteristics of Chilean institutional investors. We showed that the corporate segment is basically an investment-grade bond market and argued that this result was related to the risk investment restrictions faced by institutional investors. In this context it is not surprising that insolvency risk and legal procedures do not appear to be a real concern.

The main declared regulatory restriction is related to limitations for investing in corporate bonds. In the absence of these regulations, most of the investors declare they would increase the share of corporate bonds in their portfolios.

Finally, investors believe that a large stock of public bonds is important for the development of corporate bonds as well as for pricing them.

Explaining the Recent Corporate Bond Expansion

Three critical observations regarding the recent evolution of the domestic corporate market emerge from our analysis. First, the expansion of the domestic market began in 2000. Second, most of new bonds issued were rated AAA and AA. Third, the average maturity of new bonds issued increased significantly. In this section we try to account for these patterns.

From January 2000 to December 2004, the amount outstanding of corporate bonds expanded from US$2.5 billion to US$13.7 billion. As previously mentioned, this expansion was associated with a downward shift of the real yield curve of the economy. From 1998 to 2004, the real yield at issuance of central bank bonds decreased from 7.5% to 3.5%. This trend is mostly due to a relaxation of the monetary policy seeking to reactivate the economy. During the same period, the yield of corporate bonds with similar maturity traded in the secondary market fell from 8% to 4%.

Some observers like Zervos (2004) have argued that lower interest rates were one of the driving forces behind the observed recent expansion of the corporate bond market. However, this does not appear to be the case in Chile. Noticing that the real interest rate for bank long-term lending exhibited the same pattern, one way to test this hypothesis is to compare the evolution of bonds and long-term bank loans as substitute sources of external financing. If interest rates were the cause of the increase in the amount outstanding of corporate bonds, they should also have produced a similar relative increase in corporate bank debt. Figure 6.2 contradicts this hypothesis. From 2000, the share of bond debt over the sum of long-term bank liabilities and bonds increased. Indebted companies substituted banking loans for bonds as a source of financing. So a cyclical element like the fall in the domestic interest rate does not appear to be the reason for the recent expansion of the corporate bond market.

A second possible explanation is related to the switch from a managed (target zone) exchange rate prevailing before 1999 to the fully floating system after the Asian crisis. The resulting higher volatility could have induced the corporate sector to prepay their international bonds by means of issuing bonds domestically. Several pieces of evidence allow us to contradict this view, at least in part. First, only three out of the twelve firms, Embotelladora Andina, Endesa, and Enersis, prepaid part of their bonds issued abroad. This occurred during 2001, and the amounts involved were US$313, US$251, and US$96 million, respectively, representing just 14% of the total amount outstanding of foreign bonds at that time. (However, it is worth noting that in 2003 both Endesa and Enersis placed new foreign bonds for US$600 million and US$350 million, respectively.) At the same time, the three companies issued local debt for US$180 million, US$160 million, and US$95 million, respectively, accounting for 17% of the total corporate bonds issued domestically that year. Second, bond issuance abroad did not decline but increased from US$4,042 million between 1993 and 1998, to US$6,200 million between 1999 and 2004, in a result that also seems to contradict the view of companies facing a drier international market after the Asian crisis (see Caballero 2000). In sum, the "fear to float" argument does not appear to be particularly important in the case of Chile. On the one hand, as reported by Cowan, Hansen, and Herrera (2004) and Chan-Lau (2005), the foreign exchange exposure of the Chilean corporate sector is low compared to developed and other emerging market economies. On the other hand, after 1999, the Chilean

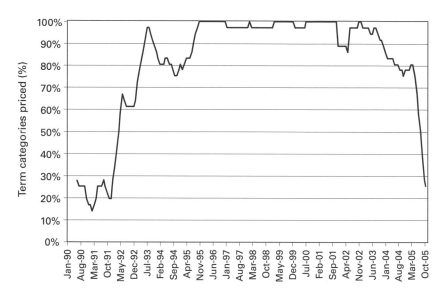

Figure 6.3
Completion of the benchmark yield curve. Source: author's database.

derivatives market experienced a solid development, thus facilitating firms managing their currency mismatches (De Gregorio and Tokman, 2004).

A third theoretical set of explanations is related to possible structural changes enhancing efficiency gains in the financial market. A lengthening of the benchmark yield curve could be a first natural candidate. However, the argument is contradicted by the fact that in the early 1990s Chile already had a complete yield curve for public bonds. This is shown in figure 6.3 where we define six term categories for central bank bonds denominated in UF and look at how many of these categories were effectively priced over time.[14] If any, changes occurring in recent years go in the opposite direction, defining a more incomplete yield curve than during the past. Since 2003, the central bank has been replacing part of its UF-denominated long-term bonds for nominal bonds. These nominal bonds represented nearly 25% of the total amount outstanding of the central bank long-term bonds in 2004, though it is still to early to evaluate the completion degree of the resulting new (nominal) yield curve.

A decrease in the issuing costs (either by increasing competition in the underwriting market or by tax reductions on bond issuances) or an improvement in the bankruptcy procedures is expected to reduce transaction costs, thus enhancing the corporate bond market. As seen in the first section, there is no evidence of a dramatic change in these regards during the most recent years.

All in all, the impressive development of the corporate bond segment does not seem to be related either to temporary factors such as a fall in the interest rate, to a switch of the Chilean exchange regime, or to exogenous shocks like the closing of international financial markets; nor to structural changes reducing the transaction costs involved in the issuance process. Based on a counterfactual experiment and regression analysis, we argue that most of the expansion appears to be related to exogenous supply factors instead of a real structural change in the determinants of bond issuance.

A Counterfactual Experiment

As previously mentioned, from 1999 to 2004 the amount outstanding of corporate bonds increased by US$12 billion, from 3% of GDP to nearly 13.7% of GDP. In accounting for the expansion of corporate bonds, one should consider structural changes in both the demand and the supply side. On the demand side, let's first consider the "natural" evolution of the two major institutional investors: the pension funds and the insurance companies, which historically have held nearly 80% of the total amount outstanding of corporate bonds. From December 1999 to December 2004, the total assets held by the pension funds increased by 74%, from US$34 billion to US$59 billion, while those of insurance companies doubled from US$10.5 billion to US$19.5 billion. The "natural" but not structural change in the demand for corporate bonds—assuming the constant share that corporate bonds historically had in their portfolios, i.e., 6% for the pension funds and 11% for the insurance companies—would have accounted for, at least, US$2.5 billion out of the US$12 billion to be explained.

Let's now consider the supply side of the story. As mentioned above, an important change that occurred from the late 1990s was the introduction of a private concession scheme for financing public infrastructure. Firms that were granted these concessions (mainly highways) largely issued long-term bonds to finance the construction of the public infrastructure. Because these firms were granted a state cash flow guarantee, 96% of the bonds they issued were rated AAA. The amount outstanding of this kind of corporate bonds jumped from nearly nil at the end of the 1990s to around US$3.5 billion in 2004, thus representing nearly 25% of the total amount outstanding. The important point to notice here is that this supply effect is not likely to be permanent, but exogenous and transitory, as most of the concession scheme is already concluded. In other words, in the future we should not expect to observe such a radical increase in supply. Taking into account this supply factor, we are left with US$6 billion to explain.

A second major change that occurred on the supply side was the important decline in the stock of central bank CPI-indexed bonds. From December 1999 to December 2004, the stock of central bank bonds fell from US$12 billion to US$7.5 billion. Needless to say, this change should be seen as exogenous and temporary instead of structural. In equilibrium, this vacuum should have been naturally filled by some kind of close bond substitute. We argue that corporate bonds undertook this supply substitution effect. Having taken into account the expansion of AAA bonds associated with the construction sector, it is important to notice that corporate bonds rated AA heavily expanded as well. Besides, the amount of AA-rated bonds almost perfectly matches the decline in the supply of the bonds from the central bank. All in all, we can assume that this supply substitution effect, not a structural change, would have accounted for nearly US$4 billion of the recent expansion of the corporate bond market. In that sense, the unexplained or real expansion of this segment of the market would be only about US$2 billion. It appears that nearly 80% of the increase in the amount outstanding of corporate bonds would not follow from any structural change.

Of course, as seen in the first section, the capital market reforms undertaken at the end of the 1990s could serve as a more structural and complementary piece of explanation, especially because these reforms lightened some of the investment restrictions faced by institutional investors.

Regression Analysis

In order to explore the issues raised above in a more formal way, we conducted a regression analysis on quarterly data. The dependent variable was defined as the change in the log of UF (CPI-denominated) corporate bonds real stock. To account for the joint determination of stocks and rates of corporate bonds, we estimated the demand and supply system by three-stage least squares. Aside from the rate of corporate bonds, demand and supply were allowed to depend on the inverse of the p/e ratio in the stock market. Supply also depends on the rate charged by banks for long-term bonds, another alternative for the issuer. This was taken as a measure of the return on alternative investments on the demand side, and the cost of raising finance via the stock market on the supply side. Two additional exogenous variables were added to the demand specification: the log change in the assets of pension funds and insurance companies, and the log change in the stock of UF-denominated central bank bonds. The first measures the captive demand of institutional investors that arises from current regulation and depends largely on past returns on their portfolio and the growth rate of wages and the labor force. Moreover, the share of corporate bonds in their portfolios is sufficiently small to safely assume that there is no reverse causality. The latter captures the existence of alternative fixed-income instruments, and can be thought of as a reduced-form variable negatively related to the rate of those instruments. Changes in this stock were due to variations in the monetary policy and the nominalization process carried out by the central bank, both largely exogenous.

Overall we do a much better job in explaining the determinants of the demand for corporate bonds. Still, most coefficients are not statistically significant. As can be seen in column (1) of table 6.7, the rate enters negatively as expected (though not significantly and not consistently across the different specifications). A low p/e ratio in the stock market increases the demand for bonds. Unexpectedly, on the supply side we get a negative sign for the rate, and a positive sign for the p/e ratio. Higher bank rates are associated with more bond financing as expected. None of these is, however, significant in statistical terms or consistent across the different specifications. Interestingly, the institutional investors' demand has the expected positive (though insignificant) sign in the demand equation. The economic magnitude is large: a 10% increase in the assets of these investors is associated with a 3.7% increase in the stock of corporate bonds.

Column (2) shows that the stock of central bank bonds enters negatively and very significantly in the demand equation. This suggests an important degree of substitution between government and corporate bonds. Column (3) confirms the effect. The economic significance is quite large: a 10% decrease in the stock of central bank bonds is associated with an increase in the stock of corporate bonds of between 12% and 20%.

Of course, the analysis can be subject to a number of criticisms in terms of the exclusion restrictions, and the lack of power of the right-side variables. Both can significantly alter the conclusions. We tried a

Table 6.7
Corporate Bonds Stock: Regression Analysis (1995–2004)

	(1)	(2)	(3)
Δ Tir BCentral t	0.017	0.016	0.009
Δ Risk Spread t	0.035	0.024	0.020
Δ Term Spread t	0.053	0.042	0.039
Δ Bank Spread t	0.023	0.018	0.017
Δ 1/P-E Ratio t	2.120	1.686	3.280
Δ log(Imacec) t	0.494		0.224
Δ log(Institutional Inv) t	0.427		0.407
Δ log(Stock BCentral) t	0.849*		1.145
Δ log(Stock BCorp) $t-1$	0.187*	0.151***	0.483
Trend t	0.000	0.002	0.002
	0.001	0.001*	0.003
Constant	0.074	−0.260	−0.345
	0.283	0.148*	0.393
R-squared	0.463	0.389	0.565
No. of observations	38	46	19

Note: Dependent variable: Δ log(Stock BCorp) t. (1) and (2) full sample. (3) pre-2001.
*, **, *** denote significance at 10%, 5%, and 1% levels, respectively.

number of different specifications and obtained similar results. We believe that the evidence is consistent with demand and substitution factors being indeed important for explaining the evolution of the stock of corporate bonds.

As for our hypothesis regarding the reasons for the impressive growth of the stock of corporate bonds since 2000, CuSum and CuSum squared tests (not reported) confirm that we cannot reject the no-structural-change hypothesis on the full model of table 6.7.

Concluding Remarks

Several interesting results have emerged from this prospective analysis of the Chilean corporate bond market. First, while the development of the Chilean capital market started during the mid-1980s, development of the corporate bond market only began by the end of the 1990s. The latter is true in terms of an increase of issuances (and a rise in the total amount outstanding) and a broadening of economic sectors that have issued bonds. This development has been impressive. The stock of corporate bonds increased from 3% of GDP in the late 1990s to 14% of GDP today, placing the country among the more developed markets, and above other Latin American countries. However, Chile's market shows low liquidity, a result in part related to the existence of a 35% tax on capital gains for bond transactions.

The size of the issuer is the more relevant factor in determining the probability of issuance, and this is even more important when deciding to issue bonds abroad. Because the main Chilean institutional investors—pension funds and insurance companies—are almost precluded from acquiring low-rated bonds, the size effect is expected to be even more important in Chile than in other countries. Rating requirements, in combination with the tremendous importance of institutional investors, and the existence of the stamp tax could explain the extraordinarily long maturities corporate bonds have in Chile. Needless to say, the natural effect of size, and the artificial rating requirements and stamp tax, are likely to have critical implications for the development of the corporate bond market for small (risky) firms.

The expansion trend observed during the last five years coincided with a declining phase of the Chilean business cycle, and an expansive monetary policy that shifted the yield curve downward. The decline of long-term interest rates, however, does not appear to be the reason why companies decided to issue more bonds. Neither the switch to a flexible exchange regime Chile undertook at the end of the 1990s nor improvements in the completion of the yield curve appears to be part of the explanation. Most of the expansion seems to be related to exogenous factors instead of a real structural change in the determinants of bond issuance, the natural growth of the assets managed by the pension funds and insurance companies in particular. The latter suggests that a similar pattern could be observed in the future in other developing countries that adopted private pension schemes later than Chile. In turn, the stringent regulations faced by these institutional investors have effectively prevented the emergence of a non-investment-grade segment. The effect is exacerbated by the existence of a 35% tax on capital gains, a disincentive for foreign investors with a more highly risk-biased investment profile. The policy implication is clear: while the new private pension schemes can have a positive effect on the size of these markets, the strong prudential regulations imposed on the managers can distort the natural development of the market. Relaxing these investment restrictions seems critical for a healthy evolution of bond markets. Eliminating the tax on capital gains is also expected to contribute to expanding the demand for more risky instruments as well as enhancing the liquidity in the secondary market. Smaller, riskier firms could benefit greatly from the elimination of the stamp tax by encouraging the demand for shorter instruments.

In a clear indication of the existence of crowding-out effects, a second major explanation of the expansion appears to be associated with an exogenous declining supply of central bank bonds, which were largely substituted by investment-grade corporate bonds. There thus appears to be a nonlinear relationship between government bond size and the development of the private bond market. A minimum level of public bonds defining a complete benchmark yield curve is required to enhance the private segment. Beyond this point, additional public bonds would lead to crowding out of private debt. The conduct of monetary policy should therefore take into account the potential effects on the private debt markets. Finally, bonds issued by construction companies participating in a large private concession scheme starting in the late 1990s also partly explain the growth of the Chilean bond market. As in the case of the pension scheme, this again suggests important links between the reform process and the development of bond markets. This knowledge is something policy makers can benefit from in countries that have adopted similar reforms.

Acknowledgments

We thank Eduardo Borensztein, Kevin Cowan, Barry Eichengreen, Ugo Panizza, Mark Seasholes, and other participants in the Latin-American Research Network on the Development of Latin American Bond Markets organized by the IDB for their comments and suggestions.

Notes

1. For an international comparison of bond markets, see Braun and Briones (2006).

2. See Meller (1996).

3. See Braun and Briones (1997).

4. Potential private buyers were allowed to borrow from the government (CORFO) up to 90% of the sale price, giving the privatized assets as collateral. See Meller (1996) for more details.

5. People willing to increase their pension contribution beyond the legal limit receive a series of tax benefits. Pension funds are no longer the sole institution allowed to manage

these voluntary funds; while they retain a market share above 80%, these voluntary savings can be done through a series of financial institutions including insurance companies (8%), mutual funds (8%), and investing banks.

6. According to the current law on pension funds, funds A-B can only invest up to 3% of their assets in corporate bonds that do not fulfill the minimum risk criteria. Funds C-D can invest at most 1% of their assets in these bonds, while this is entirely forbidden for fund E. However, the less risky fund E is allowed to invest up to 60% of its portfolio in corporate bonds, whereas funds A-B and C-D can only invest 30% and 40%, respectively.

7. We thank IM Trust, the leading bond issuance investment bank, for providing us with this information.

8. As percentage of the face value, these costs are as follows: rating agency (0.027%); road show (0.02%); legal fees (0.08%); regulatory fees (0.01%); stock exchange registration (0.01%); other (0.011%).

9. This tax is charged at a monthly rate of 0.134%, with a maximum of 1.608%. Recently, in August 2006, the government sent to the Congress a proposal to reduce the tax to 1.2% by 2009.

10. See Braun and Briones (2006).

11. Risk classification obtained from the CCR and the four private rating agencies operating in Chile.

12. Copper, subway, and railroad companies, respectively.

13. Infrastructure financing (FOI) can be taken as part of the investment-financing item. Indeed, FOI is a special category of financial investments that is given to companies participating in the infrastructure private concession scheme applied in Chile since the late 1990s (e.g., highways, ports, and airports).

14. Term categories: 0–1 years; 2–4 years; 5–7 years; 8–12 years; 13–19 years; more than 20 years.

References

Benavente, J. M., C. A. Johnson, and F. G. Morandé (2003). "Debt Composition and Balance Sheet Effects of Exchange Rate Depreciations: A Firm-Level Analysis for Chile." *Emerging Markets Review* 4(4): 397–416.

Braun, M., and I. Briones (1997). "The Chilean Capital Market 1810–1995." Manuscript, CB Capitales, Santiago.

Braun, Matías, and Ignacio Briones (2006). "The Development of Bond Markets around the World." Manuscript, Universidad Adolfo Ibáñez (February).

Caballero, R. (2000). "Structural Volatility in Chile: A Policy Report." Inter-American Development Bank, Working Paper No. 421.

Chan-Lau, Jorge A. (2005). "Hedging Foreign Exchange Risk in Chile: Market and Instruments." IMF Working Paper No. 05/37.

Corbo, V., and K. Schmidt-Hebbel (2003). "Macroeconomic Effects of the Pension Reform in Chile." In *Pension Reforms: Results and Challenges.* Santiago: FIAP.

Cowan, Kevin, Erwin Hansen, and Luis Oscar Herrera (2004). "Currency Mismatches, Balance Sheet Effects and Hedging in the Chilean Non-Financial Corporations." Paper prepared for the Eighth Annual Conference of the Central Bank of Chile, "External Vulnerability and Policies for Prevention."

De Gregorio, J., and A. Tokman (2004). "El miedo a flotar y la política cambiaria." Central Bank of Chile, Working Paper No. 302.

De la Torre, Augusto, and Sergio Schmukler (2004). "Coping with Risk through Mismatches: Domestic and International Financial Contracts for Emerging Economies." World Bank, Policy Research Working Paper No. 3212.

Gallego, Francisco, and Norman Loayza (2000). "Financial Structure in Chile: Macroeconomic Developments and Microeconomic Effects." Central Bank of Chile, Working Paper No. 75.

Hart, Oliver (1999). "Different Approaches to Bankruptcy." Manuscript, Harvard University.

International Monetary Fund (2005a). "Development of Corporate Bond Markets in Emerging Economies." *Global Financial Stability Report* (September), 103–141.

International Monetary Fund (2005b). "Corporate Finance in Emerging Markets." *Global Financial Stability Report* (April), 92–133.

La Porta, R., F. López-de-Silanes, A. Shleifer, and R. Vishny (2000). "Investor Protection and Corporate Governance." *Journal of Financial Economics* 58(1): 1–25.

La Porta, R., F. López-de-Silanes, A. Shleifer, and R. Vishny (2001). "Creditor Protection and Bankruptcy Law Reform." In Stijin Claessens, Simeon Djankov, and Ashoka Mody, eds., *Resolution of Financial Distress: An International Perspective on the Design of Bankruptcy Laws*. Washington, D.C.: World Bank.

La Porta, R., F. López-de-Silanes, A. Shleifer, and R. Vishny (2003). "What Works in Securities Law?" NBER Working Paper No. 9882.

Meller, P. (1996). *Un siglo de economía política en Chile.* Santiago: Editorial Andrés Bello.

Zervos, S. (2004). "The Transaction Costs of Primary Market Issuance: The Case of Brazil, Chile, and Mexico." World Bank, Policy Research Working Paper No. 3424.

7   Development of the Brazilian Bond Market

Ricardo P. C. Leal and Andre L. Carvalhal-da-Silva

This paper identifies the main determinants of Brazilian corporate bond financing and discusses what can be done to promote the development of that market. Although the bond market represents a large proportion of the gross domestic product (GDP) in developed countries, it seems to be underdeveloped in emerging markets. In the particular case of Brazil, it is widely known that firms do not have enough access to credit at a reasonable cost.

The Brazilian corporate bond market is small compared to the average of developed countries and even of other emerging markets, especially in East Asia (Beck 2000), but it is not small when compared to Brazil's total private debt. Demirgüç-Kunt and Maksimovic (2002) document that Brazilian firms face important financial constraints and grow slower than their counterparts in many countries. A World Bank report (De la Torre and Schmukler 2004) documents that the outstanding stock of private bonds represents 9.6% of GDP, very low when compared to the average of developed countries (40%) and to the average of other emerging markets such as Chile (22.8%), Singapore (24%), South Korea (45%), and Malaysia (58%). The same is true of the international bonds issued by Brazilian firms. When measured relative to the GDP (11%), the total seems to be small compared to developed countries (32% on average) and other emerging markets (19% in Singapore and 18% in Malaysia).

Nevertheless, when we measure the outstanding stock of private bonds relative to total private debt (instead of GDP), the Brazilian bond market seems to be larger (26% of total private debt), reaching the average of developed countries (27%) and the levels of other emerging markets (27% in Chile, 17% in Singapore, 35% in South Korea, and 36% in Malaysia), according to BIS data. This evidence suggests that the Brazilian bond market is small because the financial sector is small.

A contrasting and perhaps more interesting finding is that the use of international bonds as a proportion of domestic debt in Brazil (30%) is higher than the average of developed countries (24%) and of other emerging markets (13% in Singapore and 11% in Malaysia). In contrast to the results of the private bond data, the outstanding stock of public bonds in Brazil is high, reaching 50% of GDP, larger than the average of developed countries (41%) and of other emerging markets (27% in Chile, 34% in Singapore, 16% in South Korea, and 36% in Malaysia).

Our goal in this chapter is to provide a better understanding of the Brazilian bond market, covering both public and private debt instruments. Although the market has rapidly developed since the inception of the Real Plan in July 1994, interest rate spreads and general credit default rates remain high. Furthermore, increasing domestic credit demand by the federal government may crowd out other borrowers with a combination of attractive interest rates and favorable prudential rules treatment of government debt relative to corporate debt, providing little incentive for more credit to the private sector.

This chapter proceeds as follows. The next section presents brief background information about the Brazilian financial system. We then present the market for public sector bonds and discuss the private sector bond market. Next we present the results of our empirical analysis for the determinants of corporate bond financing and a survey of investors and issuers. We close with conclusions and policy recommendations.

The Brazilian Financial Sector

At 31.3% of GDP by the end of 2005, the Brazilian credit market is proportionally smaller than that of Chile, for example, and the credit market grew neither as a percentage of GDP nor in real terms between 1995 and 2004. In 2005, there was a substantial increase in the credit market, from 27.5% of GDP in December of 2004, especially in the personal credit segment, as a consequence of a new law allowing direct paycheck and retirement social security check deductions of consumer credit taken by individuals.

Arida, Bacha, and Resende (2005) discuss three hypotheses commonly offered to explain high interest rates in Brazil. The first is a tighter than necessary monetary policy, or the "bad equilibrium" hypothesis, while a second hypothesis emphasizes the federal government's fiscal needs and its crowding-out effect on private debt, which raises interest rates. The third hypothesis involves the general vulnerability of the Brazilian economy to international shocks.

Arida et al. conclude that the high real interest rate in Brazil is due to a large domestic currency short-term debt market with jurisdictional uncertainty. They further note that Chile has no jurisdictional uncertainty and that Colombia enjoys a reputation for responsible financing, which would explain why these countries enjoy a local currency debt market, as does Brazil, but at much lower interest rates. The interventionist nature of the Brazilian state increases jurisdictional uncertainty, and Arida et al. close by saying that jurisdictional uncertainty is the result of a historical process and can only be gradually reversed through a series of carefully thought out steps that would include ending forced savings, introducing full convertibility, the substitution of "incomeless" taxes, compulsory savings such as those that fund the National Development Bank (BNDES), and increasing financial and economic integration with low jurisdictional uncertainty economies.

In December 2005, the average corporate credit spread was 14%, down from 45% in December 1997. A study by Costa and Nakane (2004, p. 28) develops a model to identify the components of the credit spread; on the basis of data from 77 banks in December 2003, the authors find that the largest components are bank overhead costs (26%), taxes (20%), default spreads (20%), and compulsory deposits (5%). The residual corresponds to 28% of the average spread, which they attribute to the bank's profit margin. Loans for both individuals and firms were considered. Costa and Nakane comment that default spreads are very high and reflect the high legal costs of debt recovery and the overall inefficiency of the judiciary. Beck (2000) reports that Brazilian overhead costs in 1997 were almost double the Latin American average and triple the upper middle-income country average. Initiatives that lower the risk of default and reduce the administrative costs to execute bad loans could be very effective to decrease credit spreads in Brazil. As a matter of fact, a large number of initiatives have been enacted or proposed in the last few (Leal and Carvalhal-da-Silva 2006), and a great deal of discussion on the profitability of Brazilian banks has apparently taken place as well.

The Brazilian banking system was reorganized in 1988 with the adoption of universal banking. The total number of banking institutions fell from 246 in 1994 to 165 in 2002, with a much slower decline to 159 banks in August 2005. These overall figures, however, must be seen in light of two additional and possibly countervailing trends.

First, there have recently been several very high profile bank acquisitions. Second, the introduction of new forms of consumer credit has brought new and smaller players into the credit market.

Brazilian banks still earn much of their profits from holding directly or indirectly a large portion of Brazilian treasury securities, which pay very high interest rates. Arida, Bacha, and Resende (2005) document that 90% of Brazilian treasury securities are directly or indirectly in the hands of commercial banks. Of this amount, about half of treasury securities are in mutual funds managed by these banks, one third are in the bank's own free treasury operations, and the remainder are held compulsorily. The recent consolidation trend and the attractiveness of interest rates paid by the government may induce the reader to think that banks exert pressure on the government, rendering lowering the base rate difficult. However, several former central bankers have repeatedly stated in the press and in informal conversations that this is not the case, and that if future interest rates decline, they will not have an impact on the demand for treasury paper, provided the decline is not abrupt. This is certainly an issue open for debate.

Central bank statistics show that in 1995 the 20 largest banks held 72% of bank assets, and by 2003 this figure had climbed to 81%. Asset concentration rose from 49% to 54% for the five largest banks. These numbers show a lower degree of concentration than in middle-income countries where on average the three largest banks held 70% of assests (Beck, Demirgüç-Kunt, and Levine 1999). Within the region, data for the average five largest banks' share of bank assets in the 1995–99 period shows that Chile (71%) and Mexico (79%) display higher levels of concentration than Brazil (Demirgüç-Kunt, Laeven, and Levine 2004). Moreover, Brazil's concentration level is also no higher than those in many developed countries, such as Australia, the United Kingdom or Canada, and the weighted average reported by those authors for their sample of 72 countries is 57%. Brazil's concentration level should nonetheless be considered in light of evidence presented by Fajardo and Fonseca (2004), suggesting that the credit spread could be reduced given greater bank competition.

The Market for Public Sector Bonds

The Brazilian federal public debt market is one of the most liquid and sophisticated among emerging markets, offering a wide range of debt instruments (fixed-rate, floating-rate, and inflation-indexed bonds).

Leal and Carvalhal-da-Silva (2006) provide a brief historical evolution of the Brazilian public bond market. Because many major changes in the types of securities have occurred in the last 30 years as a result of high inflation and the many failed anti-inflation plans, we will primarily address the current status of the market and the security types that prevailed after the successful Real Plan of 1994 as well as recent events and possible future actions by the treasury. By the early 1990s all the main treasury debt instruments currently available had been created and established as the key national treasury financing instruments after the Real Plan: in 1970 the Letra do Tesouro Nacional (LTN), treasury bills with no stated interest coupon that trade at discounts; in 1987 the Letra Financeira do Tesouro (LFT), treasury bills with interest computed at maturity according to the daily secondary treasury securities average market rate computed by the Central Bank of Brazil at the Special System for Settlement and Custody (SELIC) rate; and in 1991 the treasury notes and bonds (Nota do Tesouro Nacional, NTN) family that includes many kinds of securities (e.g., the fixed coupon bullet bond, NTN-F; the inflation-indexed bonds, NTN-B and NTN-C; and the US dollar-indexed notes, NTN-D). All of these treasury securities, along with many others, were created before the Real Plan of 1994 but have survived since then, while many other kinds—especially some attached to inflation correction mechanisms (but not necessarily inflation indexed)—became extinct at distinct points in time during the turbulent high-inflation years. These instruments have been used more or less intensely depending on the period's economic situation and needs. Presently, LFTs are by far the most widely used instruments, followed by LTNs and two kinds of inflation-indexed NTNs. Notes indexed to the U.S. dollar exist but have not been issued since 2003. In compliance with the Fiscal Responsibility Law, the central bank has ceased to issue debt as of May 2002. All open market operations are now conducted using treasury instruments.

Recently, the government exempted foreign investors from government bond income taxation although the exemption has not been extended to corporate bonds or any other type of private sector debt. This measure is particularly directed to US investors because Brazil has no tax treaty with the United States, and tax withheld in Brazil could not be easily used as credit in their US tax filings. Immediately after its introduction in February 2006, inflow levels of foreign investment in government securities doubled relative to February of the prior year (see ANDIMA 2006, p. 4). As a policy, the Brazilian

Treasury has been trying to extend the yield curve by selling longer-term, pre-fixed interest securities, such as the LTN and the NTN-F, as well as concentrating issuance of inflation-indexed bonds on the NTN-B, which uses the official inflation index. So far, the Brazilian Treasury has been successful in extending and cleaning up the domestic yield curve, and market yields for 10-year NTN-F bonds are now observable. Going forward, the plan is more of the same, including reducing the issuance of post-fixed interest securities such as the LFT, which remains the workhorse of government securitized domestic debt.

Secondary market transactions are cleared and settled through SELIC, which is managed by the central bank on a delivery-versus-payment (DVP) basis against same-day bank reserves. Currently, there are 12 primary dealers and 10 secondary (specialist) dealers. Both foreign and domestic banks can be dealers. The volume of trade in government securities in the secondary market is very high. The total volume traded in 2005 exceeded R$3.9 trillion and the turnover ratio reached 3.96. Overall, trade on floating-rate securities has remained higher than on fixed-rate securities, reflecting the much higher amount of LFTs outstanding.

Figure 7.1 reports the level and composition of central government bonds (as a percentage of GDP) in 1999 and in 2005. We can see that the level of central government bonds increased significantly during this period. It is important to note that most bonds are issued domestically and that the amount of foreign bonds is decreasing. In the domestic market, most bonds employ post-fixed interest linked to the overnight SELIC interest rate. Domestic bonds in foreign currency are decreasing in importance, while inflation-adjusted notes are gaining ground.

In the international market, most central government bonds are issued in foreign currency and have longer maturities than domestic bonds. However, in September 2005, Brazil followed the example of Uruguay and Colombia and issued external debt denominated in the local currency. This global issue was oversubscribed several times and the distribution purchased mainly by investors from Europe and the United States. The level and composition of local government (state and municipal) bonds decreased significantly from 6.10% of GDP in 1990 to 0.11% of GDP in 2005. Detailed figures are available in Leal and Carvalhal-da-Silva (2006).

Figure 7.2 reports the amount outstanding of the total federal debt in 2005. Floating-rate bills represent 43% of the total debt, followed by

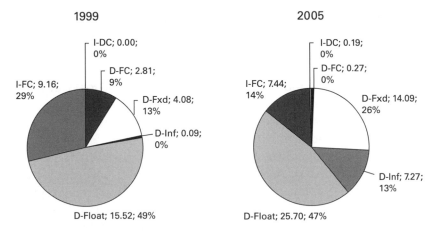

Figure 7.1
Composition of Brazilian federal government bonds outstanding in 1999 and in 2005. For each category of bond, the first number represents percent of GDP; the second number, percent of total bonds outstanding. The categories are domestic with fixed interest (D-Fxd); domestic with floating interest (D-Float); domestic inflation-indexed (D-Inf); domestic on foreign currency (D-FC); international on foreign currency (I-FC); and international on the domestic currency (I-DC).

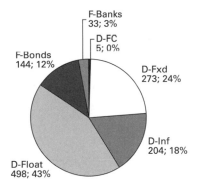

Figure 7.2
Composition of Brazilian federal government total debt in 2005. Figures are in billions of Brazilian reais (BRL 2.20 = USD 1.00 in December 2005). Debt types are foreign bonds (F-Bonds); other foreign loans, such as multilaterals, banks, etc. (F-Banks); domestic bonds in foreign currency (D-FC); domestic bonds at fixed interest (D-Fxd); domestic bonds at floating interest (D-Float); and domestic bonds inflation-indexed (D-Infl).

fixed-rate bills (24%), inflation-adjusted notes (18%), and US dollar notes (0%). The volume of fixed-rate bills has risen significantly since 2003, and the issue of inflation-adjusted notes increased from 1995 (0.62%) to 2005 (18%). In contrast, the treasury decided to decrease the issuance of US dollar-indexed notes (from 7.28% in 1995 to 0% in 2005) in order to reduce the internal debt denominated in foreign currency. Figure 7.2 also shows the external federal debt profile, which is mostly represented by bonds and notes and not by bank loans.

The average internal debt term is 2.29 years and has been decreasing since 2001 (3.32 years). As expected, fixed-rate bills have the lowest term (0.79 years), followed by US dollar notes (1 year), floating-rate bills (1.59 years), and inflation-adjusted notes (5.68 years). Despite a slight decrease since 2000, the average term of external debt is substantially higher than that of internal debt (7.19 years in 2000 and 6.32 years in 2005). In 2005, the highest average term was for global bonds (7.00 years).

In closing, we can say that things have been improving. Longer maturity in selected securities, greater demand, lower sovereign risk, friendlier policies to foreign investors, successful new issues, and securities that are less taxing on the treasury represent an increasing share of the Brazilian public debt profile. The recent trend portrayed is favorable, but nominal central government debt levels are still increasing.

The Market for Private Sector Bonds

Evolution of the Private Sector Bond Market

In talks with prominent securities lawyers, we posed the question of why the new bankruptcy law—passed in 2005 but first introduced in Congress in 1993—took so long to be approved. The answer we invariably obtained was that, although the law had no real opponents, it was simply not a priority for the executive branch, probably because fighting inflation represented a more pressing challenge. (In Brazil, 85% of new legislation is proposed by the executive branch, so Congress abides by the executive agenda.) Once inflation was tamed and new views about credit risk emerged in the central bank, a comprehensive agenda to reduce credit risk was adopted, including the new bankruptcy law. Thus legislation was finally put on the slate and passed. The lawyers we interviewed also doubt that this piece of legislation really reduces credit risk, and recent evidence suggests that very few companies, under the new law, have in fact opted for reorganization, which in our opinion remains by and large unproven. The new legislation's impact on the bond market is yet to be seen. While the law does not discriminate against bonds in any special way, real collateral bonds have priority over all other types of bonds and are paid together with all real collateral creditors. Unsecured bonds are paid together with all other unsecured credit holders, regardless of the maturity and nature of their claims.

Brazil's credit market is small compared to the average of upper middle-income countries (Beck 2000). There is plenty of evidence that Brazilian firms face important financial constraints and grow more slowly than their counterparts in many countries (Demirgüç-Kunt and Maksimovic 2000). At 31.3% of GDP by the end of 2005, the Brazilian credit market is smaller than that of Chile, for example, and the credit market has grown neither as a percentage of GDP nor in real terms between 1995 and 2004. In 2005, we observed a substantial increase in the credit market—from 27.5% of GDP in December of 2004, especially in the personal credit segment—as a consequence of a new law allowing direct paycheck and retirement social security check deductions of consumer credit by individuals. Improvements in collection time and recovery rates probably have more to do with the fall in the general level of interest rates and with the migration of part of the personal consumer credit to direct payroll deductions than with the introduction of the new bankruptcy law. Another major innovation was the introduction of new laws easing securitization.

The rule of law and the efficiency of the judiciary are related to the size of the credit and corporate debt securities market. Durnev and Kim (2005) report on the "Legality" index computed by Berkowitz, Pistor, and Richard (2003). In general, Brazil scores average in terms of rule of law, above some developing countries such as Korea, Mexico, China, and South Africa, but below others such as Chile, Malaysia, Poland, and Thailand. The story is a little worse with the "Judicial Efficiency" index obtained from the International Country Risk Guide for March 2005. Brazil ranks below the average of developing nations. Thus, in general, this situation is not helpful to the credit and debt securities markets in general and needs improvement.

As a matter of fact, a large number of initiatives have been enacted or proposed in the last few years. One of them was the reduction of reserve requirements with the central bank (for cash deposits, from 75%

to 53%). Regarding better credit information, the central bank now publishes detailed information on interest rate and fees charged by each institution and for each type of credit line on the internet. The central bank has also developed a project called Credit Risk Center that gathers information about all credits above R$5,000. While current Brazilian law gives bad debtors consumer and privacy rights that prevent their past bad credit information from being shared among financial institutions, the central bank is proposing new legislation to facilitate proper positive credit information sharing. The central bank also plans to include more information of a positive nature to turn the Center into a true credit record database. The central bank has additionally also introduced regulation allowing the portability of credit records amongst financial institutions.

There are other interesting measures enacted or being pursued. The securitization of regular bank loans through bank credit bills, for instance, represents a very important measure. These securities replace loan agreements and may be executed under the Commercial Law, which does not require proof of existence of the debt (Beck 2000), and not under the Civil Code Law, where a recognition suit to assert the existence of the debt may take years. The new provision considerably speeds collection of nonperforming loan guarantees. The central bank is further considering additional regulation on bank credit bills to stimulate their secondary market and has put in place regulation focusing on the use of credit derivatives as instruments for credit risk reduction and transfer.

Instruments to facilitate securitization are also present in recent new regulations. Banks or other financial institutions with mortgage portfolios may issue real estate credit bills or loans for the acquisition of properties put on lien. Because these securities are backed by property on lien, they are considered safer than mortgage-backed securities; they may be issued for a maximum of 36 months. Moreover, inflation indexation of real estate loans was allowed on a monthly basis to facilitate securitization, and in recent years this has stimulated tremendous growth in asset-backed securities markets—one of the major innovations in Brazilian debt securities markets.

Figure 7.3 reports the level and composition of bonds issued by the private sector in 1999 and in 2005. We can see that the amount of private sector bonds increased significantly during this period as a percentage of GDP. The issuance volumes of debentures and CPs have often been greater than those of stocks in recent years. Most domestic

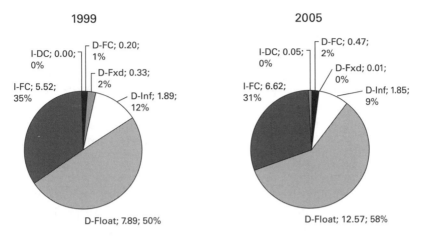

Figure 7.3
Brazilian publicly issued private sector bonds outstanding in 1999 and in 2005. For each category of bond, the first number represents percent of GDP; the second number, percent of total bonds outstanding. The categories are domestic with fixed interest (D-Fxd); domestic with floating interest (D-Float); domestic inflation-indexed (D-Inf); domestic on foreign currency (D-FC); international on foreign currency (I-FC); and international on the domestic currency (I-DC).

bonds are linked to the overnight interest rate and their interest is computed at each coupon payment anniversary according to the accumulated daily average of one-day interbank loan rate (interbank certificate of deposit rate), followed by inflation-indexed bonds and U.S. dollar-indexed bonds. The percentage of debentures with floating interest rates has significantly increased since 1999 while debentures with fixed interest rates and U.S. dollar-adjusted rates are rare. In the international market, the volume of private sector bonds also increased significantly from 0.14% of GDP in 1987 to 6.67% of GDP in 2005. Most private sector bonds are issued in foreign currency, but at the end of 2004 Brazilian private financial institutions issued external debt denominated in local currency. Despite a slight increase since 1995, the volume of corporate issue is still very small when compared to the government and to financial institutions, representing around 1% of total domestic debt. Details on all types of debt securities, as well as on the structure and practices of the bond market, prudential rules, and an analysis of bond covenants, can be found in Leal and Carvalhal-da-Silva (2006).

Debentures' priority order over the company's assets is as follows: (1) fixed-collateral debentures; (2) floating-collateral debentures; (3)

unsecured debentures; and (4) subordinated debentures. Floating collateral debentures give bondholders a general privilege over the company's free assets (i.e., those that are not a collateral for any other debt), while fixed-collateral bonds have a claim on specific assets. Of the total of bonds outstanding in December of 2005, 66.2% were subordinated debentures, 26.7% were unsecured debentures, 1.9% were floating collateral debentures, and 5.2% are fixed collateral debentures. Most debentures outstanding (94.4%) are not convertible (straight bonds).

Debentures, mortgage- and asset-backed securities, as well as credit rights funds quotas are traded in the OTC market on CETIPNet (CETIP's trading platform) or Bovespa Fix and are registered at the SND or on Bovespa Fix. Trading can be done over the phone or through computerized systems. The SND is a registration, custodial, and settlement system for debentures created in 1988 and maintained by a partnership between ANDIMA and CETIP. Bovespa Fix is an integrated framework for the trading, settlement, and safekeeping of corporate bonds created in 2001 by the São Paulo Stock Exchange (Bovespa). Most fixed-income securities are registered at CETIP because it provides a safer trading environment and guarantees the existence of the security. Prior to 1986, false securities were a serious problem.

Debenture trading volume and turnover in 2005 were, respectively, R$16.28 billion and 0.19 (relative to the amount outstanding of R$84.99 billion). Debenture trading volume and turnover are very low when compared to those of federal debt securities (R$3.9 trillion and 3.96, respectively). Almost all of the volume (98%) is still concentrated in the National Debenture System, but the volume traded on Bovespa Fix is increasing (from 0.24% in 2001 to 1.99% in 2005).

Most companies issue debentures to increase their working capital (41.02%), to invest in operations (35.88%), or to increase debt maturity (20.55%). Other minor purposes (2.55%) are changing the debt profile, purchasing fixed assets, paying previous debt, and purchasing a stake in other companies.

Brazilian firms may issue international bonds in foreign jurisdictions. As expected, most international debt securities are issued by the government (US$62.90 billion), followed by financial institutions (US$34.40 billion) and corporate issuers (US$9.80 billion), according to BIS data. The proportion of government-issued international debt securities decreased from 75.12% in 1995 to 58.73% in 2005. In contrast, foreign debt issued by financial institutions has substantially increased (from 17.25% to 32.12%), and corporate issues have enjoyed a modest increase (from 7.63% to 9.15%).

Firm and Bond-Level Sample

We collect and analyze firm and bond-level data in order to better understand the Brazilian bond market. Our sample includes all public Brazilian firms listed at Bovespa. The sample has both financial and nonfinancial institutions and does not contain companies with incomplete or unavailable information. Our 2004 sample contained 357 companies. The market and accounting data comes from the Economática database that contains financial statements and time series data of companies. The information on domestic and international bonds comes from the CVM, SND, and Bovespa Fix.

Within the sample, 36% of firms have foreign shareholders with a mean stake of 18.60%. Foreign shareholders with more than 50% of the voting capital control 18.67% of firms. Most foreign shareholders come from the United States (21.90%), Spain (10.95%), the Netherlands (7.30%), Italy (7.30%), and Japan (6.57%).

Our sample includes large firms when measured by the number of employees (mean of 7,218), total revenues (R$2.71 billion, of which 12.16% are exports), and total assets (R$5.43 billion). In general, we are analyzing firms established a long time before the study (mean of 46.67 years since incorporation). The relative financial sophistication of these firms is indicated by the fact that almost 20% issue American depositary receipts (ADRs) and 45.33% use derivatives to hedge or change their respective debt profiles.

Figure 7.4 presents the capital structure of listed Brazilian firms. The mean (median) shareholder's equity is 46.11% (31.62%) of total assets. On average, financial liabilities represent 57.29% of assets (median of 30.63%), of which 23.55% are denominated in foreign currency. On average, most debt is represented by domestic bonds (18.04% of total assets), followed by national banks (15.44%), suppliers (8.23%), international banks (5.15%), the Brazilian National Development Bank (BNDES) (4.77%), international bonds (1.45%), and asset-backed securities (1.13%). International bonds and foreign banks loans are 99.9% denominated in foreign currency, while only 0.48% of domestic bonds, 6.34% of national bank loans, 2.27% of suppliers' credit, 2.83% of

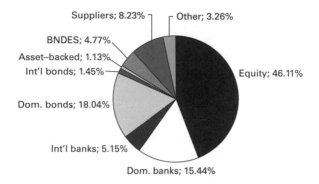

Figure 7.4
Capital structure of Brazilian listed companies. All figures are for 2005. Percentages are averages of listed Brazilian companies and do not add up to 100%. Source: Brazilian Securities Commission (CVM).

BNDES loans, and 3.73% of asset-backed securities are foreign-currency-indexed. Issuance is concentrated in a few large and more financially sophisticated listed firms, as shown by a comparison of firm characteristics in figure 7.4 and in table 7.1.

Table 7.1 reports the capital structure of listed Brazilian firms that issue domestic bonds, international bonds, and asset-backed securities. Financial liabilities of firms that issue domestic bonds average 98.51% of assets, most of which are represented by domestic bonds (60.94%), followed by BNDES (8.88%), suppliers (7.93%), international banks (6.88%), and national banks (6.58%). This gargantuan average, however, is distorted by a few firms with negative shareholders' equity. The median for financial liabilities is 44.59%. Domestic bond issuers are less financially sophisticated than international bond and asset-backed securities issuers because only about half of them use derivatives (54.95%) while most other issuers use them. In addition, domestic bond issuers are smaller (total revenues, assets, and number of employees) than international bond and asset-backed securities issuers and seem be less leveraged than other issuers. Domestic bond issuers, in turn, are larger, more financially sophisticated, and more leveraged than nonissuers.

Brazilian firms that have access to the international bond market are generally larger, more financially sophisticated, and less leveraged than firms issuing local bonds. Financial liabilities represent on average 36.60% of assets, most of which are international bonds (9.53%), followed by suppliers (6.90%), and international banks (5.60%). These

Table 7.1
Capital Structure of Firms Issuing Bonds

	Domestic bond issuers		International bond issuers		Asset-backed securities issuers	
	Mean	Median	Mean	Median	Mean	Median
Foreigner stake	18.16%	0.00%	22.41%	0.48%	12.26%	0.00%
Years since incorporation	43.84	43.00	45.20	38.50	49.32	38.00
Employees	9,083	3,466	13,797	4,314	21,247	9,242
Total revenues (R$ million)	5,471.60	1,580.61	10,266.01	4,378.10	9,862.26	5,876.52
Exports (% revenues)	10.20%	0.00%	8.46%	0.00%	14.51%	0.00%
Assets (R$ million)	10,123.00	2,263.05	26,972.55	6,975.33	42,093.36	10,130.81
Shareholders' equity (% assets)	63.24%	27.17%	22.39%	28.01%	21.76%	20.66%
Use of derivatives	54.95%	100.00%	92.98%	100.00%	80.00%	100.00%
Financial liabilities (% assets)	98.51%	44.59%	36.60%	38.28%	42.16%	38.94%
National banks (% assets)	6.58%	1.60%	4.18%	1.40%	2.28%	0.00%
International banks (% assets)	6.88%	2.51%	5.60%	2.55%	6.00%	0.85%
Domestic bonds (% assets)	60.94%	8.38%	4.58%	0.34%	5.15%	0.00%
International bonds (% assets)	2.59%	0.00%	9.53%	3.94%	2.25%	2.18%
Asset-backed securities (% assets)	0.95%	0.30%	0.53%	0.00%	16.89%	3.25%
BNDES (% assets)	8.88%	2.78%	4.31%	2.02%	4.81%	1.49%
Suppliers (% assets)	7.93%	5.60%	6.90%	5.60%	4.23%	2.84%
Other (% assets)	4.32%	0.00%	1.14%	0.02%	0.54%	0.00%

Note: Data for 2004.
Source: Economática database, and Brazilian Securities and Exchange Commission (CVM).

firms present the largest use of derivatives (92.98% of the firms) and the highest stake of foreign shareholders (22.41% of capital).

Data on the main characteristics of international bonds are available upon request. The volume issued is higher than domestic bonds (US$199.44 million). Curiously, and in contrast with the jurisdictional uncertainty hypothesis discussed earlier, maturity is slightly shorter (average original and remaining terms of 7.00 and 3.69 years, respectively). Most international bonds use fixed interest rates (80.33%), and the mean interest rate coupon is 8.14% per year (ranging from 2.92% to 13.50%). Regarding the currency, the U.S. dollar is dominant (88.96%), followed by the Brazilian real (8.20%), the yen (1.93%), and the euro (0.91%).

Asset-backed securities are generally issued by large Brazilian firms (total revenues, assets, and number of employees are generally higher than those of other companies), which present the highest proportion of exports in total revenues (14.51%). This is not surprising, since most of these asset-backed securities are related to export receivables. Asset-backed securities represent 16.89% of total assets, followed by international banks (6.00%) and domestic bonds (5.15%). Derivatives are used by 80% of the firms, and foreign shareholders have on average a lower stake (12.26%) when compared to the other two groups of companies.

Financial institutions have issued R$125.90 billion or 70.17% of the total volume of public bond offers between 1995 and 2005, followed by electricity, gas, and water supply (12.90%) and manufacturing firms (7.26%). In general, financial firms are leasing companies. Banks cannot issue bonds, but they are allowed to buy bonds from associated leasing companies. Although the amount issued is higher for financial firms, the number of issues is relatively low (36) when compared to electricity, gas and water supply (152), and manufacturing (83), which means that the average amount issued by financial firms is high.

Table 7.2 shows the main characteristics of domestic bonds issued by the listed firms in our sample, and table 7.3 shows the main characteristics of privately placed bonds. Note that the results are somewhat different from those in table 7.2. The average volume issued is lower, but the maximum volume issued is higher for privately placed than for publicly placed bonds, and the turnover is low. However, the average original maturity is 8.83 years, and the average remaining term from 2004 is similar to publicly issued bonds.

In contrast with publicly placed bonds, most privately placed bonds are convertible (71.76%) and secured (34.12% of floating collateral

Table 7.2
Characteristics of Domestic Bonds

Domestic bonds by public and private offer

Type of offer	% of domestic bonds
Publicly placed bonds	72.93
Privately placed bonds	27.07

Descriptive statistics of publicly placed bonds

Descriptive statistics	Issued volume (R$ thousands)	Turnover in the secondary market	Original term (years)	Remaining term (years)
Mean	227,189.26	0.23	8.37	4.65
Median	120,000.00	0.02	7.00	3.92
Standard deviation	268,545.22	0.44	5.91	3.29
Minimum	2,000.00	0.00	2.00	0.09
Maximum	1,500,000.00	3.45	31.34	15.42

Publicly placed bonds by collateral, type, and interest rate

Category	% of publicly placed bonds
Collateral:	
Fixed	20.52
Floating	12.66
Unsecured	37.55
Subordinated	29.26
Type of bond:	
Straight	85.59
Convertible	14.41
Interest rate:	
Fixed	0.44
Floating	45.85
Inflation-adjusted	34.50
Long-term ("TJLP")	13.10
% earnings or revenues	3.06
US dollar-adjusted	3.06

Note: Data for 2004.
Source: Brazilian Securities and Exchange Commission (CVM), National Debenture System (SND), and Bovespa Fix.

Table 7.3
Characteristics of Privately Placed Bonds

Descriptive statistics of privately placed bonds

Descriptive statistics	Issued volume (R$ thousands)	Turnover in the secondary market	Original term (years)	Remaining term (years)
Mean	146,047.20	0.00	8.83	4.17
Median	25,702.50	0.00	7.00	2.62
Standard deviation	354,984.31	0.01	5.41	5.23
Minimum	60.00	0.00	3.00	0.08
Maximum	2,693,080.00	0.10	25.00	24.99

Privately placed bonds by collateral, type, and interest rate

Category	% of privately placed bonds
Collateral:	
Fixed	25.88
Floating	34.12
Unsecured	15.29
Subordinated	24.71
Type of bond:	
Straight	28.24
Convertible	71.76
Interest rate:	
Fixed	7.06
Floating	15.29
Inflation-adjusted	12.94
Long-term ("TJLP")	55.29
% earnings or revenues	9.41

Note: Data for 2004.
Source: Brazilian Securities and Exchange Commission (CVM), National Debenture System (SND), and Bovespa Fix.

bonds and 25.88% of fixed collateral bonds). Furthermore, most privately placed bonds use long-term interest rate (55.29%), followed by floating rates (15.29%) and inflation-adjusted rates (12.94%). These differences among publicly and privately placed domestic bonds are not surprising. Most privately placed bonds are generally subscribed by the BNDES, which uses the long-term interest rate (TJLP) as the basic cost of credit, requires fixed or floating collateral in order to finance companies in Brazil, and prefers convertible bonds in order to enjoy the upside in case of success of the financed project.

Dynamics of Bond Financing

We produce an analysis of firm leverage and analyze, in particular, the use of bonds relative to other types of debt. We control for some possible determinants of leverage in general and use total leverage, bank loans, domestic bonds (debentures and commercial papers), international bonds, and asset-backed securities as endogenous variables. We use an econometric and a survey method. The econometric model is employed to determine the dynamics between the use of different types of debt by public Brazilian firms. The survey is designed and conducted among selected market participants, representing issuers and investors, in order to identify the main motivations and potential obstacles to bond investing and financing.

Econometric Model

We begin with a brief discussion of our control variables. In Brazil, Leal and Saito (2003) review the Brazilian empirical evidence on the determinants of capital structure. Booth et al. (2001) present evidence of capital structure in developing countries. Harris and Raviv (1991) provide evidence that leverage increases with fixed assets, non-debt tax shields, investment opportunities, and firm size and decreases with volatility, the probability of bankruptcy, profitability, and the uniqueness of the product. Our empirical analysis includes five of these variables: tangibility of assets, firm size, investment opportunities, profitability, and volatility.

Our measure for tangibility of assets is the ratio of fixed to total assets. Warner (1977) and Ang et al. (1982) document that smaller firms tend to have relatively higher bankruptcy costs, while Titman and Wessels (1988) argue that larger firms tend to be less risky because they can diversify. We use the natural logarithm of total assets as a proxy for firm size. We expect that larger firms are able to use more debt, particularly bonds.

Firms with more investment opportunities are expected to be less leveraged. The market-to-book ratio is our proxy for investment opportunities. Alternatively, we will also use the Tobin's Q, constructed as the market value of assets (total assets minus book equity plus the market value of equity) divided by the book value of assets. Forms of computing Q are described in DaDalt, Donaldson, and Garner (2003), but they find that simpler computations of Q should be preferred over more complex estimators, particularly when data availability is a concern, which is our case.

According to the trade-off theory, more profitable firms should have higher leverage as bankruptcy costs are lower when profitability is higher, and interest tax shields induce them to finance with debt. In contrast, the pecking order theory suggests that more profitable firms should be less leveraged because they should prefer raising capital from retained earnings first, before turning to debt, and lastly to new equity. The empirical evidence on this hypothesis, however, is ambiguous. Our measure of profitability is the return on assets (ROA), measured as operating income over total assets.

Bolton and Freixas (2000) propose a model of financial markets and corporate finance where equity, bank debt, and bond financing coexist in equilibrium. They suggest that riskier firms prefer bank loans, safer firms issue bonds, and those in the middle prefer to issue both equity and bonds. More volatile firms are generally associated with a higher probability of default, implying a negative relationship between leverage and volatility. Because of the lack of suitable time-series data for the volatility of cash flows or earnings, we measure volatility as the standard deviation of daily returns in the year of analysis.

In Brazil, there is a huge separation of voting and cash flow rights (Leal and Carvalhal-da-Silva 2007), mainly through deviations from the one-share-one-vote rule. Because this separation may affect firm valuation and consequently its cost of capital, we will include three variables to attempt to capture the effect of ownership and control on leverage: the controlling shareholder's stake of voting shares (control), of total shares (ownership), and the ratio of these two variables (separation of ownership from control).

Carvalhal-da-Silva and Leal (2005) construct a firm-level corporate governance practices index (CGI). They find that the CGI maintains a positive, significant, and robust relationship with corporate value. We construct a reduced version of their CGI with 15 questions, including those that are more discriminating among firms. We believe that better-governed firms provide better protection to outside financiers, whether shareholders or bondholders. The greater the CGI score, the greater the firm's leverage.

We include year dummies in order to control for differences in macroeconomic variables (such as GDP growth, interest rates, volatility of interest rates, and inflation) during our time period. There is evidence that macroeconomic factors may be important in determining the size and currency denomination of the domestic bond market, although they do not seem to have a significant effect on the currency composition of international bonds (Eichengreen, Hausmann, and Panizza 2005).

Our basic econometric model was estimated for a sample of firms listed at Bovespa with available information between 1998 and 2004, according to the following equation:

$$Lev = \beta_0 + \beta_1 Tang + \beta_2 Size + \beta_3 Price/Book + \beta_4 Tobin'sQ + \beta_5 ROA$$

$$+ \beta_6 Vol + \beta_7 Control + \beta_8 Own + \beta_9 Control/Own + \beta_{10} CGI$$

$$+ \beta_{11} Industry \mid \beta_{12} Year + \varepsilon$$

where *Lev* denotes the ratio of total (nonequity) liabilities to total assets, *Tang* is the tangibility of assets (the ratio of fixed to total assets), *Size* is the natural logarithm of total assets, *Price/Book* is the market-to-book ratio, *Tobin'sQ* is the market value of assets divided by the book value of assets, *ROA* is the return on assets (profitability), *Vol* is the standard deviation of the daily returns of stock prices in a calendar year, *Control* is the controlling shareholder's stake of voting shares, *Own* is the controlling shareholder's stake of total (voting and nonvoting) shares, *Control/Own* is the ratio of voting shares to total shares owned by controlling shareholder, *CGI* is the reduced version of the corporate governance index, *Industry* are industry dummy variables in order to control for the firm's industrial classification, and *Year* are year dummy variables in order to control for differences in macroeconomic variables during the time period.

In order to analyze the different types of debt issued by Brazilian firms, we also estimate the same regression using four alternative dependent variables: *Bank* (ratio of bank loans to total assets), *Bond* (ratio of domestic bonds to total assets), *IntBond* (ratio of international bonds to total assets), and *AssetBacked* (ratio of asset-backed securities to total assets). Our four additional regressions are similar to the one above.

We also included some additional variables that may be useful in explaining the choice of the international bond market: *Export* (a dummy variable indicating if the firm exports goods or services), *ADR* (a dummy variable indicating if the firm list its shares in the United States), *ForeignControllingShareholder* (a dummy variable indicating if the firm has a foreign shareholder with more than 50% of the voting capital), and *ForeignShareholder* (a dummy variable indicating if the firm has a foreign shareholder).

OLS panel regressions do not deal with the potential endogeneity of the variables in the system of equations, which may cause bias in the OLS estimation. One way to address this problem is to use an instrumental variables estimator such as two-stage least squares (2SLS) or three-stage least squares (3SLS). Both models attempt to account for the endogeneity that exists in the simultaneous equation model. While 2SLS estimates the model parameters of each equation one at a time, full-system estimators such as 3SLS estimate all parameters simultaneously.

2SLS is a method of using instrumental variables to replace the endogenous variables where they appear as explanatory variables in the simultaneous equation model. It is important to note that the 2SLS estimates will still be biased, but they will be consistent. Zellner and Theil (1962) show that 3SLS produces consistent and more efficient estimates than those produced by the 2SLS procedure. In this paper, 3SLS is adopted, since it is likely to have an efficiency advantage over single-equation methods such as 2SLS. The endogenous variables in the system are *Lev*, *Bank*, *Bond*, *IntBond*, and *AssetBacked*. Thus, these variables are expected to be endogenous within our simultaneous equations framework. The endogenous model can be represented using the following simultaneous equation notation:

$$d_j = \alpha + \sum_{i \neq j} \phi_i d_i + \sum_{i=1}^{N} \varphi_i X_i + \varepsilon$$

where d is as a vector of debt measures, such as *Lev*, *Bank*, *Bond*, *IntBond*, and *AssetBacked*, and X is a vector of control variables that are associated with debt measures as well. If the coefficients of d, simultaneously determined, are still significant, this will be an indication that the net effect of alternate debt measures is significant. In order to allow for nonlinear relationships, we also include quadratic versions of some control variables. Except for size, we find no significant relationship with the square of the other control variables.

Table 7.4 shows the results of our simultaneous equations analysis. We do not report the results for the quadratic variables (except for size), since none is significant. The sign of the size coefficient is generally positive and the sign of squared size is negative, suggesting that large firms tend to use more debt in all forms but that, as they become larger, their debt use increases at a slower rate. Asset tangibility is always positive and sometimes significant. Other control variables show significance in some cases without sign consistency. The ownership controls show no significance.

Table 7.4 shows that domestic bonds are used together with international bonds and asset-backed securities and are substitutes for bank loans. However, the dynamic between international bonds and banks is not clear. Asset-backed securities tend to be used together with all forms of debt. Exporting firms use export receivables-backed securities as substitutes for international bonds. ADR issuing firms tend to issue fewer international bonds and asset-backed securities. Firms with foreign shareholders use more international bonds.

Survey

We conducted a survey among selected market participants representative of firms (financial and nonfinancial) and investors (mutual funds, insurance companies, pension funds, etc). The purpose of this survey is to identify the main determinants and potential obstacles of the bond financing choice for a typical Brazilian firm (supply side) and the main reasons that drive investors to buy corporate bonds (demand side).

We conducted the survey on a statistically valid sample, covering different firms' characteristics: industry, firm, size, access to the international market (ADR and Eurobonds, among others), as well as users and nonusers of commercial papers and bonds. This allowed us to have broad coverage of Brazilian firms and draw valid conclusions about the sample and possible extensions to other public companies in Brazil.

A brief survey that took no more than 15 minutes to answer was proposed. The questionnaires, made available through the Internet, are available upon request. Some questions could be objectively

Table 7.4
Three-Stage Least Squares Regressions

Independent variable	Dependent variable				
	Lev	Bank	Bond	IntBond	AssetBacked
Tang	0.27***	0.00	0.01	−0.05*	0.01**
	(0.00)	(0.96)	(0.79)	(0.07)	(0.04)
Size	7.56***	3.02	0.83*	0.23	0.45***
	(0.00)	(0.12)	(0.07)	(0.68)	(0.00)
$(Size)^2$	−0.15**	−0.13	−0.05**	0.00	−0.02***
	(0.04)	(0.19)	(0.04)	(0.93)	(0.00)
ROA	−1.92***	−0.97***	−0.13	−0.07	0.07***
	(0.00)	(0.00)	(0.14)	(0.45)	(0.01)
Vol	−0.14***	−0.09***	−0.02	0.03***	0.00
	(0.00)	(0.02)	(0.11)	(0.00)	(0.41)
Tobin'sQ	0.07	0.24*	−0.02	−0.06*	0.03***
	(0.53)	(0.07)	(0.60)	(0.10)	(0.00)
Price/Book	1.18	2.80**	−0.77***	0.60**	0.09
	(0.24)	(0.03)	(0.00)	(0.05)	(0.35)
Control	−0.16				
	(0.13)				
Own	0.08				
	(0.58)				
Control/Own	2.36				
	(0.51)				
CGI	−1.89***			0.19	
	(0.01)			(0.19)	
Bank			−0.08*	−0.16**	0.02
			(0.10)	(0.00)	(0.15)
Bond		−1.42**		0.73***	0.12
		(0.04)		(0.00)	(0.17)
IntBond		2.29***	0.62***		0.07
		(0.00)	(0.00)		(0.31)
AssetBacked		4.00	1.17*		
		(0.17)	(0.10)		
Export				−1.43**	0.62***
				(0.03)	(0.01)
ADR				−1.70*	−0.25***
				(0.08)	(0.01)
ForeignShareholder				0.34*	0.15
				(0.06)	(0.26)
Number of observations	460	460	460	460	460
Adjusted R^2	0.25	0.34	0.55	0.45	0.18

Note: All variables are defined in the text. Industry and year dummies are omitted to conserve space. ***, **, * denote significance at 1%, 5%, and 10% levels, respectively; p-values in parentheses.

answered from publicly available data, but others were subjective and depended on the respondents' views. The 38 institutional investors suggest that the main problems of the local bond market are low liquidity of the secondary market (97% of the respondents), low market capitalization (74%), absence of a complete benchmark yield curve (68%), and low quality of legal recourse in the event of default (63%).

Half of the investors surveyed are subject to constraints in their portfolio's asset allocation. In case constraints are relaxed, they would increase the weight of asset-backed securities (44%), foreign assets (55%), and domestic bonds issued by private-owned companies (38%). If their portfolios increased in value by 50%, their asset allocation would mostly remain unchanged. Nevertheless, some investors would increase the weight of domestic government bonds (50%), asset-backed securities (55%), and certificates of deposit (39%). Most investors (more than 70%) would be interested in holding Brazilian real-denominated bonds or inflation-indexed bonds issued by AAA multilateral institutions (World Bank and Inter-American Development Bank, among others).

Overall, investors agree that the yield curve provided by public bonds is crucial for pricing corporate bonds. Furthermore, if the yield on government bonds were to increase significantly and that of private bonds remained constant, they would sell private bonds and buy government bonds. They feel that a large stock of public sector bonds is not necessarily important for the development of the corporate bond market and that government and corporate bonds are not substitutes in their portfolios.

Results for the firm survey, covering a sample of 30 firms, indicate that most firms (83%) have outstanding bonds and have issued bonds over the last three years, so answers may be biased in favor of bond financing. However, respondents are not sure about issuing bonds in the next two years. The main reason (33%) to change the funding strategy from bonds to other types of financing is associated with high issuance costs. Another reason pointed out by most firms (56%) is that cash flow from operations is high enough that they do not need other types of financing.

High interest rates are a major problem associated with banks located in Brazil, and collateral requirements and a slow lending process are problematic for both domestic and foreign bank borrowings. Different types of fees (for underwriters, credit rating agencies, lawyers, and registration) represent obstacles to issuing domestic and international bonds. Domestic bond issues additionally have the following problems: small market (40%) and low liquidity in the secondary market (43%). Regulatory requirements represent a problem for both domestic (30%) and international (27%) bonds.

As expected, long-term lending is only available in the international bond market. Suppliers' credit is generally a short-term financing choice. There is no substantial difference in the non–interest rate costs among the financing instruments. Domestic bonds have the most favorable tax treatment, while international bank loans present the worse tax treatment. The advantage of suppliers' credit when compared to bank or bond financing is the possibility of renegotiation in the case of economic difficulties. In contrast, asset-backed securities have the lowest possibility of renegotiation in case of economic difficulties.

The costs related to disclosure requirements are lower for domestic bank borrowings and higher for international bond issues. The size of the potential market relative to the firm's financing needs is higher in the international bond market and lower for suppliers' credit. Complete survey tabulations are available in Leal and Carvalhal-da-Silva (2006).

Conclusions and Recommendations

The federal government's gargantuan financing needs induce it to pass regulation favoring its own debt to the detriment of the development of the corporate financing market. The recent foreign investor exemption of income tax withholding on government debt investments only, while corporate debt is still taxable, is a clear example of the government's "self-dealing." Capital adequacy rules, pension fund prudential rules, and mutual fund prudential rules, among others, all favor treasury debt. While this is not surprising per se, it is hard to say if a local AAA corporate bond issued by a Brazilian firm is really less risky than the federal government's debt. In any event, ceilings for corporate securities are arbitrary and could have been set with an anti-creditor or "self-dealing" mind-set on the part of regulators.

Consequently, our first recommendation is for a revision of capital adequacy and prudential rules to reduce their bias toward government debt. While we do not claim that portfolios should be unconstrained, ceilings for holdings in managed funds or weights used in capital adequacy calculations appear to be biased toward treasury paper. Of course, this will take some pressure on regulators from market organizations. Because regulations in different areas are issued by different branches of the government—the Central Bank of Brazil (commercial banks), the Securities and Exchange Commission (Comissão de Valores Mobiliários, CVM) (mutual funds), the Ministry of Social Security (closed pension funds), and the Ministry of Finance (open pension funds and insurance companies)—this is no easy task.

We know that the CVM, however, is actually planning to go in the opposite direction. They are holding public discussions of a potential new norm that will limit holdings of private debt in mutual funds marketed for retail investors to 30% of the portfolio with several "sub-limits," such as no more than 20% in stocks or corporate bonds. This ruling does not apply to stock funds but to non-stock funds (that is, multimarket or fixed-income funds). We believe that this is a step in the wrong direction. The new regulation, motivated by several recent financial institution debacles that hurt retail investors, for the time being defines mutual funds directed to retail investors as those with a minimum initial investment of R$300,000 or less. Their intent is to protect retail investors because they do not have the ability to evaluate credit risk. The CVM also argues that the vast majority of funds hold much less than 30% in private debt and that the measure will not change current practices. We believe that this will put a limit where no limit exists and may signal to individual investors that private securities in general are very risky and are a bad thing.

Specifically, in the case of the bond market in Brazil, ending the biased tax treatment in favor of government debt (such as extending the tax exemption of foreigners to corporate debt) and lifting the financial transactions tax (CPMF) on securitization structures could be very helpful. The question of accrued taxes on coupon payments, however, remains unresolved. In order for the secondary market to be friendlier to individuals, there should be a mechanism to compensate bond buyers from the tax they paid on interest accrued on behalf of the seller. This issue seems simple and would provide the right signal to the market.

Reducing restrictions for institutional investors to hold foreign assets is another step that can only be taken gradually. Raising the ceiling for foreigner-issued asset holdings, particularly for noncompulsory savings funds such as mutual funds and open pension funds, could allow the introduction of globally, albeit imperfectly, diversified portfolios in the domestic market, helping to reduce jurisdictional uncertainty. Along those same lines, the CVM opened for public discussion a new ruling that will allow some types of mutual funds—loosely called hedge funds or, in a literal translation, multimarket funds—to have up to 10% of their holdings in foreign-issued securities. This is an important first step that should be extended in the future to all types of institutional investors.

Great uncertainties in the Brazilian economy in the last 20 years have certainly led a substantial amount of funds into foreign countries. It is quite possible that a significant part of these funds was gained lawfully but has subsequently become undeclared and untaxed wealth following those funds' irregular remittance abroad. The creation of funds for the repatriation of those moneys—that could be invested in corporate as well as in government debt markets, with a hold on withdrawals for some time and taxation as the money comes in to fund the principal, as compensation for unpaid past-due taxes—could help ease any potential tax losses of allowing foreign securities to be part of existing institutional investors' portfolios. One possibility is that these funds are managed by financial institutions operating in Brazil but are located in foreign jurisdictions. The funds could hold Brazilian debt securities indexed to reais, and the money would not have to be repatriated. If the main motivation for the money to be abroad was jurisdictional uncertainty, then it would still be under foreign jurisdiction. Naturally, some procedure would be necessary to ascertain that the money in those funds does not originate from unlawful activities.

As noted above, our survey pointed out problems in the local bond market such as low liquidity of the secondary market, low market capitalization, the absence of a complete benchmark yield curve, and low quality of legal recourse in the event of default; all of the measures that have been suggested could contribute to improving the current situation. Initiatives that lower the risk of default and reduce the administrative costs of writing off bad loans could be very effective in reducing credit spreads in Brazil. While lowering the costs of writing off bad loans involves many initiatives, these initiatives are highly feasible. The central bank proposal to reduce the anti-creditor bias of lower court judges is very important. Market representatives as well as government regulators should promote seminars with judges to clarify why their pro-debtor rulings, particularly when contract terms are ignored, is very important to reduce the costs of unnecessary appeals and injunctions and shorten the legal process.

Market organizations such as ANDIMA and ANBID (Associação Nacional dos Bancos de Investimento) are pushing for a simplified standard bond indenture. The simplified bond would hopefully reduce issuance costs, increase market volume and maybe reduce underwriting fees, which are relatively high in Brazil when compared to Mexico's and those in developed countries. Simplified bonds would be approved on some sort of a fast track by the CVM, reducing legal processing costs as well. No bond with this new feature, however, has yet been offered. BNDES has additionally been called upon to advocate simplified bonds in the market and to help induce liquidity in the secondary bond market—the latter because its sizable portfolio is comprised largely of privately issued bonds. To date, no concrete measures have been undertaken.

Another important initiative has been the consolidation of Brazilian yield curves in strategic markets (US dollar, euro, and yen) with liquid benchmarks, thus paving the way for other borrowers to access long-term financing and broadening the investor base in Brazilian public debt. The Brazilian government has also pursued a strategy of buying back restructured debt (Brady bonds) and replacing them with new bonds (global bonds and Eurobonds). The same strategy is intended for domestic markets. In our survey we found that market participants believe the absence of a full yield curve hurts the market for bonds. Recently, BNDES has announced that it will act as market maker for selected bonds in the secondary market, and it is also pushing for the promotion of simplified indentures as well as for the dispersion of bonds amongst individual investors. Pursuant to the latter, BNDES was recently successful in issuing inflation-indexed bonds with a large portion of the issue reserved for individuals through an issue discount bidding process.

No priority is given to short-term debt over long-term debt in the Brazilian bankruptcy laws, and this has not helped the Brazilian commercial paper market. In fact, many potential issuers that are not in the market today could benefit from more privileged treatment under the bankruptcy law. Our results show that issuance is concentrated in a few larger and more financially sophisticated listed firms; for other firms, commercial paper could represent an easier entry mode into the market than other means. Even nonpublic firms are allowed to issue them.

In closing, we review our main econometric findings on the determinants of bond use. Asset-backed securities are used more often by exporting firms and replace international bonds in these firms, while size is positively related to debt use in general. Larger firms tend to borrow more but at a decreasing rate as they get larger. Interestingly, corporate governance variables show little influence over debt issuance in general, and the domestic bond market and the bank loan market seem to be substitutes. However, firms that issue abroad also tend to use more bank loans and domestic bonds, suggesting that more sophisticated and larger firms use every kind of debt at their disposal. Firms that use bank loans are smaller and less financially sophisticated than those that issue domestic bonds, which in turn are smaller and less sophisticated than those that issue bonds internationally. Finally, our results suggest that smaller and less financially sophisticated firms resort to bank loans, in contrast to larger and more financially sophisticated firms.

Acknowledgments

We thank Antonio Filgueira for his excellent insightful comments and research assistance; Eduardo Borensztein, Kevin Cowan, Barry Eichengreen, Márcio Garcia, Ugo Panizza, and several ANDIMA professionals for their comments; the Inter-American Development Bank for their grant; and the National Association of Financial Institutions (ANDIMA) and the Coppead Graduate School of Business at the Federal University of Rio de Janeiro for additional support.

References

ANDIMA, 2006. *Sinopse*. March issue.

Ang, J., J. Chua, and J. McConnell (1982). "The Administrative Costs of Corporate Bankruptcy: A Note." *Journal of Finance* 37: 219–226.

Arida, P., E. Bacha, and A. Resende (2005). "Credit, Interest, and Jurisdictional Uncertainty: Conjectures on the Case of Brazil." In F. Giavazzi, I. Goldfajn, and S. Herrera, eds., *Inflation Targeting, Debt, and the Brazilian Experience, 1999 to 2003*. Cambridge, MA: MIT Press.

Beck, T. (2000). "Impediments to the Development and Efficiency of Financial Intermediation in Brazil." World Bank, Policy Research Working Paper No. 2382.

Beck, T., A. Demirgüç-Kunt, and R. Levine (1999). "A New Database on Financial Development and Structure." World Bank, Policy Research Working Paper No. 2146.

Berkowitz, D., K. Pistor, and J. Richard (2003). "Economic Development, Legality, and the Transplant Effect." *European Economic Review* 47(1): 165–195.

Bolton, P., and X. Freixas (2000). "Equity, Bonds, and Bank Debt: Capital Structure and Financial Market Equilibrium under Asymmetric Information." *Journal of Political Economy* 108: 324–351.

Booth, L., A. Aivazian, A. Demirgüç-Kunt, and V. Maksimovic (2001). "Capital Structure in Developing Countries." *Journal of Finance* 56: 87–130.

Carvalhal-da-Silva, A., and R. Leal (2005). "Corporate Governance Index, Firm Valuation and Performance in Brazil." *Revista Brasileira de Finanças* 3(1): 1–18.

Costa, A., and M. Nakane (2004). *Economia bancária e crédito—avaliação de 5 anos do projeto juros e spread bancário*. Brasília: Banco Central do Brasil.

Dadalt, P., J. Donaldson, and J. Garner (2003). "Will Any Q Do?" *Journal of Financial Research* 26: 535–551.

De la Torre, Augusto, and Sergio Schmukler (2004). *Whither Latin American Capital Markets?* Washington, DC: World Bank.

Demirgüç-Kunt, A., and V. Maksimovic (2002). "Funding Growth in Bank-Based or Market-Based Financial Systems: Evidence on Firm Level Data." *Journal of Financial Economics* 65(3): 337–363.

Demirgüç-Kunt, A., L. Laeven, and R. Levine (2004). "Regulations, Market Structure, Institutions, and the Cost of Financial Intermediation." *Journal of Money, Credit, and Banking* 36(3): 593–622.

Durnev, A., and E. H. Kim (2005). "To Steal or Not to Steal: Firm Attributes, Legal Environment, and Valuation." *Journal of Finance* 60(3): 1461–1493.

Eichengreen, B., R. Hausmann, and U. Panizza (2005). "The Mystery of Original Sin." In B. Eichengreen and R. Hausmann, eds., *Other People's Money: Debt Denomination and Financial Instability in Emerging Market Economies*. Chicago: University of Chicago Press.

Eichengreen, B., and P. Luengnaruemitchai (2004). "Why Doesn't Asia Have Bigger Bond Markets?" NBER Working Paper No. 10576.

Fajardo, B., J. S., and M. M. Fonseca (2004). "Concentração bancária brasileira: uma análise microeconômica." Ibmec Finance Lab Working Paper.

Harris, M., and A. Raviv (1991). "The Theory of the Capital Structure." *Journal of Finance* 46: 297–355.

Leal, R., and R. Saito (2003). "Finanças corporativas no Brasil." *RAE Eletrônica* 2. http://www.rae.com.br.

Leal, R., and A. Carvalhal-da-Silva (2007). "Corporate Governance and Value in Brazil (and in Chile)." In F. Lopez-de-Silanes and A. Chong, org., *Investor Protection and Corporate Governance—Firm Level Evidence Across Latin America*. Stanford University Press and Inter-American Development Bank Research Network Working Paper #R-514.

Leal, R., and A. Carvalhal-da-Silva (2006). "The Development of the Brazilian Bond Market." Working paper, Inter-American Development Bank.

Titman, S., and R. Wessels (1988). "The Determinants of Capital Structure Choice." *Journal of Finance* 43: 1–19.

Warner, J. (1977). "Bankruptcy Costs: Some Evidence." *Journal of Finance* 32: 337–347.

Zellner, A., and H. Theil (1962). "Three Stage Least Squares: Simultaneous Estimation of Simultaneous Equations." *Econometrica* 30: 63–68.

8 The Fixed-Income Market in Uruguay

Julio de Brun, Néstor
Gandelman, Herman Kamil,
and Arturo C. Porzecanski

Capital markets in Uruguay have remained underdeveloped despite the growth and internationalization of the onshore and offshore banking industry following liberalization in the 1970s. Not even the development of a lively, liquid market for government securities has been able to nurture the parallel growth of a corporate bond market, and thus virtually all companies continue to rely mostly on financing from banks and suppliers rather than from the capital markets (de Brun, Gandelman, and Barbieri 2003). Laws passed in the mid-1990s specifically intended to promote the development of the local capital markets did boost the issuance of corporate debt, particularly on the part of banks. However, after some corporate defaults and near-default episodes took place in the late 1990s, the confidence of investors was shattered and the fledgling corporate bond market shriveled up.

In 2002, Uruguay suffered a profound financial crisis triggered by contagion effects from a depositor run on banks, massive currency devaluation, and large-scale default on sovereign debt that took place in next-door Argentina. In the wake of a run on its own exceedingly dollarized banking system, Uruguay's government was forced by the ensuing loss of international reserves to let the currency depreciate rapidly. The government subsequently had to provide support to state-owned financial institutions while intervening in several failing private sector banks, which involved obtaining massive financial backing from the Washington-based multilateral agencies. In addition, the government eventually had to arrange for a market-friendly restructuring of the public debt. The fallout of this crisis on the local capital markets was such that the volume of securities traded in its traditional and electronic exchanges collapsed. Starting in late 2003, however, the Uruguayan economy staged a vigorous recovery and the government regained access to domestic and international capital markets. In contrast, the local equity and fixed-income markets have not revived, and there has been lingering damage to investor confidence in firms, regulators, auditors and credit-rating companies. Nonetheless, as we demonstrate, these are not the only impediments to the growth of the domestic fixed-income market.

Origins of the Fixed-Income Market

Between the 1930s and 1950s, Uruguay's economy grew strongly based on an import-substitution strategy made viable by booming international demand for its agricultural and livestock products during World War II and the Korean War. However, the potential for investment growth under this strategy was limited by the rise of agricultural protectionism in Europe and the United States, the small size of the domestic market, increasingly inflationary public financing, and the distortions generated by various forms of state interference. The Uruguayan economy thus experienced high inflation, massive currency depreciation, and economic stagnation between the mid-1950s and the mid-1970s, with grave social and political consequences.

The surge of domestic inflation in the 1950s eroded the value of the public debt issued up to the 1930s to finance the development of national and local public infrastructure. Moreover, as of the late 1950s an inflationary environment and weak tax structure (based primarily on export taxes and import tariffs applied to a shrinking base of foreign trade) closed the government's access to financial markets. Inflation-induced distortions in corporate financial statements further diminished the reliability and attractiveness of private sector securities, and turnover in the local stock exchange decreased steadily until the mid-1970s.

After stabilization policies and structural reforms were implemented starting in 1973, inflation decelerated and economic growth resumed, accompanied by an increase in foreign trade and private investment. Those reforms included tax structure modernization, trade liberalization, and full convertibility of the capital account of the balance of payments. Specifically, a value-added tax was introduced, nontariff barriers to trade were mostly eliminated, import tariffs were gradually reduced, interest rate caps became nonbinding, exchange-rate controls were abolished, and financial intermediaries' access to capital markets was liberalized.

Subsequent improvement in the fiscal situation allowed the government to return to financial markets, and it did so by issuing securities via the local stock exchange. Given the full convertibility of the Uruguayan peso, the government was able to issue long-term debt denominated in U.S. dollars (USD), which was accepted by domestic and regional investors eager to protect themselves from the ravages of inflation. It was thus through domestic issues of short- and medium-term (up to 8-year) government debt that the local capital market was given a new lease on life after the mid-1970s.

Indeed, the government's financing needs and liability-management operations have set the tone for most of the activity in local capital markets ever since the financial reforms of the 1970s. The debt crisis of the 1980s, for example, spurred the issuance of public debt in the domestic capital market as a substitute for the financing that was no longer forthcoming from foreign banks—the main source of new funds for the public sector during the second half of the 1970s. In the second half of the 1980s, short-term treasury bills represented a high and increasing share of the market for government debt. Starting in 1991 and following the successful debt restructuring under the Brady Plan, however, the government pursued a strategy of extending maturities including via the issuance of Eurobonds. This is reflected in the decreasing share of short-term debt during the 1990s all the way until 2001, when adverse developments in Argentina and then in Brazil scared investors—and bank depositors—away.

Recent Developments in the Government Bond Market

During the mid-1970s, when the domestic market for public debt began to develop, the Banco Central del Uruguay (BCU) acted as the government's financial agent, issuing securities through the Montevideo Stock Exchange (Bolsa de Valores de Montevideo, BVM), giving stockbrokers a premium on the face value of the securities. The bonds were usually issued at par, and they were distributed proportionally among shareholders. This practice was maintained until the early 1990s, when the BCU began to issue public debt through auctions on an over-the-counter (OTC) market.

Public debt instruments have been by far the most actively traded on the secondary market, in both the BVM and the Electronic Stock Exchange (Bolsa Electrónica de Valores, BEVSA). In fact, government

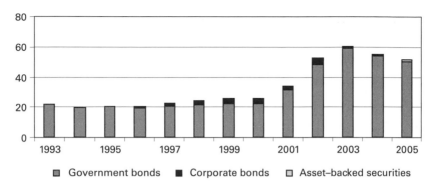

Figure 8.1
Fixed-income debt (percent of GDP).

securities have usually represented more than 90% of total transactions in the secondary market.

After the government gained access to international financial markets, bonds issued under foreign jurisdiction (mostly New York law) have been the main driver of transactions in local exchanges. This was especially true after 1998, when Uruguay obtained an investment-grade rating for its sovereign debt from all the leading credit-rating agencies. The participation of domestic end-investors in the secondary market for public debt issued overseas—particularly pension funds following a reform of the social security system—greatly stimulated turnover in years like 1998 and 2001.

The attractiveness of government securities issued abroad for participants in the secondary market has been their relatively higher liquidity, at least in comparison with securities issued domestically, which usually have lower amounts outstanding. This effect was markedly reinforced after the debt restructuring exercise of 2003, when many of the existing bonds submitted were exchanged under the "liquidity option" for three benchmark bonds, each of which qualified (because of its size) for inclusion in the J. P. Morgan Emerging Market Bond Index.[1]

The financial crises of 2002 and the debt exchange of 2003 seem to have had enduring consequences for transactions on the domestic capital market. Not only are the amounts traded in both domestic and external bonds lower in recent years than those observed in 2001, but the composition of the instruments has also shifted toward shortened maturities. While in 2001 trading in domestic bonds amounted to US$440 million and in short-term treasury bills a mere US$32 million, in 2004 transactions involving domestic bonds dropped to US$195 million while trading in short-term securities increased to US$270 million. Even though the successful, investor-friendly debt restructuring of 2003 has allowed the government to regain access to the domestic and international financial markets and sovereign spreads have compressed a great deal, the 2002–2003 experience has reinforced the traditional hold-to-maturity strategy of Uruguayan bondholders, reducing turnover in the secondary market and increasing the attractiveness of short-term instruments.

A visible characteristic of Uruguay's public debt is its extremely high degree of dollarization—now as well as before the 2003 debt restructuring. This long-standing willingness of the public sector to run a massive currency mismatch has had repercussions throughout the local financial system and remains one of its main sources of fragility (Licandro and Licandro 2003; de Brun and Licandro 2006). A critical step toward increasing the presence of domestic currency in the financial system and in capital markets is the development of a yield curve for sovereign instruments in domestic currency, which is to be used as a benchmark for the introduction of private sector securities likewise denominated in local currency, with the potential start of a market for derivative products.

Indeed, in recent years the government has been trying to pave the way for a financial market in peso-denominated instruments, featuring nominal, fixed-rate securities as well as inflation-adjusted debt. The issuance of debt instruments in pesos was kick-started when the BCU began to deal in short-term treasury bills in pesos for monetary policy purposes—and that issuance grew rapidly during 2003–2004, although the trend slowed down somewhat in 2005. Meanwhile, the introduction of inflation-adjusted instruments denominated in pesos got a boost from the international issue of Uruguay's first inflation-linked bond in October 2003 for an amount equivalent to US$200 million (latter expanded to US$300 million). This was the first placement in the markets after the debt restructuring, and the first international issue of a Latin American sovereign bond denominated in local currency—a transaction emulated by Colombia and Brazil in 2004 and 2005, respectively. The catalytic effect of that international placement is reflected in the increased interest of domestic investors—and presumably foreign investors acting through domestic intermediaries—in local placements of UI bonds (where UI stands for *unidad indexada*, namely, debt indexed to consumer prices). Since late 2004, the real interest rate on UI bonds with 10-year maturities has fallen below 5% per annum.

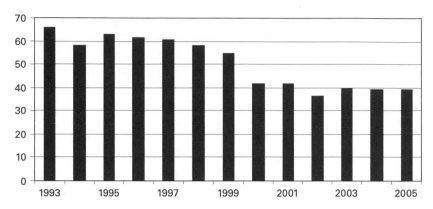

Figure 8.2
Government debt issued domestically (percent of total public debt).

The successful placement of peso-denominated instruments on the local OTC and international markets generated increased participation of these securities in the local secondary market for public debt. Transactions involving government debt securities in pesos increased to 12% of total transactions in 2003 (from almost zero before that) and to above 20% in 2004 and 2005. The lesser impulse in the development of the secondary market for peso-denominated instruments in 2005 reflects the present government's strategy of emphasizing longer debt maturities, if need be via long-term, USD-denominated debt in local and foreign markets. Nevertheless, the larger amount outstanding of inflation-linked notes issued by the BCU and the government has helped to increase turnover in the secondary market from a mere 1.5% of public debt transactions in 2003 to 6% in 2004 and 15% in 2005.

Genesis of the Corporate Fixed-Income Market

During the 1990s, new legislation was enacted in an attempt to spur the development of a domestic capital market, particularly on the back of a deepening primary and secondary market for government securities. Many of the new rules were devoted to dealing with lingering issues of corporate transparency; the most important piece of legislation was the Securities Market Law of 1996. In addition to government backing, the law also enjoyed the strong support of interested parties, particularly stockbrokers trading on the BVM. The government explicitly sought to facilitate economic development through deepening financial access for Uruguayan firms, and stockbrokers welcomed the

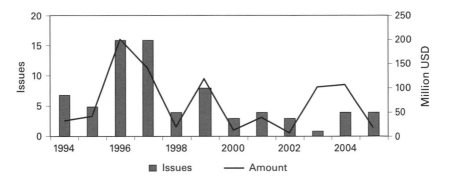

Figure 8.3
Corporate bond issues (excluding financial intermediaries).

idea because they foresaw greater turnover on domestic exchanges. For their part, local banks viewed securitization as a useful way of earning underwriting fees and reducing portfolio concentration risks. In fact, local banks have since acted as intermediaries in the public placement of corporate debt, with the main purpose of reducing their own exposure to particular corporate debtors.

In addition, financial intermediaries supported the new legislation because of its highly liberal regulatory and supervisory approach. Although the BCU's powers included the regulation and supervision of exchanges, issuers, and intermediaries, OTC transactions were explicitly excluded from the Securities Market Law provisions. The exchanges became in effect self-regulating, and this laxity played a role in some irregularities observed during the 2002 financial crisis. Subsquently, a December 2002 attempt by the BCU to include OTC transactions involving intermediaries in Securities Market Law regulations met strong opposition from interested parties, who successfully lobbied against congressional discussion of the BCU proposal.

Nonetheless, only a limited number of companies have tapped the markets for fresh capital since the Securities Market Law was passed, and in most cases they have issued bonds rather than equities. The issuance of new corporate bonds (excluding those of financial intermediaries) reached its peak in 1996–1997, when 16 different firms issued corporate debt in the form of *obligaciones negociables* (ONs) in each of those two years, raising nearly US$200 million and US$140 million, respectively (figure 8.3). Since that time, each year has brought no more than eight new corporate bond issues, and as few as one, and the total amounts raised have averaged less than US$60 million per annum.

Virtually all bonds sold have been denominated in USD, and during 2000–2004 their maturity averaged a little more than four years. The financial crisis of 2002, which affected among others two of the largest private sector banks—both issuers of Eurobonds, no less—reinforced negative investor sentiment. A recent law for asset-backed securities (ABS, or *fideicomisos*) approved in 2003, however, has recognized a new type of private sector debt instrument that would seem to address most of the concerns of private investors. Firms now have the possibility of issuing securitized debt that is backed by specific cash flows or assets. Still, the development of an ABS market has so far been limited.[2]

In sum, Uruguay lacks a developed market for corporate obligations, and as detailed below, financing for companies still comes mainly from retained earnings, bank loans, and suppliers' credit. The primary market for corporate securities is currently dominated by the issuance of certificates of deposit issued by banking institutions, which have accounted for almost 80% of total primary issuance in recent years. The issuance of a first ABS by the state-owned electricity concern represented 11% of total issuance in 2004, while corporate bonds accounted for a mere 6% of primary-market activity. The secondary market, for its part, has become mainly a vehicle for transactions involving public debt instruments, which represented 94% of total turnover in 2004. The absence of state-related issuance in 2005 explains that year's sharp contraction of corporate bond activity in the primary market.

Corporate Governance Issues

In Uruguay, minority shareholders have generally fared very badly in business failures as majority owners have abused their rights, squeezing out minority players and forcing them to take heavy losses. A high-profile business failure that took place in the late 1990s, which later proved to be an organized swindle, led to new regulations requiring greater corporate transparency. However, more recent bankruptcies suggest that the problem is not solely one of lack of transparency, since "agency problems" may also be playing a significant role. Boards of directors in Uruguay are very much linked to the principal shareholders, and independent persons rarely serve on boards. In practice, managers who work for companies rather than boards of directors generally exercise decision-making authority. Additional features include the presence of integrated economic groups and the existence of financial links among related companies. The existing legislation on corporate structures (Law 16.060) includes some elements of protection for minority shareholders, but they are not sufficient to address present practices and circumstances.

The country also has in place detailed regulations on the operations of credit-rating agencies, an activity that has come under scrutiny in recent years because of a series of failures in the assessment of corporate creditworthiness, as seen in episodes of default during the 2002 crisis. Uruguay's experience with rating agencies does not greatly differ from that observed in other countries hit by systemic financial crises. As pointed out below in our summary of the institutional investor survey, the local market has come to accept the outcome of those default episodes, even though they damaged rating agencies' reputations.

The absence of a single depository agent and a less-than-adequate clearing and settlement process represents a further technical issue that introduces a high degree of risk into the operation of Uruguay's capital markets, the difficulty of measuring that impact notwithstanding (Clarke 2004). The BCU is the depository agent of securities included in the portfolios of the pension funds, as it is in general when it comes to government securities issued in the domestic market on a book-entry basis. However, there is no regulation in place concerning the custody of physical bonds or securities issued by other financial and nonfinancial corporations. Moreover, the compensation process takes place in the first instance in the corresponding exchanges, and after that net balances are settled bilaterally through the accounts that agents maintain at the BCU. Because no guarantees are demanded on credit lines of the different market operators, there is always a risk that the transaction will not be completed—as in fact happened in 2002 after four financial institutions were suspended.

Supply-Side Analysis: The Corporate Sector

Pioneering analytical work by Pascale (1978, 1982, 1994), and subsequently by Robledo (1994), was based on surveys conducted periodically by the BCU among dozens of companies engaged in manufacturing. However, the sample and the nature of the information gathered by these surveys during the 1970s, 1980s, and early 1990s changed so that the results are not entirely comparable over time. Nevertheless, the available data shows that manufacturing firms in Uruguay tended to be highly indebted, even by the standards of developing countries. Ratios of corporate debt to assets averaged around 60% in the early 1970s and about 70% during the 1980s and early 1990s.

In terms of the maturity structure of these corporate obligations, the proportion of long-term debt tended to be low but rising over time, from less than 15% of total prior to 1980 to nearly 40% of total by the early 1990s. This ability to obtain longer-term funds may have been related to the sharply increased dollarization of liabilities over time: corporate debt in foreign currencies represented less than 20% of total liabilities until the mid-1970s but accounted for more than 60% by the early 1980s, averaging two-thirds of total during 1989–1991. As a result of this liability dollarization, most companies began to run large currency mismatches, since their sales were largely booked in local currency and their foreign-currency-denominated assets were small (e.g., 10% of total assets during 1982–1984). This exposed them to financial losses every time the exchange rate suffered a major depreciation—at least once a decade.

Banks have been by far the principal source of financing for manufacturing companies in Uruguay, with obligations to them representing more than half, and sometimes more than two-thirds, of total corporate liabilities. Access to a local bond market has never been a realistic option for most firms, except for the few years during the mid-1990s when new debt instruments such as the previously mentioned ONs became popular in the wake of new legislation, raising the amount of debt that firms could issue relative to their capital. However, nearly 70% of the securities traded were issued by private sector banks, and, as noted above, the market dried up in the late 1990s following the 1998 bankruptcy filing of one of the corporate issuers, the poultry firm Moro (Bentancor 1999).

Munyo (2005) found that 60% of corporate financing needs were met through borrowing (and therefore 40% from retained earnings), none of which included the issuance of equity or debt securities. Reliance on bank credit was on average as great as on trade credit, although larger companies with greater tangible assets tended to rely proportionally more on bank rather than trade financing and had greater access to long-term financing.

For the purposes of this study, we enlisted the collaboration of the National Statistics Institute (Instituto Nacional de Estadística, INE), which agreed to conduct a special survey during August and Septem-

Table 8.1
Summary Statistics for Firms Surveyed, 2004

Structure of liabilities (% of total)

	Bonds	Bank loans	Suppliers' credit	Other liabilities
Median	0.0	16.1	21.8	38.2
Mean	0.6	26.2	27.8	45.2
Standard deviation	4.5	28.0	24.2	33.8
Number of cases	453	452	453	451

Financial ratios

	Solvency	ROA	Leverage
Median	0.5	6.5	0.8
Mean	0.4	9.1	2.4
Standard deviation	0.9	81.7	9.9
Number of cases	459	457	459

Note: Solvency = equity/(equity + liabilities); ROA = net operating income/assets; Leverage = liabilities/equity.
Source: Authors' calculations based on INE survey.

ber of 2005 that targeted potential issuers of securities. The INE conducts an annual survey of economic activity that encompasses most sectors of the economy. Because the capital markets are not a real option for small firms, our sample includes all firms regularly surveyed by INE that have more than 50 employees. The response rate for 463 firms was 100%, which adequately covered most sectors.[3] Given Uruguay's economic structure, the most important omission from the sample is that of individuals and firms engaged in activities such as farming and livestock.

Table 8.1 reports summary statistics on corporate finance patterns for the firms surveyed by INE in 2004. Consistent with Munyo's results discussed earlier, the two main sources of external funds for the surveyed firms were bank loans and suppliers' credit. Bond and equity financing, on the other hand, accounted for only a minuscule portion of total liabilities (0.8% for the average firm).[4] Indeed, of the 463 firms in our sample, only 10 firms had bonds outstanding and only 9 firms (2%) were listed in the local stock exchange. This evidence reflects the stunted development of Uruguay's capital markets: while business ventures in Uruguay are usually organized as corporations, most of them remain closed.

Table 8.1 presents three oft-reported financial indicators. The solvency ratio is defined as the ratio of equity over the sum of equity and total liabilities. A second indicator is ROA (return on assets), defined as the ratio between net operating income before interest payments and total assets. The median ROA is 50% lower than the mean ROA, implying that the distribution of this statistic is heavily skewed to the left. Given the implicit risk present in investment projects taking place in Uruguay, a median ROA of 6.5% strikes us as somewhat low. As a rule of thumb, we could take this figure as the maximum interest rate that Uruguayan firms could afford to pay. The leverage indicator is defined as the ratio between total liabilities and total equity.[5]

Using data for 2004 from the INE survey, we can confirm that Uruguayan firms suffer from severe currency and maturity mismatches. For the median firm in the INE survey, 76% of its financial liabilities are denominated in US dollars. The INE survey included one specific question targeted to determine whether firms take any precautions with regard to their currency and maturity mismatches. Only 7% of firms used derivatives to change the profile of their liabilities, and thus most ran their foreign currency exposures largely unhedged.

In terms of maturity, 84.4% of the average firm's liabilities were short term. Although suppliers' credit generally had shorter maturities than bank credit, on average 77% of financial credit was nevertheless short term. These results confirm that Uruguayan firms have great difficulty in accessing long-term credit, even via the issuance of USD-denominated corporate bonds. Smaller firms tend to have even less access to long-term credit. The correlation of long-term liabilities with various measures of firm size (e.g., assets, equity, and employees) is positive and significant.

Uruguay's dollarization experience, as in the case of many other countries in Latin America and beyond, is the legacy of several decades of high and unstable rates of inflation, which eroded trust in the national currency as a store of value, a medium of exchange, and even a unit of account. In the absence of widespread indexation to inflation, economic agents became unwilling to enter into any medium-term contracts unless the payment amounts specified were protected from currency depreciation—and indirectly from the ravages of inflation—by being indexed to or expressed in USD. As a result, firms increasingly realized that any obligations to banks or suppliers not subject to correction for inflation or currency depreciation necessarily would be of a very short-term nature. Practically the only way to obtain longer-term funds—other than through the issuance of equity stakes, of course—was to do so via contracts in USD, with the accompanying risks of a currency mismatch. For these reasons, between 90% and 100% of all corporate bonds issued during 1994–2004 were denominated in USD. Indeed, the currency and maturity composition of any obligation contemplated by borrowers or lenders came to be determined jointly as part of the same portfolio decision.[6]

Two key objectives of our research were to quantify the potential for financial stress arising from unhedged currency mismatches in firms' balance sheets and to determine whether firms issuing corporate debt were better prepared than others to withstand exchange rate shocks. The results indicate that Uruguayan firms remain vulnerable to a sudden currency devaluation, given high levels of unhedged, short-term foreign currency borrowing—liabilities in foreign currency that are not fully backed by assets or income streams in foreign currency. Furthermore, 93% of the firms without a natural hedge fail to purchase protection by engaging in any financial hedging. In this sense, there is no evidence that the corporate sector is more sheltered from exchange rate risk than it was on the eve of the 2002 crisis. Although these mismatches may not be a concern in the current external environment of low interest rates and a stable domestic currency, they may become a source of financial instability in future years, once international conditions become less benign.

To assess a firm's financial health, we used two criteria: the debt-service coverage ratio (the fraction of financial liabilities coming due in less than a year covered by cash flow); and the net-worth position of the firm (total assets minus total liabilities). For the purpose of the stress test, we defined a firm as financially stressed whenever an exchange-rate depreciation made it unable to meet its amortization and interest payments falling due (liquidity effect) and/or whenever it pushed the firm into a negative equity position (balance sheet effect). We thus assessed the effect that different exchange rate shocks could have on interest-coverage ratios and the proportion of firms that are at greater risk of defaulting. To assess the downside exchange rate risk of the corporate sector, we stress-tested the portfolio of each firm to a sudden 5%, 10%, 20%, 40%, 60%, 80%, or 100% increase in the peso price of USD (table 8.2).

Estimates on the contractionary effects of a sudden devaluation are conservative (i.e., they provide a lower bound) for four reasons. First, we only considered a sudden depreciation of the domestic currency,

Table 8.2
Systemic Effects of a Sudden Devaluation

If the price of the USD were to increase by:	Number of firms under financial distress	Share of economy-wide:		
		Short-term supplier liabilities (effect on interfirm chain of payments)	Employment (effect on unemployment)	Total assets
5%	6	11%	1%	2%
10%	11	11%	2%	4%
20%	24	32%	12%	11%
40%	45	50%	15%	17%
60%	74	67%	21%	33%
80%	90	71%	26%	38%
100%	109	72%	29%	43%

If the price of the USD were to increase by:	Share of economy-wide:		
	Total financial liabilities (credit risk effect on banking system)	Total dollar financial liabilities	Sales (growth and tax revenue effects)
5%	4%	4%	2%
10%	9%	11%	3%
20%	17%	20%	7%
40%	28%	33%	12%
60%	45%	54%	36%
80%	51%	61%	41%
100%	60%	71%	47%

Source: Authors' calculations based on INE survey.

excluding other simultaneous effects, such as an increase in interest rates or a recession, which typically accompany a depreciation. Second, to assess the vulnerability to foreign-currency borrowing, we only considered financial obligations, assuming that USD trade credit liabilities could be rolled over through negotiations with suppliers in the event of financial distress. Third, the exercise was static in nature in that we only considered the direct or first-round effect on each firm, excluding spillover or dynamic effects—a breakdown in the chain of payments among firms, for instance. Finally, we only considered firms that as of 2004 had an initially healthy financial position in order to avoid contaminating the results with data from weak firms that may be close to bankruptcy.

The results of the stress test show whether different scenarios featuring a significant depreciation of the peso would have a large effect on corporate capital and ability to service bank debt. For every possible static scenario, the number expressed in percentage terms represents the fraction accounted for by the group of distressed firms in the total value of each variable for the whole sample. The results suggest that Uruguayan firms still face the potential for financial stress arising from sizable and unhedged balance sheet currency mismatches—liabilities in foreign currency that are not fully backed by assets or income streams likewise in foreign currency. Moreover, we found no significant difference on simulated short-term responses across firms that issued bonds versus those that did not issue them.

The high proportion of financial liabilities accounted for by the pool of firms in distress suggests significant vulnerability of the banking system to corporate credit risk. For prudential reasons, bank balance sheets are protected from the direct impact of a devaluation, as their net assets in foreign currency adequately reflect the dollarization of both their assets and liabilities. Commercial banks, of course, are exposed to devaluation-induced credit risks from loans granted to non-USD earners or to firms with significant currency mismatches.[7] Thus, the high proportion of unhedged foreign currency borrowing can render Uruguayan firms—and by extension, their bank creditors—highly vulnerable to a sharp increase in the cost of foreign exchange.

Survey of Potential Issuers: The INE Database

One of the hypotheses that we wanted to check was whether potential issuers lack knowledge about the prerequisites and feasibility of issuing corporate debt. We included a specific question allowing respondents to classify themselves as knowing enough, something or nothing about the use of bonds and ABS as financial sourcing alternatives. Although this survey targeted the CFOs (or equivalent) of firms, only about one quarter of respondents reported having a good knowledge of bonds and ABS.

Another aspect is the decision process of many firms that, though organized as corporations, tend to follow the traditional family-business structure. In spite of what will be presented in the following paragraphs, this conservative structure may prevent managers from considering financing alternatives that could make proprietary information public. The reluctance of surveyed firms to use nontraditional financial instruments is quite notable: only 13 firms (7%) in the whole sample reported that they had used derivative instruments to manage or change the profile of their liabilities.

Of the 463 firms in our sample, 10 firms had bonds outstanding and 21 report having issued ABS. Approximately the same number of firms had in the past issued bonds and ABS, and—at least according to firms' future plans as revealed in this survey—one should not expect many new issuers in the future. Of those firms that used to issue bonds in the past and no longer do so, 12 firms reported specific reasons for stopping. There is no one reason that clearly predominates over others: high costs of issuance were reported 3 times; high interest rates were mentioned 2 times; low investor demand was reported 4 times; other issuance requirements were mentioned twice; and bad reputation of the firm was admitted twice.

Uruguayan firms have two main sources of external funds: bank loans and suppliers' credit. Naturally, most bank financing is provided by financial institutions located in-country: about 300 firms report that they obtain credit from local banks, and only 20 firms report having access to credit from banks abroad. More than 90% of the sample was able to evaluate whether collateral requirements, bank monitoring, slow approval processes, high interest rates in pesos, or access to credit only in USD affected access to bank credit from institutions operating in Uruguay. On the other hand, only 40% of firms were able to evaluate these factors with respect to banks located outside Uruguay.

In spite of the currency mismatches of Uruguayan firms mentioned above, availability of credit only in USD is not considered a problem per se. According to the results of this survey, the problem is not the availability of peso-denominated loans, but rather their relatively high cost. Other important problems include collateral requirements and, to a lesser extent, the speed of loan approval and disbursement. Interestingly, 45% of respondents have the perception that local banks are not willing to lend. This contradicts the view of banks according to our survey of market makers (see next section), where they stress their willingness to lend but voice concerns regarding the high risks involved in financing local firms.

As in the case of banking obstacles, the survey found that replies on the factors affecting issuance of bonds outside Uruguay were much fewer than replies on the issuance of corporate debt in Uruguay. More-over, the response rate for bond financing was smaller than the re-sponse rate for bank financing, revealing a lesser degree of familiarity with the subject. Overall, half of the surveyed firms provided feedback on the factors affecting the issuance of bonds in Uruguay and only 26% spoke upon the factors affecting the issuance of bonds abroad. The potential obstacles mentioned were underwriters' fees, credit-rating agencies' fees, disclosure requirements, minimum issue requirements, the small size of the market, the absence of "junk bonds" and other reg-ulatory requirements.

There are notable similarities in the problems associated with most factors for bonds issued in Uruguay and abroad; the only significant difference is with respect to market size—perceived to be small in Uru-guay but not abroad. Moreover, this is the factor most often mentioned as a problem in terms of issuing bonds domestically (62%). This lack of perceived investor demand again stands in contrast with the results of the institutional investors' survey. (Institutional investors reported their willingness to invest in corporate debt but expressed the view that there were no worthwhile projects to be underwritten.) This contradiction may in part be solved by the fact that the second-most-reported problem is the nonexistence of a market for low-rated, specu-lative bonds (55% and 52% for bonds issues domestically and abroad, respectively). The fees charged by credit-rating agencies are also con-sidered an obstacle by about 49% of respondents.

About 47% of respondents considered disclosure requirements to be something that discourages the issuance of bonds domestically. In our questionnaire, we added an extra question to assess the willingness of firms to disclose information. The question was: "Are you willing to disclose the necessary information in order to be rated by a credit agency as a preliminary step to an eventual issuance of bonds?" Of the total respondents, 33% were willing to disclose information; 31% said they were probably willing to do so; and only 36% of respondents had a negative inclination toward information disclosure (answering "No, probably" and "No, for sure"). Most firms do not consider the other factors as important impediments to issuing bonds. In particular, this is true with respect to underwriters' fees, minimum issue require-ments, and disclosure requirements.

In evaluating the obstacles to obtaining financing in Uruguay through the banking system or through the issuance of corporate debt, we again had very different response rates. More than 90% of

Table 8.3
Best Financing Alternatives

	Uruguay		Outside Uruguay		Suppliers' credit
	Banks	Bonds	Banks	Bonds	
Interest rate cost	12	2	3	15	68
Local-currency lending	29	1	0	14	56
Indexation alternatives	29	6	1	11	53
Long-term lending	42	20	12	10	15
Non-interest rate costs	9	2	2	14	72
Tax treatment	19	7	2	14	58
Possibility of renegotiation	9	1	1	21	68
Costs related to disclosure requirements	8	1	1	13	77
Size of potential market relative to firm's financing needs	31	6	9	16	38

Source: Authors' calculations based on INE survey.

respondents were able to discuss access to bank credit, while only 46% were able to comment on bond financing. In comparative terms, banks were viewed more positively with respect to speed of access to the required financing and in terms of the information requirements involved. Also, the relatively high minimum amount required to make a bond issuance worthwhile was considered a disadvantage. On the other hand, bonds were viewed more favorably in terms of the possibility of accessing longer-term funds and with respect to guarantee requirements, though the latter were considered an important obstacle in both alternatives. The most frequent complaint was the cost of borrowed capital, and the least common was again information requirements.

We asked firms to consider five financing alternatives: banks in Uruguay or abroad, issuance of bonds in Uruguay or abroad, and suppliers' credit from any source (table 8.3). Suppliers' credit was perceived as by far the best alternative in almost all dimensions. In fact, long-term lending and the size of loans with respect to the firm's financing needs are the only two aspects in which suppliers' credit does not clearly dominate the other financial alternatives. With respect to long-term lending, the preferred option is credit from a Uruguayan bank. It is surprising that in our sample only 34% of bank credit is long term, as many firms have ongoing relations with banks and are constantly renewing short-term credits. Therefore, although these credits are

Table 8.4
Costs of a Plain-Vanilla Domestic Bond Issue

	Face value issued (thousand USD)				
	1,500	3,000	10,000	20,000	50,000
Underwriting fees (1%)	15,000	30,000	100,000	200,000	500,000
Arranger fees (0.75%)	11,250	22,500	75,000	150,000	375,000
Distribution costs	22,500	45,000	150,000	300,000	500,000
Legal fees	5,000	5,000	8,000	8,000	10,000
Stock exchange registration[1]	3,000	6,000	15,000	20,000	40,000
Rating agency	10,000	10,000	12,000	12,000	15,000
Total costs	66,750	118,500	360,000	690,000	1,440,000
Issue size (%)	4.45%	3.95%	3.60%	3.45%	2.88%
Brazil			n/a	4.20%	2.78%
Chile			4.76%	4.20%	2.85%
Mexico			n/a	1.99%	1.58%

[1] Assuming registration in both bourses.
Source: Authors' calculations, and Zervos (2004) for Brazil, Chile, and Mexico.

nominally short term, they may be perceived as a long-term financing alternative on the assumption that they can be rolled over. Naturally, the risk exposure of firms to sudden credit crunches is enormous.

We applied the methodology of Zervos (2004) to address the costs of issuing debt in the Uruguayan corporate bond market. These costs only apply to the private sector, since the government issues debt in the domestic market at no cost. Among the main costs detected are bank fees, the most important being underwriting fees.[8] The range is wide, depending on the complexity of the issue and the characteristics of the issuer. They usually vary between 0.5% and 1.5% of the issue amount, with "plain-vanilla" corporate bonds issued by well-established firms at the lower bound and more sophisticated financial structures, like ABS, at the upper bound (table 8.4).

The arrangement costs of the issue can be charged to the issuer by the intervening bank or any other financial advisor. According to the interview results, they are usually close to 0.75%, while distribution costs have a range of 0.75–1.50%. Another important cost related to the issue comes from legal fees associated with the preparation of a legal document, usually accompanied by a prospectus and an offering memorandum. These costs are more difficult to estimate, but according to information provided by local issuers, they range between US$5,000 and 10,000.

In the case of Uruguay, no regulatory fees apply. The two exchanges (BVM and BEVSA) apply registration fees that vary from 0.04% to 0.10%, depending on the size of the issue. The higher fee applies to issues less than US$1.5 million while the lower is charged for issues higher than US$20 million. The Uruguayan regulatory agency does require at least one credit rating for all issuers. The fees charged by credit rating agencies usually vary from US$10,000 to US$15,000, and there are other costs charged during the life of the bond. For instance, a fiduciary agent, when needed, usually applies annual fees of 0.15–0.25%; the exchanges charge, besides the initial registration cost, an annual maintenance fee of 0.005–0.020%. Credit rating agencies also apply annual fees, usually around 10% of the initial fee.

For an issue of US$20 million, the costs in Uruguay (3.45%) compare reasonably well with those in Chile and Brazil (both 4.20%) but are much higher than in Mexico (1.99%). Problems arise when the costs are adjusted for maturity. Until recently, the maturity of Uruguayan corporate bonds was very short, and thus the impact of issuance costs was quite significant in the overall decision. For instance, a 3% issuance cost is equivalent to an increase of 76 basis points (bps) in the interest rate for a 4-year bond, while it only adds 30 bps to the cost of a 10-year bond.

Demand-Side Analysis: Institutional Investors

The principal institutional investors in Uruguay's capital market are the pension funds (AFAPs) created after the 1996 reform of the country's social security system. These funds are managed by four companies: the state-owned República AFAP and the three asset managers—Afinidad AFAP, Integración AFAP, and Unión Capital AFAP—that are owned by private sector banks operating in Uruguay.

Pension fund investments are highly regulated in terms of types of securities, currency denomination, and jurisdiction, which leads to numerous restrictions on their portfolio allocation (figure 8.4). Pension funds are not allowed to make any investments outside Uruguay, and investments in foreign currencies cannot exceed 60% of the portfolio's value. The same limit applies to securities issued by the central government. Likewise, securities issued by the state-owned mortgage bank (Banco Hipotecario del Uruguay, BHU) and the BCU itself may not exceed 30% of pension fund assets. Pension fund time deposits in financial institutions must be represented by certificates of deposit and

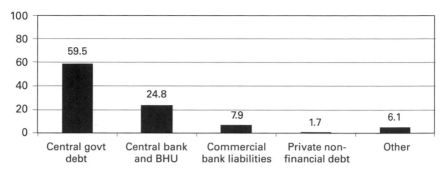

Figure 8.4
Pension funds' portfolio investments (percent of total assets as of December 2005).

cannot exceed 30% of assets; securities issued by private sector corporations are constrained by a 25% limit. In addition, the BCU does not allow securities issued by any particular company to amount to more than 3% of total assets or to constitute more than 50% of the amount outstanding of each security. This limit applies to both corporate bonds and stocks. Asset-backed securities may not amount to more than 20% of pension fund assets and are likewise constrained by the 3% ceiling on any given issuer; this applies to both so-called certificates representative of investments (CRIs) and to financial trusts (*fideicomisos financieros*). Exposure to beneficiaries of the pension system is limited to 15% of pension assets, and the latter three exposures cannot exceed a combined total of 40% of total pension assets.

At present, pension fund holdings of sovereign debt are close to the current ceiling imposed by law: at the end of 2005, 59.5% of the value of the portfolio of the pension funds was allocated to securities issued by the Uruguayan central government (figure 8.4). The pension funds are also heavily invested in securities issued by the monetary authority, with a concentration in newly issued inflation-linked securities, which represent more than 20% of the total portfolio. The sum of holdings of securities issued by the BCU and the BHU (24.8% of total assets) are nonetheless below the maximum of 30% established by law.

In contrast, pension fund exposures to nonfinancial, private sector instruments are well below the limits: corporate bonds, stocks, CRIs, and financial trusts combined represented a mere 3.4% of total assets as of end-2005. Interestingly, the aggregate cash position of the four pension funds was as large as their holdings of private sector securities issued by nonfinancial enterprises. Given their relatively recent vintage, most of their liabilities are long-term in nature.

Pension funds have contributed greatly to the development of a market for peso-denominated instruments, at least through their participation in the primary market for debt. Prior to the financial crisis of 2002, the holdings of peso-denominated instruments represented around one-fourth of the total portfolio of the pension funds. The crisis induced a run from domestic currency, however, and instruments in pesos decreased to less than 5% of the value of pension assets by mid-2002. The country's economic and financial stabilization has since supported a rebound in demand for peso instruments, and by mid-2006 their share in pension funds had jumped to 56.3% of total assets, mostly in the form of inflation-linked securities.

With the cooperation of BEVSA, we carried out a survey among the 4 pension fund managers and the 14 banks authorized by the BCU and also surveyed the 35 stockbrokers registered at the BVM. We received answers from 12 banks and 16 stockbrokers, encountering strong resistance among the latter for "confidentiality" reasons.

As the figures on the composition of the pension funds suggest, the legal constraints on their capacity to invest in private sector, nonfinancial issuers are not binding. Not only is the allocation of resources to these instruments well below the extreme bounds allowed by legislation, but recent history also shows that new funds arising from contributions to the pension system and the reduction of cash holdings have been invested in other investments—basically, CDs issued by banking institutions.

According to the survey made among the pension funds, managers feel that the regulations imposed by law and the regulatory agency (the BCU) are especially binding with respect to their ability to invest abroad. Indeed, when pension fund managers are asked how they would allocate their assets if they did not face any regulatory constraints, they consistently point to a desired increase in the share of foreign assets in their portfolios. As can be expected from the behavior revealed in the composition of the portfolios, no binding legal restrictions are emphasized on the side of their ability to invest in the securities of private sector, nonfinancial firms.

The survey reveals a perception of high risk entailed in investments in corporate bonds. Among the factors affecting the decision to invest in those instruments, the answer to the criterion "high risk of insolvency" was "Yes" in all the answers obtained. In three of the four cases, the criterion "limited legal recourse in the event of default" was considered relevant as well. This perception may be based on the recent history of defaults involving issuers of corporate bonds.

The availability of information does not seem to be a limiting factor in the demand for corporate bonds. Only one of the four managers answered "Yes" to the criterion "lack of timely information about the issuer," suggesting that default risks are viewed as related more to sudden changes in the macroeconomic environment than to lack of appropriate information on the issuer. Similarly, only one manager considered the credit rating system to be of "low quality" or too costly—the same single manager that pointed to inadequate information about issuers. In sum, pension fund managers are far more concerned about the vulnerability of Uruguayan companies to macroeconomic shocks and the difficulties of enforcing creditor rights in the event of a default than they are about the lack of adequate information on issuers.

All the managers of pension funds surveyed considered "low market capitalization" a limiting factor, but the absence of a deep secondary market does not seem to be relevant for the decision to invest in corporate bonds. In three of the four cases, the answer to concerns about "low liquidity/poor functioning of the secondary market" was "No," revealing that pension funds generally behave as hold-to-maturity investors.

When fund managers are asked about the allocation of additional funds in their portfolio, they say they would like to reduce the share of government securities in their portfolios (except in one case) and to increase the participation of domestic private sector securities and foreign assets. Asked about the apparent contradiction of being ready to increase investments in domestic corporate bonds in a context where they can do this already, managers say that any marginal availability of funds would likely be directed to CDs issued by banks.

The evidence on the perception of either a "crowding-out" effect or a positive externality effect between government and corporate bonds is mixed. The reaction to the statement "A large stock of government bonds is important for the development of the corporate bond market" is tilted to "disagreement," suggesting that, from the point of view of the pension funds, the underdevelopment of the capital market is not a constraint on allocating resources to private sector projects. At the same time, the statement "Government and corporate bonds are substitutes in your portfolio" had a reaction also tilted to disagreement.

The apparent contradiction with the expectation that government debt will serve as a benchmark for capital market development, facilitating issuance by private sector firms once transactions costs are reduced, can be explained by the special characteristics of pension funds as institutional investors. As noted above, pension funds in Uruguay seem to behave as hold-to-maturity investors. They are therefore mostly concerned with adequate assumption of risk through appropriate design of financial instruments and with access to the primary market, rather than with the extent of liquidity in the secondary market or the eventual impact of public debt on returns on private sector securities. This explanation is consistent with the good reception among pension funds of some ABS deals issued recently; in fact, in some instances these instruments were placed solely among pension funds. A feature shared by those successful placements was appropriate contract design aimed at facilitating the recovery of the investment in case of default.

Besides the pension funds, there are other institutional investors involved in the management of sector-specific pension systems, such as those funds serving self-employed professionals and bank employees. Given that those other pension systems also have some participation in the Uruguayan capital market, we extended the survey to cover these secondary pension funds as well.

As in the case of the pension funds considered above, government securities represent most of the portfolios managed by these institutional investors. Like the main pension fund managers, these smaller pensions are concerned with "high insolvency risk" on the part of corporate bond issuers. In contrast to the larger funds, however, they are more consistently concerned with problems of appropriate information on issuers—including the role of credit-rating agencies and the reliability of their judgments—and with the extent of liquidity in the secondary market, perhaps because these funds are much older and their portfolio managers put a higher premium on liquidity considerations. All the investors surveyed considered important problems such as "low market capitalization" and "low liquidity/functioning of the secondary market." And as in the case of the managers of the main pension funds, there was no clear consensus about the role of government debt in the development of the capital market.

Given the absence of a great variety of institutional investors and the important presence of retail investors in the Uruguayan capital market, we considered it useful to extend the survey to include some important market makers, such as banks and stockbrokers, whose opinions are also influential in the investment decision of their customers.

There are no significant differences between the opinions of market makers and those of other institutional investors. Among the banks that provided information on the composition of their portfolios (nine of twelve reported their own and third-party positions), only two (of nine) reported a significant (around 10%) share of corporate bonds. In the rest, the share was almost zero. There is much more dispersion in the case of stockbrokers, among which the share of corporate debt in their customers portfolios ranges from zero to almost one third. There are in fact many coincidences in terms of risk-return considerations regarding limitations on investing in corporate bonds. The perception is that returns are often too low given the default risks involved, or that default risks are unacceptably high given the returns available.

The concerns of stockbrokers are biased toward insolvency risks rather than high returns, and 70% of stockbrokers in the sample do not list "low returns" as a relevant consideration. This outcome suggests low demand for "junk" bonds among Uruguayan investors, given that investment in corporate bonds is mostly led by diversification objectives rather than by the search for high yields. As in the case of other institutional investors, there are more concerns about liquidity in the secondary market than in the case of the main pension funds, though opinions among brokers are more mixed. This finding is complemented by a generalized view that "low market capitalization" is a determinant factor in discouraging investment in corporate debt.

However, in contrast to other financial intermediaries, there is a great deal of dispersion in reactions to the eventual lack of good quality in the services provided by credit-rating agencies, but most of the banks and stockbrokers surveyed agree that the "lack of timely information about the issuer" discourages investments in private sector corporate bonds. When financial intermediaries other than stockbrokers were asked about the allocation of increased resources, they offered a particularly negative view of corporate debt. In fact, only one of twelve banks showed a consistent interest in augmenting the share of corporate debt under this scenario. The majority of stockbrokers said they would maintain the present share of corporate debt in their suggested portfolios (given that there are no supply restrictions), and some would even increase their share of corporate bonds. In explaining the different views of stockbrokers and banks, it must be taken into account that these market participants have a pecuniary incentive to defend the development of financial instruments other than government debt.

Conclusions

Uruguayan capital markets have functioned well in terms of allowing for secondary-market transactions of government debt, but they remain notably undeveloped in regard to fixed-income securities issued by the private sector. After a short period of encouraging growth in the mid-1990s, the market for corporate bonds shriveled up prior to the 2002 economic crisis. The financial fragility of Uruguayan firms, made obvious during that crisis and amplified by preexisting deficiencies in corporate governance, represents the main reason for this stunted development.

A lingering result of government macroeconomic mismanagement during the 1960s and 1970s is that Uruguay became the most dollarized country in Latin America as well as the market where corporate debt has featured the shortest average maturities. This situation has generated currency and maturity mismatches that have exposed the country's firms—most of which are not export-oriented—to dangerous currency and refinancing risks. Although some regulatory deficiencies remain, they cannot account for the extent of underdevelopment in the financial markets. Instead, the leading reasons for this underdevelopment are the vulnerability of the country and its firms to macroeconomic shocks as well as practical obstacles in the enforcement of creditor rights in cases of default.

Potential corporate debt issuers say they are willing to disclose the information necessary to obtain a credit rating in order to access the fixed-income market, but the legacy of errors in judgment by rating agencies and the legacy of past fraud and default episodes still linger, inducing great caution among potential investors. Moreover, there is a surprisingly low level of sophistication among corporate managers about alternatives to borrowing from traditional sources such as banks and suppliers.

Currently, the only actively traded issues in the market are those sold by the government and its state-owned companies. Since there was no political consensus in favor of privatizations during the 1990s, local capital markets lack the kind of liquid, widely held corporate debt and equity benchmarks that jump-started the financial markets of so many other Latin American countries. The granting of further concessions and the establishment of joint ventures between state-owned and private companies could lead to additional debt issuance in the markets. Until then, we expect that those few firms that have maintained a good reputation, and have been successful in raising funds from the capital markets, will be the main ones continuing to do so. The arrival of asset-backed transactions may allow investors to overcome financial fragility and corporate governance concerns, allowing new issuers to arise, but the small size of typical firms makes it difficult to find assets or claims on future income streams large enough to make ABS issuance worthwhile.

Acknowledgments

The authors express their gratitude to Giorgina Piani for help in designing the survey; Griselda Charlo, Graciela Basañez, and Susana Picardo of the National Institute of Statistics (INE) for the survey's implementation; Eduardo Barbieri of the Electronic Stock Market (BEVSA) for his support with the survey of financial intermediaries; Bruno Gili and Ignacio Munyo for sharing relevant corporate financial data they had previously collected; and Daniel Sieradzki, Gabriel Moszkowicz, and Hernan Berro for excellent research assistance. All remaining errors are the sole responsibility of the authors.

Notes

1. The Uruguayan debt exchange of 2003 gave bondholders two choices: (a) under the "extension option," an existing bond could be exchanged for a new one with same principal, currency and coupon, but with an extended maturity (5 years, on average); (b) under the "liquidity option," existing bonds could be exchanged for so-called benchmark bonds, under which many small bonds could be aggregated. There were benchmark bonds both in the international and the local debt exchange transactions, but the size of the domestic benchmarks was much lower than the international ones.

2. Realistically, it takes time for the introduction of new financial instruments in an emerging market lacking expertise in the management of these more sophisticated products. In the case of Chile, their securitization law was passed in 1994, but the first securitized bond was issued there in 1996, and the market for this kind of instrument took off only in 1999.

3. Because INE was responsible for the field survey, this made answering the survey a legal obligation, and firms risked being fined if they failed to comply.

4. The main component of the "Other liabilities" column in table 8.1 is internally generated funds, with securities accounting for a very small fraction of total liabilities.

5. In de Brun et al. (2007) we present a more detailed analysis of the financial structure of Uruguayan firms, differentiating publicly traded from non–publicly traded companies and how their financial structure changed before and after the 2002 crisis.

6. There is some evidence of a systematic relationship between the two key dimensions of a firm's financial structure: the maturity structure of its total liabilities, measured as the fraction of long-term debt in total debt, and its degree of liability dollarization, measured as the percentage of total liabilities that are denominated in, or indexed to, USD. Kamil (2004) reports a statistically significant correlation coefficient between the maturity of corporate debt and its dollarization of 0.35. This empirical evidence suggests that the observed dollarization of liabilities may well be motivated by a desire to extend the maturity structure of obligations—and not necessarily by a given currency preference.

7. This is especially true in the case of Uruguay where most domestic foreign-currency deposits are offset by domestic foreign-currency loans and not by assets held abroad. The banking sector's net foreign asset position is generally positive but close to balance.

8. In fact, it is not strictly necessary to have a bank as underwriter or even an underwriter of any kind. The firms that have a well-established reputation as issuers usually do not pay underwriter fees. In some cases, the stockbroker assumes the role of underwriter, and their fees are similar to those of the bank.

References

Bentancor, A. (1999). "Estructura financiera de las empresas en Uruguay." *XIV Jornadas Anuales de Economía*. Montevideo: Banco Central del Uruguay.

Clarke, Álvaro (2004). "Uruguay—fuentes de crecimiento: un análisis del mercado de capitales uruguayo." Background paper for the report "Uruguay: Sources of Growth." World Bank, Regional Office for Latin America and the Caribbean.

De Brun, J., N. Gandelman, and E. Barbieri (2003). "Investment and Financial Restrictions at the Firm Level in Uruguay." In Arturo Galindo and Fabio Schiantarelli, eds., *Credit Constraints and Investment in Latin America*. Washington, D.C.: Inter-American Development Bank, 259–291.

De Brun, H., N. Gandelman, H. Kamil, and A. C. Porzecanski (2007). "El mercado de renta fija en Uruguay." *Revista de Economía* 14(1).

De Brun, J., and G. Licandro (2006). "To Hell and Back: Crisis Management in a Dollarized Economy, the Case of Uruguay." In Adrián Armas, Alain Ize, and Eduardo Levy Yeyati, eds., *Financial Dollarization: The Policy Agenda*. New York: Palgrave MacMillan, 147–176.

Kamil, H. (2004). "A New Database on the Currency Composition and Maturity Structure of Firms' Balance Sheets in Latin America: 1990–2002." Mimeo, Inter-American Development Bank.

Licandro, G., and J. A. Licandro (2003). "Building the De-dollarization Agenda: The Case of Uruguay." *Money Affairs* (CEMLA) 16(1) (July–December).

Munyo, I. (2005). "The Determinants of Capital Structure: Evidence from an Economy without [a] Stock Market." Mimeo.

Pascale, R. (1978). *Inversión, financiamiento y rentabilidad de la industria manufacturera uruguaya.* Montevideo: Banco Central del Uruguay.

Pascale, R. (1982). *Comportamiento financiero de la industria manufacturera uruguaya.* Montevideo: Banco Central del Uruguay.

Pascale, R. (1994). *Finanzas de las empresas uruguayas.* Montevideo: Banco Central del Uruguay.

Robledo, I. (1994). "Estructura financiera de la empresa e inversión: el caso uruguayo." CERES, Montevideo, Documento de Trabajo No. 14.

Zervos, S. (2004). "The Transaction Costs of Primary Market Issuance: The Case of Brazil, Chile, and Mexico." World Bank, Policy Research Working Paper No. 3424.

9 Prospects for Latin American Bond Markets: A Cross-Country View

Barry Eichengreen, Ugo Panizza, and Eduardo Borensztein

What is the state of bond markets in Latin America? What are the main determinants of market development? While a cursory look at measures of market capitalization relative to GDP would suggest that Latin America is lagging, the answers to these questions are in fact more nuanced. For one thing, it is the aggregate capitalization of all financial markets—comprising bonds, bank loans, and equities—that is small in Latin America relative to other regions. Furthermore, while the volume of bond markets is a function of a country's level of economic and institutional development, among other things, the scope of bond markets may also be limited by the small scale of potential borrowers and of the overall market.

Thus, identifying the determinants of market development can help to form expectations about the prospects for market development and identify weaknesses that may hinder their growth. This chapter addresses these issues with the information that can be gleaned from a broad cross-country econometric analysis.

Even in the advanced industrial countries, bond markets in general and corporate bond markets in particular have been relatively late to develop, reflecting the existence of substantial institutional prerequisites. Prior to the 1980s corporate bond markets in most advanced economies were essentially nonexistent, with the United States being a notable outlier (IMF 2005, p. 106). US exceptionalism reflected restrictions on the banking industry (the separation of commercial and investment banking, restrictions on interstate branching, and so on), together with the creation of a relatively robust regulatory environment and a bankruptcy code that facilitated reorganization and thus encouraged firms to rely on debt finance (Bolton 2003). The US corporate bond market then expanded further in the 1980s with the relaxation of regulatory restrictions and improvements in the information environment encouraging securitization, which facilitated the creation of the junk bond market. It then expanded further in the 1990s as strong economic growth encouraged corporate debt issuance. In Japan, the bond market grew rapidly from the second half of the 1980s as a restrictive regulatory environment gave way to widespread liberalization, in turn precipitating institutional innovation (the start of bond futures trading, the establishment of rating agencies, and so forth). The "big bang" reforms of the mid-1990s—which eliminated the securities transactions tax, deregulated brokerage commissions, and introduced a legal framework for securitization—then facilitated further growth even in the face of a stagnant economy (IMF 2002). In Europe, meanwhile, corporate bond markets remained small, reflecting the continent's traditional dependence on bank finance.[1] This is now changing with the advent of the single market, which intensified competition in the financial sector, compressing underwriting fees and—especially following the advent of the euro in 1999—suggesting that exchange rate risk and problems associated with the small scale of national markets may have played a role (Eichengreen 2000; Nierop 2006).

The story is similar in Latin America and in emerging markets generally. As late as the early 1990s, Latin America still had essentially no corporate bond markets, although local issuance by governments was extensive. At that point macroeconomic stabilization and the adoption of strengthened securities market and corporate governance regulations ignited the takeoff of local markets. The period since the middle of the 1990s has seen rapid growth in bond markets in a number of Latin American countries. Figure 9.1 shows the growth of the bond market in the decade ending in 2004 (with market capitalization scaled by GDP). Chile, where the process began somewhat earlier, has seen domestic market capitalization grow in line with the economy, while Peru, Colombia, Mexico, and above all Brazil—where there was more scope for catch-up—have seen the bond market grow even faster than the output of goods and services. This exceptional growth, especially in Brazil, has been due mainly to budget deficits and the use of bond finance by governments. By comparison, corporate bond markets have lagged behind. An exception again is Chile, where the market in public bonds has grown more slowly than GDP while that in corporate bonds has grown more quickly.

On balance, Latin America continues to lag behind not just the advanced countries but also emerging East Asia, when bond markets are measured relative to GDP. While Latin America has a larger stock

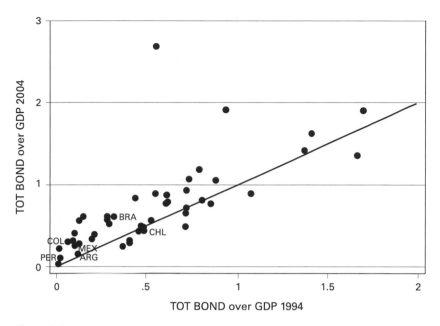

Figure 9.1
Growth of the domestic bond market, 1994–2004. Source: Authors' calculations based on
BIS data.

of government bonds so measured, reflecting the region's history of
budget deficits, the segments of the bond market accounted for by
issues of financial institutions and corporations are noticeably smaller
than in East Asia. Interestingly, this differential in the growth of local
markets is less pronounced when capitalization is scaled by the size of
the financial sector—that is, by stock of domestic credit (compare figures 9.2 and 9.3).[2] In short, Latin American financial sectors overall—
and not merely bond markets—are underdeveloped.

That the different segments of the financial market seem to grow together suggests that bond market development is a corollary of the
larger process of financial development. This hypothesis is consistent
with the observation that the development of banking systems and the
development of bond markets have prerequisites in common. In both
cases, investor participation requires a reasonable level of information
disclosure. In turn, mandating such disclosure and solving "lemons
problems" may require regulation by a supervisory agency or securities commission. The development of both a bond market and a
sound banking system will require strong creditor rights and an effective system of corporate governance so that small creditors can be

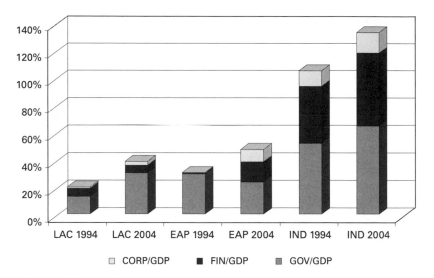

Figure 9.2
Domestic bonds as a share of GDP (weighted average). Source: Authors' calculations based on BIS data.

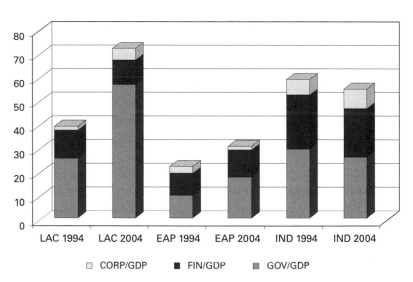

Figure 9.3
Domestic bonds as a share of domestic credit (weighted average). Source: Authors' calculations based on BIS data.

assured of being dealt with fairly. In both cases, confidence on the part of market participants requires macroeconomic stability so that depositors and investors do not fear that the value of their claims will be inflated away, and strong creditor rights so that they are confident that they will be treated fairly in the event of a debt crisis or banking crisis.

In addition, the fact that bond markets grow in tandem with the rest of the financial system (which means in practice with the banking system) suggests that banks and bond markets are complements rather than substitutes. Banks provide underwriting services for domestic issuers, advising them on the terms and timing of the offer. Banks provide bridge finance in the period when the marketing of bonds is still under way, as well as distribution channels for government and corporate bonds, and form an important part of the primary dealer network. Their institutional support may also be conducive to secondary-market liquidity. Most directly, banks, owing to their relatively large size, can be major issuers of domestic bonds themselves.[3] While some of these services can be purchased from foreign banks, the costs of doing so can be substantial, and for some functions, such as the provision of a distribution network to local retail investors, foreign banks may lack the relevant institutional capacity.

All this suggests that bond market development should not be seen as an alternative to the development of an efficient banking system but rather as part of a single organic process. Conversely, there are fears that an inefficient banking system may hinder bond market development and that an imperfectly competitive system—in which banks have significant market power—may allow banks to use their incumbency advantage to hinder the advance of securitization and disintermediation by slowing the growth of the bond market.[4] In Chile, the Latin American country with the most active corporate bond market, fully 26 investment banks have been active in underwriting and helping to place domestic debt securities (see chapter 6); Brazil has 20 different commercial and investment banks that act as lead underwriters (see chapter 7). Mexico is a counterexample: three large banks have dominated the underwriting and sell side of the domestic market (see chapter 3).

This perspective is rather different from the "pecking order model" in which bank finance develops first because the information and contracting environments are highly imperfect. According to this model, banks in long-term relationships with their clients have a comparative

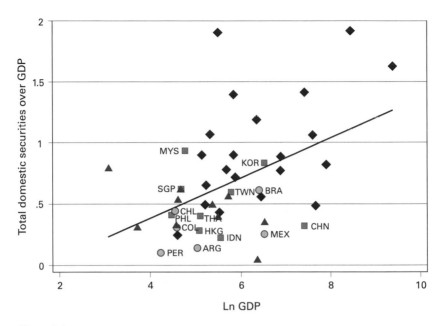

Figure 9.4
Domestic bond markets and the size of the economy. Source: Authors' calculations based on BIS and World Bank data.

advantage in bridging information gaps, enforcing repayment and reorganizing problem loans. Bond markets only develop later, once the economy has acquired strong institutions of information disclosure, corporate governance, and insolvency reorganization.

Recent research (e.g., Rajan and Zingales 2003b), however, suggests that the actual sequencing of external finance, starting with banks and moving to bond markets and finally equity markets, is not so clear-cut in practice. The precise form of this sequencing differs across countries and over time. While not denying the special role of banks in the kind of imperfect information and contracting environment that is characteristic of many emerging markets, the perspective here suggests that the development of banking systems does not simply precede the development of bond markets; instead, the two are complementary processes.

Determinants of Bond Market Development

The country studies included in this volume suggest that bond market development has multiple causes. In some countries the problems are

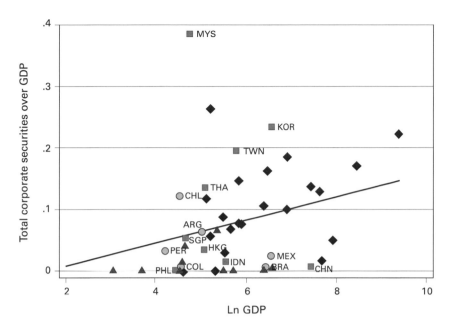

Figure 9.5
Domestic corporate bond markets and the size of the economy. Source: Authors' calculations based on BIS and World Bank data.

the small size of the economy, which makes it difficult to develop secondary liquidity, and the small size of potential corporate issuers, who may not be able to spread the fixed costs of placement over an adequately sized bond placement. This is evident in figures 9.4 and 9.5, which show that larger countries have better-capitalized bond markets. Some of the country studies in this volume highlight that, given fixed costs, small firms are unlikely to use bonds, and there is in fact a positive correlation between adjusted firm size and the size of the corporate bond market.[5] Still, in several Asian countries, such as Korea, the corporate bond market is much larger than firm size alone would predict.[6]

In some countries the problem is relatively low saving rates and their implications for developing an adequate investor base. In Asia, on the other hand, high saving rates create a considerable pool of funds for investment in locally issued bonds. A classic case in point is Japan, where a significant saving surplus has kept spreads narrow, which has resulted in the dominance of domestic investors in the bond market (Ma, Remolona, Jianxiong 2006, p. 4). In Latin America, by

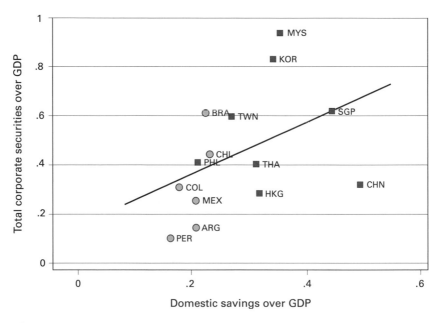

Figure 9.6
Savings and domestic bond market capitalization.

comparison, saving rates are lower. Figure 9.6 suggests that this is at least one factor contributing to differential bond market development.[7]

Given Latin America's relatively low savings rates, it is all the more important to promote the participation of institutional investors— pension funds, mutual funds, insurance companies, and banks. Banks demand government bonds in order to satisfy prudential requirements. Pension funds and insurance companies have long-term liabilities in domestic currency; it therefore makes sense for them to match these with long-term domestic-currency investments. Mutual funds enable individual investors to diversify away the idiosyncratic risk associated with individual bonds by holding claims on a broad underlying investment portfolio. In cross-country regressions, we find that the number of years since a country privatized its pension system has a strongly positive impact on the capitalization of its bond markets.[8]

To be sure, the importance of institutional investors is not limited to Latin America; pension funds and provident funds play a prominent role in local markets in East Asia as well. Latin America's low savings rates, however, arguably render institutional investors even more indispensable to the development of local markets in the region. Pension funds hold a very significant fraction of government bonds in countries like Chile, Colombia, and Mexico, where the reform of pension systems began relatively early. In Brazil the mutual fund industry is the most important holder of government securities (along with the banking system and the state development bank, BNDES), although it focuses mainly on the short end of the market. The role of life and other types of insurance companies is smaller in Latin America than in Asia, with the notable exception of Chile where insurance company assets under management approach 20% of GDP. In Mexico and Chile, institutional investors hold upward of 90% of corporate bonds; in Peru they hold more than 70% (IMF 2005). In Asian countries with higher savings rates, such as Thailand, retail investors who purchase bonds directly through bank branches play a larger role in the local bond market.

Latin American governments have taken a variety of steps to encourage the participation of institutional investors. Chile has relaxed limits on the investment portfolios of insurance companies, raised limits on individual voluntary contributions to pension funds, and standardized capital requirements for mutual funds (see chapter 6). It has put in place safeguards and procedures to facilitate the investment of pension funds in corporate bonds: bonds first must be reviewed by the securities commission, accepted for listing by the stock exchange and, in the case of corporate bonds, approved by the Risk Classification Commission.[9] Companies issuing bonds must be registered with the supervisory authority and meet demanding disclosure requirements, mainly by submitting detailed balance sheets quarterly. Mexico reformed its Mutual Fund Act in 2001 to facilitate the development of additional collective investment vehicles. Rules governing the portfolio allocation decisions of pension funds were relaxed (although these funds are still prohibited from taking positions in sub-investment-grade bonds); for details, see chapter 3. Peru is seeking to relax regulations limiting pension fund investments in corporate bonds. Brazil's new bankruptcy law, designed to speed reorganization and strengthen creditor rights, should work in the same direction.

Relying on institutional investors, however, has costs as well as benefits. Pension funds and insurance companies follow buy-and-hold strategies.[10] Hence liquidity, at least as measured by turnover, tends to be lower in markets dominated by a few large institutional investors. Less liquidity makes participation even less attractive for retail investors, and the lower levels of demand that result raise required rates of

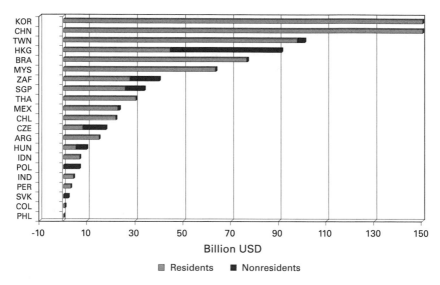

Figure 9.7
Domestic currency corporate bonds issued by residents and nonresidents (2004). Includes bonds issued by financial and nonfinancial corporations, state agencies, and international organizations. It assumes that all bonds issued domestically are issued by residents and are in local currency.

return and placement costs for issuers. While these dilemmas are formidable, higher savings rates may be an important part of the solution.

The other way of enhancing market liquidity is by encouraging foreign participation in local markets.[11] This can be done by eliminating capital controls and relaxing or eliminating withholding taxes on interest payments that foreign investors regard as particularly onerous.[12] Figure 9.7 shows the role of resident and nonresident issuers of bonds in the currencies of 21 emerging market countries. While in most cases the local currency market is completely dominated by residents, nonresidents play an important role in Hong Kong, South Africa, Singapore, and the Czech Republic. Overall, 99% of bonds issued in Latin American currencies are issued by residents as are 92% of bonds issued in East Asian currencies.[13]

Participation by investors from outside the region appears to be particularly important for the development of deep and active bond markets in Latin America.[14] However, foreign investors are most inclined to take positions in countries with larger bond markets, such as Brazil, where the costs of closing out positions are lowest (i.e., where liquidity is already greatest). The Brazilian authorities have sought to capitalize

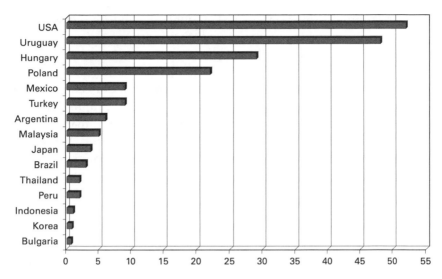

Figure 9.8
Share of domestic bonds held by foreign investors.

on this interest by retiring foreign debt from the market and replacing it with domestic-currency (interest-rate- and inflation-indexed) issues. Mexico, where foreign participants are reported to hold more than 50% of the government's 10-year bonds and more than 80% of its 20-year bonds, has sought to take advantage of foreign participation by issuing exclusively on the domestic market (IMF 2005, p. 113). To be sure, there is also a foreign demand for "exotics," or the less liquid bonds of smaller countries (figure 9.8 shows that, after the United States, the bond markets with the largest foreign participation are those of Uruguay, Hungary, and Poland).[15] But this phenomenon is quantitatively limited; for most investors, the restricted liquidity of exotics, together with a lack of hedging instruments and fixed costs of obtaining information about issue quality, currency risk, withholding tax regimes, etc. in smaller markets, limits foreign demand. Foreign investors prefer the bonds of larger countries and of their governments in particular, because these government bonds already display the most liquidity.

This raises the possibility that the globalization of bond markets and the growing participation of foreign investors in Latin America's local markets in particular may be creating a bifurcation between the region's larger and smaller markets by further enhancing the already greater liquidity of the larger markets while having little discernible impact on their smaller counterparts.[16] Similarly, these developments may be enhancing the liquidity of government bond markets relative to corporate bond markets, which encourages smaller countries to borrow by issuing global bonds in extra-regional financial centers as an alternative to developing their domestic markets. In turn, this activity may further limit the development and liquidity of local markets, discouraging foreign participation even more.[17] On the other hand, one can argue that international issues are useful for familiarizing foreign investors with a country's situation and its debt instruments and that domestic and international issues are complements rather than substitutes. One can further argue that the two influences coexist.

The most popular class of explanations for cross-country variations in bond market development, alluded to earlier, is surely market infrastructure (the reliability of custodial services; the efficiency of payment and settlement systems), legal infrastructure (speed of judicial proceedings; efficiency of national bankruptcy and insolvency procedures), and the effectiveness of information disclosure and corporate government requirements (which are in turn functions of the effectiveness of regulation). The slow pace and unpredictable result of judicial proceedings in Brazil are said to render investors reluctant to hold private debt securities, whereas in Chile the efficiency of the judicial system is sometimes invoked as an explanation for the development of the private bond market. More broadly, there are wide variations in these measures of legal infrastructure both within Latin America and between Latin America and other regions. Latin America tends to fare poorly in terms of both investor and creditor protection: the highest-ranked Latin American country (Chile) has values that are lower than the Asian average.

Similar arguments are made regarding the development of new financial instruments enabling firms and financial institutions to securitize their receivables and other assets and allowing them to access bond markets more easily. In some countries the government and leading financial institutions have aggressively promoted the development of these instruments and markets, for example, by using regulation to encourage issuers and investors to focus on standard formats. In Brazil the development of mortgage-backed securities (*certificados de recebiveis imobilarios*, or CRIs) and receivables investment funds (*fundos de investimentos em diretos creditorios*, or FIDCs)—with impetus from the central bank and the securities and exchange commission—was a significant step in widening the market.[18] Uruguay has similarly sought to facilitate the issuance of securitized debt instruments backed by receivables or other assets through provisions included in its Law of Trust Funds approved in 2003 (see chapter 8).

The problem is that the development of the relevant legal and economic infrastructure is to some extent endogenous. In other words, countries that develop relatively deep and liquid bond markets for other reasons have an incentive to invest in the relevant legal and market infrastructure and to develop innovative debt instruments. One can register the same objection to statements to the effect that the low liquidity of the secondary market makes holding some assets unattractive.[19] Market liquidity will be enhanced by other initiatives that will make investing in corporate bonds more attractive. This suggests, at a minimum, controlling for those other determinants of bond market development when making comparative statements.

Previous Literature

We know of only three studies examining empirically the determinants of overall local bond market capitalization in a broad cross section of countries. Burger and Warnock (2004, 2006) were first to use Bank for International Settlements (BIS) data to analyze the determinants of local bond market capitalization as a share of GDP. They use a cross section of up to 49 countries and consider GDP, GDP per capita, the average level of inflation, inflation variability, and rule of law as potential determinants of market cap. All of these variables except the first enter with statistically significant coefficients (inflation and inflation variability, negatively; the others, positively). Burger and Warnock's results also suggest that there are important complementarities between the development of the bond market and that of the banking system.

Eichengreen and Leungnaruemitchai (2004) similarly use BIS data to study the determinants of capitalization in 41 countries in the period 1990–2001. They find that the development of bond markets has multiple determinants, a number of which have important implications for Latin America. The authors find that larger countries have better-capitalized bond markets where capitalization is measured relative to GDP. They argue that these scale effects reflect the fixed costs of creating the relevant bond market infrastructure, including clearing and settlement systems and a reliable legal framework for issuing and trading, and that scale may also be important for the liquidity of secondary markets. Their results also suggest that countries with more competitive, better-capitalized banking systems have larger markets, as if bond and bank intermediation are complements rather than substitutes—consistent with the observations of the previous section. Institutional quality (low levels of corruption; adherence to internationally recognized accounting standards) appears to be important for the development of bond markets, particularly private markets.[20] Stable exchange rates additionally appear to be conducive to the existence of larger bond markets, presumably by lowering currency risk and encouraging foreign participation; so too is the absence of capital controls. Finally, while a history of budget deficits results in a larger outstanding stock of government debt, which in itself is not surprising, the authors find little evidence that this affects the corporate segment of the market one way or the other.[21] Large amounts of government bond issuance seem to have cross-cutting implications for the development of the private bond market that on balance cancel out: on the one hand, a large government bond market makes for a benchmark asset or yield curve off which other credits can be conveniently priced; on the other hand, large amounts of government bond issuance may crowd private bonds out of investors' portfolios.

Braun and Briones (2006) adopt a similar approach except that they analyze BIS data only for the end of 2004. Their strongest result is that bond market development increases with GDP per capita as a measure of economic development. A recent history of budget deficits is associated with a larger domestic debt stock overall because of its impact on the outstanding stock of government debt; once more, however, fiscal policy has no discernible impact on the domestic stock of nongovernmental issues. The authors' findings on threshold or market-size effects are ambiguous: the overall size of the economy as measured by aggregate GDP is positive and significant in their regressions for overall bond market capitalization but not in the separate regressions for bonds issued by the government, private financial firms, and private nonfinancial firms. They also report insignificant coefficients for the presence or absence of capital controls and the exchange rate regime, again in contrast to the results in Eichengreen and Leungnaruemitchai. It is hard to know whether these contrasts reflect their limited number of observations (as few as 34) or a substantive difference in findings.

Braun and Briones also find that a wide range of institutional variables seem to have relatively little effect. An exception is creditor rights, which enter negatively in the equations for overall bond market capitalization, government bond market capitalization, and corporate bond market capitalization alike.[22]

In addition, their dummy variable for Latin American countries enters with a negative coefficient in the regressions for overall bond market capitalization. Specifically, the Latin dummy is still significantly negative even though variables like creditor rights enter with significant coefficients and have a lower average value in Latin America than other parts of the world. This suggests that there is something else about Latin American countries not fully captured by the range of included explanatory variables that causes bond market development to lag. The authors find negative coefficients on this regional dummy variable not just in their regressions for overall domestic market capitalization but also in regressions for government and private bonds. Interestingly, however, that negative coefficient is significantly less than zero only in the equation for public sector bonds, as if there are particular problems stunting the growth of government bond markets in the region that appear only once one controls for the size of budget deficits and the general level of economic development, among other things.

Braun and Briones consider a number of other dimensions of bond market development besides capitalization by aggregating data on the characteristics of individual corporate bonds issued in the period 1995–2004. They analyze, inter alia, currency of denomination (own currency versus foreign), mean maturity (and share of bonds with a maturity of more than five years), mean yield to maturity, mean spread (in basis points), and the share of corporate bond issues that are investment grade. The limitation of this analysis is that their source, SDC Platinum, incompletely captures the issuance of government bonds, short-term government bonds in particular. Still, there are a number of suggestive findings. The maturity of corporate bond issues depends not only on the general level of economic development (proxied by per capita GDP) but also on macroeconomic stability (maturity declines with inflation and budget deficits).[23] A more efficient and competitive banking system—as measured by the spread between bank deposit and lending rates and by banks' average overhead costs—seems to be associated with longer maturities of corporate bond issues, as if the underwriting role of banks shows up in this aspect of market development. Once more, the dummy variable for Latin America is negative and significant, as if the maturity of Latin American bonds is also shorter for other reasons not fully captured by the explanatory variables.

Other studies have considered subsets of these issues and markets. Burger and Warnock (2004) distinguish total, government, and private local-currency bonds, finding that countries with more variable inflation rates issue fewer local currency bonds. Stronger rule of law is positively associated with the capitalization of local-currency markets but does not obviously increase the local currency share (the ratio of local currency bonds to total bonds). Conversely, stronger creditor rights appear to affect the local currency share without affecting the overall size of the local-currency market. Finally, a stronger fiscal balance reduces issuance of local currency government bonds but, interestingly, does not appear to affect private issuance in local currency or the total size of the local currency market.

Claessens, Klingebiel, Schmukler (2003) consider the determinants of government bond market development, distinguishing local-currency- and foreign-currency-denominated bonds.[24] Consistent with Eichengreen and Luengnaruemitchai (2004), the authors find that country size is important for local-currency bond issuance. They also discover that countries with larger banking systems have larger domestic currency bond markets, as if efficient banking systems and bond markets are complements rather than substitutes. Inflation as a measure of macroeconomic instability enters negatively as a determinant of market capitalization for domestic- and foreign-currency bonds alike. These authors consider a measure of political institutions (the extent of institutionalized democracy) rather than creditor rights (as in previous studies) as a measure of institutional strength and find that this is positively related to market development.

Finally, the exchange rate regime appears to have different effects on domestic- and foreign-currency issuance. Countries with more flexible exchange rates, either de facto or de jure, have larger domestic-currency bond markets but smaller foreign-currency bond markets. This suggests that pegged exchange rates encourage governments to issue more foreign currency debt to take advantage of short-run reductions in debt-servicing costs and to signal the credibility of their commitment to the peg. Of course, this view is also consistent with moral-hazard arguments about the adverse effects of currency pegs.[25]

Hausmann and Panizza (2003) and Mehl and Reynaud (2005) focus on the share of domestic government debt that is in local currency and bears a fixed interest rate on the grounds that this is a particularly desirable form of funding—and one that governments in emerging markets have historically found difficult to obtain. They find that lower inflation is positively associated with this form of funding. There is also some evidence of a positive association with the size of the investor base (proxied by the private-savings-to-GDP ratio). The two studies disagree on the impact of capital-account liberalization on countries' ability to issue long-term domestic currency bonds: Mehl and Reynaud find a positive effect, as if liberalization encourages the issuance of long-term domestic currency bonds, while Hausmann and Panizza find the opposite.

Burger and Warnock (2003) also focus on foreign participation, using data on US investors' holdings of foreign bonds as of the end of 2001 (their measure includes both bonds floated on the issuing country's local market and Bradies and global bonds placed in, inter alia, New York). They find that US investors favor bonds issued by countries with greater bilateral trade with the United States, more open capital accounts, and less correlated returns.[26]

In sum, previous empirical studies suggest roles in bond market development for scale effects (country and/or issuing firm size), institutional development (the strength of legal and political rights), and macroeconomic policy (inflationary history in particular). They point to the importance of the regulation and development of the financial system more broadly (bond markets are larger in countries that have been able to relax capital controls and that also possess efficient and well-developed banking systems). Studies of the market in domestic currency-denominated, long-maturity issues, the market segment that policy makers are most anxious to foster, find that this market segment is particularly sensitive to the size of the investor base and to the country's inflation history.[27] A number of other results, however, are still disputed and uncertain. We attempt to shed more light on these in the following section.

Econometric Analysis

In this section, we follow Burger and Warnock (2004), Eichengreen and Luengnaruemitchai (2004), and Braun and Briones (2006) in testing for the determinants of bond market development. In contrast to these previous studies, we distinguish the determinants of the development of markets in government, corporate, and financial sector bonds, rather than considering the bond market as a single aggregate. In addition to standard regression analysis, we use a difference-in-differences methodology suitable for identifying the differential effects of country characteristics on the development of these market segments.

Cross-Country Results for the Full Sample of Countries

Like Eichengreen and Luengnaruemitchai (2004), we use annual data from BIS and estimate the model using generalized least squares with corrections for heteroskedasticity and panel-specific autocorrelation. In the regressions with the full set of controls, we have as many as 491 additional observations.[28] In addition, we explore what happens when we restrict our analysis to emerging market countries. We allow for nonlinear effects of GDP, GDP per capita, and credit extended by the banking sector; control for the size of domestic savings, the de facto exchange rate regime, the level and volatility of the interest rate, the size of total public debt (as opposed to the size of domestic government debt financed by issuing bonds), the interaction between capital controls and public debt, and a variable measuring the number of years since a country privatized its pension system; and we include a full set of region and year fixed effects.

The results, which are displayed in table 9.1, refer to four definitions of the bond market. Column 1 refers to government bonds, column 2 to private (financial plus corporate) bonds, column 3 to corporate bonds, and column 4 to bonds issued by financial institutions. While these markets are closely related, the variables affecting their development may have differential impacts on each of them. Many of our results confirm those of Eichengreen and Luengnaruemitchai (2004), but further details also emerge. (Columns 5–8 are discussed in the following section, "Cross-Country Results for Emerging Markets.")

In line with previous studies, we find that country size is significantly correlated with the size of bond market (scaled by GDP). However, the relationship is nonlinear and, in the case of government bonds, the point estimates imply that the level of GDP that maximizes the size of the government bond market relative to GDP is US$6 trillion (which is twice the GDP of Japan). We also find a positive and concave relationship of bond markets with per capita GDP, suggesting that the government bond market reaches a maximum when GDP per capita is around US$34,000, while the private bond market reaches its maximum when GDP per capita is well above US$40,000. As regards the level of private savings (scaled by GDP), we do not find a statistically significant relationship in any market, although the signs of the coefficients are at least positive in the case of corporate and financial bond markets.

Trade openness, measured as the ratio of exports to GDP (EXP), has a uniformly positive and significant effect on bond market development. The channels are probably both direct (a healthy export industry is likely to be creditworthy and pursue large investment projects) and indirect (openness tends to help economic dynamism and institutional development in ways not completely captured by other variables). One would suspect, then, that the exchange rate regime may also have an impact on market development, and to check this assumption we utilize the effect of the index of de facto exchange rate arrangements of Levy Yeyati and Sturzenegger (2005). We include a dummy variable taking a value of one when a country has a de facto fixed exchange rate regime (FIX) and a dummy variable taking a value of one when a country has an intermediate regime (INTER); thus, a floating exchange rate is the excluded alternative. Although exchange rate policies are surely relevant for both investors and borrowers who may have alternative opportunities in foreign currency instruments available in international markets, the regressions do not identify significant effects arising from the (de facto) exchange rate systems themselves.

The level of the domestic interest rate (IRATE) is negatively correlated with market capitalization, but the relationship is statistically significant only for government bonds.[29] The results for the volatility of the interest rate are less clear; we find that volatility is negatively correlated with the size of the government bond market, as expected, but positively correlated with the size of the private bond market.[30] A possible interpretation is that countries with less liquid financial markets see smaller changes in interest rates because trading is infrequent; it would then appear that volatility stimulates market development. This conjecture is supported by the results for the sample of emerging economies only (to be discussed later), where the anomalous coefficient signs disappear.

We find a concave relationship between the size of the market in bonds issued by financial institutions (and private total bonds in general) and domestic credit provided by the banking sector (DOMCR).

Table 9.1
Determinants of the Size of Government and Private Bond Markets Relative to GDP

	(1) GBOND/GDP	(2) PBOND/GDP	(3) CBOND/GDP	(4) FBOND/GDP	(5) GBOND/GDP	(6) PBOND/GDP	(7) CBOND/GDP	(8) FBOND/GDP
GDP	4.935 (5.12)***	7.821 (5.93)***	0.842 (1.61)	5.762 (5.02)***	-1.943 (0.76)	3.252 (2.63)***	0.863 (1.72)*	4.282 (4.51)***
GDP2	-0.407 (4.73)***	0.139 (0.84)	0.056 (1.01)	0.081 (0.63)	0.317 (0.75)	-0.358 (1.85)*	-0.213 (2.93)***	-0.350 (2.37)**
GDP_PC	1.296 (2.60)***	2.288 (6.66)***	0.566 (3.95)***	1.765 (7.01)***	2.236 (2.28)**	1.328 (2.77)***	1.073 (5.66)***	-0.227 (0.93)
GDP_PC2	-0.019 (1.97)**	-0.028 (3.91)***	-0.007 (2.31)**	-0.018 (3.01)***	-0.110 (3.76)***	-0.063 (3.09)***	-0.055 (8.18)***	0.013 (1.60)
EXP	0.199 (4.93)***	0.218 (7.15)***	0.032 (2.54)**	0.141 (6.37)***	0.228 (3.21)***	0.163 (4.55)***	0.061 (4.18)***	0.034 (2.27)**
PRSAV	-16.657 (2.38)**	1.563 (0.41)	1.409 (0.94)	0.999 (0.31)	-18.876 (1.73)*	-0.496 (0.12)	1.411 (0.72)	2.137 (1.17)
FIX	-0.369 (0.69)	-0.495 (1.37)	0.040 (0.30)	-0.436 (1.46)	2.637 (2.54)**	0.662 (1.39)	0.064 (0.27)	0.161 (0.74)
INTER	0.861 (1.59)	0.140 (0.48)	0.016 (0.15)	0.141 (0.58)	1.497 (1.96)*	0.155 (0.53)	-0.046 (0.30)	0.043 (0.28)
IRATE	-0.178 (4.67)***	-0.013 (0.89)	-0.003 (0.47)	-0.013 (1.03)	-0.115 (2.67)***	0.023 (1.59)	0.011 (1.39)	-0.004 (0.55)
SD_IRATE	-0.702 (6.52)***	0.146 (2.10)**	0.091 (2.46)**	0.132 (2.21)**	-0.804 (4.14)***	-0.266 (3.39)***	0.061 (1.90)*	-0.173 (3.43)***
DOMCR	-0.478 (0.15)	10.894 (3.66)***	0.538 (0.56)	7.106 (2.99)***	-2.443 (0.29)	3.881 (1.22)	3.277 (2.15)**	-0.023 (0.01)

	(1)	(2)	(3)	(4)	(5)	(6)	(7)	(8)
DOMCR2	-0.127	-3.576	-0.024	-2.221	-1.885	-0.777	-0.995	-0.054
	(0.12)	(2.92)***	(0.06)	(2.31)**	(0.48)	(0.59)	(1.48)	(0.08)
CONC	-11.029	0.825	0.671	-0.616	16.850	4.564	-0.130	1.020
	(3.34)***	(0.33)	(0.67)	(0.29)	(1.98)**	(1.29)	(0.08)	(0.58)
SPREAD	-0.004	-0.152	0.080	-0.142	-0.054	0.270	0.103	0.030
	(0.05)	(1.97)**	(3.42)***	(2.29)**	(0.22)	(0.95)	(1.02)	(0.23)
KAPCON	6.783	-0.653	0.308	0.506	8.687	-1.188	-1.034	0.586
	(6.16)***	(0.96)	(0.98)	(0.91)	(3.92)***	(1.87)*	(2.40)**	(1.38)
PUBLICDEBT	0.376	0.004	-0.003	0.012	0.272	-0.009	-0.010	-0.000
	(18.83)***	(0.34)	(0.69)	(1.41)	(5.54)***	(0.68)	(1.39)	(0.05)
DEBT_KCON	-0.162	0.005	-0.000	-0.008	-0.162	0.013	0.011	-0.001
	(9.06)***	(0.62)	(0.13)	(1.11)	(4.13)***	(1.32)	(1.79)*	(0.18)
YR_PR	1.049	0.731	0.179	0.697	0.561	0.773	0.174	0.339
	(3.73)***	(5.09)***	(2.15)**	(6.90)***	(1.78)*	(7.42)***	(2.70)***	(4.54)***
RULEOFLAW	0.483	0.504	0.129	0.431	1.157	-0.239	0.046	0.002
	(1.09)	(2.00)**	(1.31)	(2.08)**	(1.72)*	(0.79)	(0.33)	(0.02)
INVPROT	3.541	2.803	0.317	0.438	4.061	3.314	0.629	2.334
	(5.78)***	(5.44)***	(1.27)	(0.83)	(3.56)***	(5.56)***	(2.40)**	(8.67)***
CRIGHT	-3.087	-1.877	-0.219	-1.639	-1.106	-0.433	0.077	0.475
	(6.37)***	(4.29)***	(0.85)	(3.77)***	(0.69)	(0.62)	(0.25)	(1.25)
CONTR_COST	-0.204	-0.100	-0.067	-0.012	-0.350	-0.079	-0.023	-0.086
	(5.55)***	(3.97)***	(3.49)***	(0.60)	(6.19)***	(2.77)***	(1.99)**	(5.76)***
FRENCHLAW	16.794	13.010	0.481	6.840	42.266	6.839	-1.613	9.521
	(5.05)***	(5.43)***	(0.40)	(3.31)***	(7.46)***	(2.81)***	(1.50)	(6.54)***
SOCLAW	-2.499	8.078	-2.761	3.744	23.792	5.948	-3.383	7.274
	(0.52)	(2.80)***	(2.07)**	(1.37)	(3.92)***	(2.28)**	(3.22)***	(4.22)***
GERSCANLAW	1.631	32.515	3.468	19.255	10.100	39.877	10.490	22.996
	(0.48)	(15.74)***	(3.18)***	(9.44)***	(1.42)	(11.49)***	(4.29)***	(13.46)***

Table 9.1
(continued)

	(1) GBOND/ GDP	(2) PBOND/ GDP	(3) CBOND/ GDP	(4) FBOND/ GDP	(5) GBOND/ GDP	(6) PBOND/ GDP	(7) CBOND/ GDP	(8) FBOND/ GDP
LATITUDE	-4.252	-26.997	-1.499	-24.483	-11.096	-14.233	3.124	-14.141
	(0.59)	(4.72)***	(0.71)	(5.06)***	(0.60)	(1.94)*	(0.81)	(2.96)***
EAP	-5.731	7.963	8.309	-1.519	-33.146	-1.538	2.891	-2.504
	(1.24)	(2.90)***	(5.05)***	(0.65)	(5.64)***	(0.64)	(2.79)***	(2.10)**
LAC	-20.484	-6.791	1.499	-6.755	-55.847	-4.217	-1.059	-2.774
	(4.31)***	(2.72)***	(1.24)	(2.94)***	(7.58)***	(1.54)	(0.79)	(2.03)**
ECA	3.305	-2.321	1.831	-2.183	-36.640	-3.909	-2.589	-1.305
	(0.70)	(0.69)	(1.25)	(0.91)	(4.64)***	(1.35)	(2.06)**	(1.00)
OTH	13.463	10.518	5.851	5.584				
	(2.49)**	(3.53)***	(3.38)***	(3.00)***				
Constant	3.856	-30.910	-6.160	-9.563	-1.744	-20.065	-7.528	-12.137
	(0.43)	(4.98)***	(2.08)**	(1.93)*	(0.12)	(3.12)***	(2.34)**	(3.27)***
Observations	491	481	485	478	222	224	216	224
Number of cc	43	43	43	42	21	21	21	21
F test: EAP = LAC	15.37	37.46	24.49	5.71	17.95	1.34	13.94	0.05
Prob > F	0.000	0.000	0.000	0.017	0.000	0.247	0.000	0.823

Note: Absolute value of z statistics in parentheses. Estimation method: generalized least squares with correction for heteroskedasticity and panel-specific autocorrelation. All regressions include year-fixed effects. *, **, *** denote significance at 10%, 5%, and 1% levels, respectively.
Source: Authors' calculations.

The point estimates indicate that the market in bonds issued by financial institutions reaches a maximum when domestic credit provided by the banking sector is about 160% of GDP, which is well above the levels of domestic credit in Latin American economies.[31] This suggests, plausibly, that banks that operate in more developed markets fund a larger share of their operations by issuing bonds instead of taking deposits.

Unlike Eichengreen and Luengnaruemitchai (2004), we detect no significant correlation between banking spreads (SPREAD) and the size of the government bond market. Instead, we find that the spread is positively correlated with the size of the corporate bond market. However, the opposite is true for financial bonds: these tend to be smaller when banks have higher spreads. The first result indicates, somewhat surprisingly, that the corporate bond market is more likely to develop in countries where banks have market power. This would contradict the widespread presumption that banks with market power will discourage the development of alternative sources of external finance. Our results suggest that they may in fact have limited ability to do so. On the supply side, firms are more likely to utilize bond finance when bank lending rates are high; on the demand side, investors are more likely to be interested in buying bonds when bank deposit rates are low.[32] The second result suggests that, insofar as high spreads are associated with low deposit rates, banks do not have incentives to fund their operations by issuing bonds.

We find that stricter capital controls are correlated with larger government bond market capitalization. (Our measure of capital controls ranges between -1, indicating no capital controls, and $+1$, indicating a high level of capital controls.) But we find that capital controls do not seem to increase the size of private bond markets in a significant way. These results, however, should be taken with caution. It may be that governments that need to issue large volumes of debt impose controls in an attempt to create a captive investor base. That is, causality may run in the opposite direction. We include a variable measuring the interaction of the level of public debt and the degree of capital controls (DEBT_KCON) as a way of testing whether in the presence of a large public debt, capital controls are more effective in creating a captive investor base, but the regression results do not support this conjecture.[33]

As expected, we find that a larger public debt is associated with a larger market for government bonds. (The variable PUBLICDEBT measures total public debt, regardless of how it is financed.) Public debt does not have a discernible effect on private bond markets, suggesting that any negative "crowding out" effect is not significant.

Given that a variety of emerging markets privatized their pension systems in the 1980s and 1990s, we ask whether pension privatization stimulates the growth of the bond market. We construct a variable (YR_PR) measuring the number of years since the beginning of the privatization process. (YR_PR takes a value of zero for countries that have never privatized their pension systems.) We find that the coefficients are always large, positive, and statistically significant. Not surprisingly, the effect is largest for government bonds (pension funds often being subject to regulations preventing them from purchasing speculative-grade corporate paper). Each extra year after the privatization of the pension system adds about 1 percentage point to the size of the market in government bonds, compared to about 0.7 percentage points for the markets of bonds issued by financial institutions and 0.2 percentage points for corporate bonds.

While there is no doubt that a strong institutional framework and high standards of corporate governance are essential pillars of bond market development, identifying the appropriate indicators of the quality of institutions and measuring their impact is not necessarily straightforward. We do find that the index of rule of law (RULEOF-LAW), lower contract enforcement costs (CONTR_COST), and the index of investor rights protection (INVPROT) show the right signs although they are not always robust. We focus here mainly on private bond markets and their breakdown between the corporate and financial sectors because government bond defaults follow a more complicated resolution process. Higher levels of creditor rights (CRIGHT), however, result in smaller private bond markets. A possible explanation is that some of the provisions that strengthen creditor rights may in fact discourage managers from issuing bonds. This could be the case, for example, of the loss of control of the company by management during bankruptcy reorganization, a provision that raises the score of the creditor rights variable. Regarding the origin of the legal code, our results are not in line with predominant views. We find that, compared with countries with a British legal code (the excluded alternative), countries with a French legal code tend to have larger bond markets (both private and corporate), while countries with a socialist legal code tend to have smaller private bond markets. Countries with a German or Scandinavian legal code have the largest private bond markets. These results are puzzling insofar as they indicate that the well-known positive effect of British legal origin on the size of the domestic financial system does not translate to the size of the bond market. Finally, latitude (often used as a proxy for institutional development) also presents a puzzling result, as it is negatively correlated with the size of the private bond market (a result driven by the market for bonds issued by financial institutions).[34]

The coefficients on the region dummies indicate that, after controlling for all factors enumerated above, Latin America still has significantly smaller government and private bond markets than the advanced economies (the excluded region). In fact, Latin America has the smallest government bond market of all regions, and the "OTHER" emerging market group has the largest government bond market (a result driven by South Africa). This result, however, is not robust to the case of corporate bonds, where the sign is positive although not statistically significant. The other emerging markets groups also have positive signs and, in fact, larger corporate bond markets than Latin America on the basis of the point estimates.

Overall, this result tells us that standard determinants of bond market development explain only part of the difference in development between the advanced and emerging economies. In other words, something else in addition to the effect of the obvious variables is going on—and that "something else" is most dramatically visible in the case of Latin America.

Cross-Country Results for Emerging Markets

Columns 5–8 of table 9.1 restrict the sample to 21 emerging market economies to see if this more homogeneous group presents the same results. The main differences between these regressions and those in the full sample can be summarized as follows. Country size no longer appears to matter for government bonds. Emerging markets with a fixed exchange rate tend to have larger government bond markets. However, the exchange rate system has no impact on the size of the private bond market. Contrary to the results for the full sample, we find a more plausible negative association between the volatility of the interest rate and the size of the private bond market and that bank credit to the private sector is more important for corporate than for financial bonds.

The results for public debt are also interesting. For government bonds we still find a positive and statistically significant coefficient.

Table 9.2
Determinants of the Size of Government and Private Bond Markets Relative to Domestic Credit

	(1) GBOND/CR	(2) PBOND/CR	(3) CBOND/CR	(4) FBOND/CR	(5) GBOND/CR	(6) PBOND/CR	(7) CBOND/CR	(8) FBOND/CR
GDP	3.184	8.592	−0.076	3.961	−6.523	4.905	0.706	3.854
	(2.03)**	(6.49)***	(0.18)	(4.97)***	(1.55)	(3.45)***	(1.20)	(3.55)***
GDP2	−0.283	−0.993	0.038	−0.141	1.772	−0.611	−0.136	−0.399
	(2.11)**	(4.00)***	(0.94)	(1.47)	(2.90)***	(2.77)**	(1.60)	(2.29)**
GDP_PC	−0.737	2.370	0.797	1.457	−0.468	1.392	1.246	−0.291
	(1.14)	(6.99)***	(5.51)***	(6.49)***	(0.30)	(3.76)***	(6.82)***	(0.98)
GDP_PC2	0.016	−0.033	−0.010	−0.013	−0.014	−0.080	−0.061	0.006
	(1.11)	(4.59)***	(3.56)***	(2.72)***	(0.28)	(6.58)***	(11.36)***	(0.60)
EXP	0.183	0.212	0.028	0.109	−0.054	0.102	0.048	0.002
	(3.31)***	(5.53)***	(2.24)**	(5.22)***	(0.60)	(3.71)***	(3.12)***	(0.09)
PRSAV	−23.194	3.966	2.846	2.198	−39.637	5.843	5.321	7.124
	(2.21)**	(0.77)	(1.80)*	(0.66)	(2.25)**	(1.45)	(2.67)***	(2.69)***
FIX	0.209	−0.288	0.238	−0.408	2.089	0.532	−0.006	0.128
	(0.24)	(0.62)	(1.54)	(1.40)	(1.28)	(1.12)	(0.02)	(0.43)
INTER	2.244	0.436	0.163	0.158	4.538	0.397	0.143	0.222
	(2.61)***	(1.23)	(1.11)	(0.65)	(3.66)***	(1.32)	(0.90)	(1.07)
IRATE	−0.233	−0.039	−0.017	−0.039	−0.139	−0.024	−0.014	−0.032
	(3.53)***	(1.65)*	(1.93)*	(3.25)***	(1.96)**	(1.50)	(1.71)*	(3.04)***
SD_IRATE	−1.911	0.339	0.083	0.232	−3.316	−0.245	0.070	−0.199
	(9.25)***	(3.08)***	(1.70)*	(4.27)***	(9.18)***	(3.15)***	(2.04)**	(3.18)***
DOMCR	−87.586	−2.392	−5.489	7.094	−118.897	−2.571	0.077	−4.341
	(17.08)***	(0.74)	(6.30)***	(3.17)***	(9.19)***	(0.86)	(0.05)	(2.09)**

DOMCR2	17.539	−3.464	1.117	−3.889	24.320	−0.065	−0.355	1.160
	(10.31)***	(2.93)***	(4.09)***	(4.30)***	(4.53)***	(0.05)	(0.58)	(1.31)
CONC	−15.181	0.551	1.611	0.539	43.446	6.530	2.932	2.029
	(3.11)***	(0.17)	(1.52)	(0.28)	(3.20)***	(1.73)*	(1.64)	(0.78)
SPREAD	−0.426	−0.090	0.016	−0.063	−0.140	0.926	0.060	0.163
	(3.59)***	(1.41)	(1.01)	(1.39)	(0.29)	(2.51)**	(0.33)	(0.88)
KAPCON	4.950	1.714	0.272	1.320	6.616	−1.423	−1.505	0.170
	(3.01)***	(1.96)*	(0.77)	(2.31)**	(1.91)*	(1.95)*	(3.08)***	(0.28)
PUBLICDEBT	0.323	0.038	0.009	0.018	0.342	0.007	−0.001	−0.005
	(11.25)***	(2.82)***	(1.69)*	(2.03)**	(6.39)***	(0.47)	(0.09)	(0.54)
DEBT_KCON	−0.115	−0.021	−0.001	−0.019	−0.151	0.012	0.013	0.005
	(4.75)***	(1.84)*	(0.29)	(2.44)**	(3.02)***	(1.00)	(2.05)**	(0.56)
YR_PR	2.394	1.155	0.431	0.720	1.687	0.900	0.319	0.534
	(5.89)***	(7.65)***	(4.33)***	(7.75)***	(3.13)***	(8.33)***	(4.05)***	(5.34)***
RULEOFLAW	0.157	0.872	0.282	0.520	0.874	0.388	0.283	0.192
	(0.24)	(2.64)***	(2.63)***	(2.64)***	(0.80)	(1.31)	(1.86)*	(0.95)
INVPROT	2.738	2.121	0.209	0.832	11.191	3.930	0.289	2.623
	(2.46)**	(2.98)***	(0.98)	(2.47)**	(5.65)***	(7.90)***	(1.13)	(7.83)***
CRIGHT	−4.076	−1.401	−0.324	−0.815	−2.936	0.555	0.204	0.986
	(5.54)***	(2.26)**	(1.62)	(2.46)**	(1.10)	(0.85)	(0.60)	(1.95)*
CONTR_COST	−0.550	−0.142	−0.067	−0.039	−1.012	−0.133	−0.035	−0.120
	(8.88)***	(4.38)***	(4.17)***	(1.76)*	(11.60)***	(5.28)***	(2.20)**	(6.48)***
FRENCHLAW	8.755	14.588	−0.540	9.671	63.818	11.862	−0.184	12.014
	(1.76)*	(5.07)***	(0.49)	(4.63)***	(6.94)***	(5.49)***	(0.15)	(7.12)***
SOCLAW	−17.265	0.986	−3.279	3.460	9.729	6.467	−3.671	9.707
	(0.83)	(0.28)	(2.37)**	(1.80)*	(0.91)	(2.38)**	(3.07)***	(4.04)***
GERSCANLAW	−7.876	32.006	0.333	18.900	−3.217	53.646		30.914
	(1.68)*	(11.19)***	(0.32)	(8.85)***	(0.23)	(17.64)***		(11.61)***

Table 9.2
(continued)

	(1) GBOND/ CR	(2) PBOND/ CR	(3) CBOND/ CR	(4) FBOND/ CR	(5) GBOND/ CR	(6) PBOND/ CR	(7) CBOND/ CR	(8) FBOND/ CR
LATITUDE	2.477	-3.707	-3.206	-10.145	-19.941	-14.880	2.311	-16.938
	(0.24)	(0.52)	(1.34)	(2.36)**	(0.59)	(1.83)*	(0.54)	(2.40)**
EAP	-18.564	19.833	9.148	1.983	-1.777	-0.437	2.762	-2.690
	(2.98)***	(6.46)***	(4.85)***	(0.74)	(0.21)	(0.20)	(2.44)**	(1.57)
LAC	-51.670	-3.415	2.666	-4.982	-65.284	-1.765	-1.229	-2.147
	(7.53)***	(1.25)	(1.98)**	(2.73)***	(6.04)***	(0.71)	(0.87)	(1.16)
ECA	1.203	-3.802	1.743	-3.364	13.381	-3.629	-2.784	-2.274
	(0.06)	(1.02)	(1.10)	(1.46)	(0.93)	(1.40)	(2.12)**	(1.22)
OTH	-0.739	20.448	7.232	6.048				
	(0.12)	(6.42)***	(4.80)***	(2.64)***				
Constant	135.263	-34.848	-2.418	-18.172	65.249	-26.644	-6.619	-11.792
	(11.03)***	(4.70)***	(0.89)	(3.34)***	(2.74)***	(4.22)***	(1.79)*	(2.35)**
Observations	491	475	471	471	222	224	205	224
Number of cc	43	42	42	42	21	21	20	21
F test: EAP = LAC	21.18	55.34	19.93	8.40	49.09	0.43	11.70	0.14
Prob > F	0.000	0.000	0.000	0.004	0.000	0.513	0.001	0.705

Note: Absolute value of t statistics in parentheses. * , ** , *** denote significance at 10%, 5%, and 1% levels, respectively.
Source: Authors' calculations.

However, the point estimate is about one third lower than that of the whole sample, indicating that emerging market countries tend to finance a larger share of their public debt by borrowing abroad (in fact, if we restrict the sample to industrial countries we find a point estimate that is almost three times as large). Finally, the institutional variables have broadly similar impact in terms of the signs of the coefficients, but their statistical significance tends to be lower.

Table 9.2 repeats the analysis but scaling the size of the bond market by domestic credit instead of GDP. Interestingly, we find that the size of the government and corporate bond markets are negatively correlated with domestic credit, which indicates that when domestic credit grows, these segments of the bond market grow at a slower rate. We also find a concave relationship between domestic credit and the size of the market for bonds issued by financial institutions. The point estimates indicate that this segment of the bond market grows faster than domestic credit until the latter reaches about 90% of GDP (close to the median value of DOMCR), and then it starts growing at a slower rate. We always find that capital controls are associated with larger bond markets (however, only the coefficients for government bonds are statistically significant). This seems to indicate that the presence of capital control favors the switch from bank credit to bonds. We also find that public debt is always positively correlated with bond market development, indicating that when we use the domestic credit metric, the market development effect of having a larger public debt clearly dominates the crowding-out effect. Rule of law, the cost of enforcing a contract and investor protection continue to be significant in the regressions for private bonds.

It is noteworthy that, when scaled by domestic credit, Latin America's government and financial bond markets continue to appear to be unwarrantedly small, but corporate bond markets are in fact larger than expected, and this effect is statistically significant. This reinforces the view that it is financial markets available to private corporations overall that are lagging in Latin America, and not the relative importance of corporate bond markets.

When we focus on our sample of emerging market countries, we find no significant relationship between domestic credit and the size of the private bond market, except for the case of financial bonds. Finally, we find that Latin American countries tend to have smaller bond markets than other emerging regions although, contrary to results for the

Table 9.3
Differences-in-Differences Analysis

	(1) Government bonds as excluded interaction		(2) Financial bonds as excluded interaction		(3) Corporate bonds as excluded interaction	
CORP	4.013 (0.55)		32.637 (4.47)***			
FIN	−28.624 (3.91)***				−32.637 (4.47)***	
GOV			28.624 (3.91)***		−4.013 (0.55)	
	CORP	FIN	CORP	GOV	FIN	GOV
GDP	−2.384 (1.55)	3.004 (1.92)*	−5.388 (3.42)***	−3.004 (1.92)*	5.388 (3.42)***	2.384 (1.55)
GDP2	0.484 (2.96)***	0.475 (2.76)***	0.008 (0.05)	−0.475 (2.76)***	−0.008 (0.05)	−0.484 (2.96)***
GDP_PC	−0.339 (0.82)	−0.255 (0.62)	−0.085 (0.21)	0.255 (0.62)	0.085 (0.21)	0.339 (0.82)
GDP_PC2	0.004 (0.41)	0.012 (1.13)	−0.007 (0.72)	−0.012 (1.13)	0.007 (0.72)	−0.004 (0.41)
EXP	0.034 (0.77)	0.108 (2.57)**	−0.073 (1.63)	−0.108 (2.57)**	0.073 (1.63)	−0.034 (0.77)
PRSAV	21.098 (1.70)*	25.876 (2.09)**	−4.777 (0.39)	−25.876 (2.09)**	4.777 (0.39)	−21.098 (1.70)*
FIX	3.957 (2.57)**	−2.552 (1.66)*	6.509 (4.21)***	2.552 (1.66)*	−6.509 (4.21)***	−3.957 (2.57)**
INT	3.425 (1.95)*	0.954 (0.55)	2.471 (1.42)	−0.954 (0.55)	−2.471 (1.42)	−3.425 (1.95)*
IRATE	0.126 (1.99)**	0.192 (3.03)***	−0.066 (1.05)	−0.192 (3.03)***	0.066 (1.05)	−0.126 (1.99)**
SD_IRATE	1.053 (7.47)***	1.041 (7.32)***	0.011 (0.08)	−1.041 (7.32)***	−0.011 (0.08)	−1.053 (7.47)***
YR_PR	0.071 (0.28)	0.016 (0.06)	0.055 (0.21)	−0.016 (0.06)	−0.055 (0.21)	−0.071 (0.28)
RULEOFLAW	0.136 (0.19)	1.057 (1.51)	−0.921 (1.32)	−1.057 (1.51)	0.921 (1.32)	−0.136 (0.19)
INVPROT	−3.091 (4.94)***	−2.201 (3.48)***	−0.890 (1.41)	2.201 (3.48)***	0.890 (1.41)	3.091 (4.94)***
CRIGHT	1.750 (3.17)***	2.164 (3.91)***	−0.414 (0.75)	−2.164 (3.91)***	0.414 (0.75)	−1.750 (3.17)***
CONTR_C	0.173 (3.43)***	0.155 (3.06)***	0.018 (0.36)	−0.155 (3.06)***	−0.018 (0.36)	−0.173 (3.43)***
DOMCR	−10.643 (2.29)**	6.997 (1.49)	−17.640 (3.75)***	−6.997 (1.49)	17.640 (3.75)***	10.643 (2.29)**

Table 9.3
(continued)

	(1) Government bonds as excluded interaction		(2) Financial bonds as excluded interaction		(3) Corporate bonds as excluded interaction	
DOMCR2	2.988	−4.354	7.343	4.354	−7.343	−2.988
	(1.81)*	(2.64)***	(4.45)***	(2.64)***	(4.45)***	(1.81)*
CONC	4.949	3.470	1.478	−3.470	−1.478	−4.949
	(1.21)	(0.85)	(0.36)	(0.85)	(0.36)	(1.21)
SPREAD	0.110	−0.294	0.404	0.294	−0.404	−0.110
	(0.80)	(2.16)**	(2.94)***	(2.16)**	(2.94)***	(0.80)
LATITUDE	−11.768	−13.484	1.717	13.484	−1.717	11.768
	(1.75)*	(1.98)**	(0.25)	(1.98)**	(0.25)	(1.75)*
KAPCON	1.745	−0.687	2.432	0.687	−2.432	−1.745
	(1.70)*	(0.66)	(2.37)**	(0.66)	(2.37)**	(1.70)*
PUBLICDEBT	−0.530	−0.439	−0.091	0.439	0.091	0.530
	(23.53)***	(19.06)***	(3.97)***	(19.06)***	(3.97)***	(23.53)***
FRENCH	−13.058	0.484	−13.541	−0.484	13.541	13.058
	(4.19)***	(0.16)	(4.35)***	(0.16)	(4.35)***	(4.19)***
SOC	−4.033	0.938	−4.971	−0.938	4.971	4.033
	(1.14)	(0.26)	(1.39)	(0.26)	(1.39)	(1.14)
GER	3.636	29.949	−26.312	−29.949	26.312	−3.636
	(1.26)	(10.14)***	(8.89)***	(10.14)***	(8.89)***	(1.26)
Constant	35.251		15.701		5.055	
	(93.25)***		(40.78)***		(13.25)***	
Observations	1454		1454		1454	
R-squared	0.91		0.91		0.91	

Note: Absolute value of ± statistics in parentheses. *, **, *** denote significance at 10%, 5%, and 1% levels, respectively.
Source: Authors' calculations.

whole sample, the differences are not statistically significant for the private bond market and its breakdown.

Differences-in-Differences Analysis

While the preceding provided an idea of how country characteristics affect the development of the private and government bond markets, it did not allow us to easily identify the differential effects of these characteristics on the various segments of the bond market. We now do this by estimating an equation of the form:

$$BOND/GDP_{j,i,t} = \alpha_{i,t} + \beta TYPE_j + \gamma(X_{i,t} * TYPE_j) + \varepsilon_{j,i,t}$$

where $BOND/GDP$ is the ratio of outstanding type j bonds to GDP (we have three types of bonds: government, financial, and corporate) in country i and year t; $\alpha_{i,t}$ is a country-year fixed effect; $TYPE$ is a dummy variable taking value 1 when the bond is of type j; and X is a matrix of country characteristics (we use the same set of variables as in table 9.1). While this "differences-in-differences" approach cannot tell us about the determinants of the absolute size of the bond market, it can help us estimate what factors affect the relative size of a type of bond market, holding constant all country-year characteristics.

Column 1 of table 9.3 estimates the above equation with government bonds as omitted alternative. The first subcolumn reports the coefficients of the $X*CORP$ interactions indicating how the various country characteristics affect the size of the corporate bond market *relative* to that of the government bond market, while the second subcolumn reports the coefficients of the $X*FIN$ interactions indicating how the various country characteristics affect the size of the financial bond market relative to that of the government bond market. Columns 2 and 3 estimate similar models with financial institutions' bonds and corporate bonds as excluded dummies.[35]

The main messages of table 9.3 can be summarized as follows. It is not clear that high levels of institutional quality are associated with relatively larger private bond markets. In fact, the government bond market seems to be relatively large in countries with high levels of investor protection and low contract enforcement costs. We also find no significant relationship between the relative size of the private bond market and GDP per capita. However, countries with higher and more volatile interest rates tend to have larger private bond markets. Pension privatization has no differential impact on the different types of bonds.

When we compare the market in bonds issued by nonfinancial corporations with the market for bonds issued by financial institutions, we find that the corporate bond market tends to be particularly large in countries with less efficient banking sectors (i.e., countries with high banking spreads and high levels of bank concentration) and in countries with English legal codes. The first finding is straightforward; the second one presumably reflects the fact that the countries that adopted a legal code in the English tradition have market-based financial systems while countries with legal systems based on civil law are more likely to have bank-based financial systems (Demirgüç-Kunt and Levine 1999). We also find that the presence of capital controls and fixed exchange rates (which often go hand in hand) are associated with relatively large corporate bond markets. As one may expect, we find that a larger financial system is associated with a relatively larger share of financial bonds but, interestingly, this effect reverses in countries with very large financial systems.

Table 9.4 repeats the experiment but now restricting the sample to emerging markets. It appears that the financial and corporate segments of the private bond market are more homogenous in emerging markets (the only differences are for investor protection and French legal code, which are associated with more issuance by financial institutions.) But there are still important differences between private and government bond markets. For example, the level of private savings and rule of law are important for the relative size of the private bond market.[36] Again, the relationship between the size of the financial sector and the relative development of the private bond market is nonlinear. The point estimates suggest that the relative size of the private bond market initially tends to decline with the growth of the financial sector, but this relationship reverses in countries with highly developed financial systems. An interpretation is that development of the banking system initially enables financial institutions to gain ground relative to securities markets (banks gain a larger share of total private intermediation), but further development of the banking system (and an efficient, competitive, well-functioning banking system in particular) leads to a rising share of market-based (bond-based) finance in the total, as if an efficient banking system and a liquid private bond market are complements in the long run (as we suggest in this chapter).

Conclusions

This chapter has documented the underdevelopment of Latin American financial markets, and Latin American corporate bond markets in particular. Our statistical analysis shows that a limited number of observable policy variables and country characteristics explain 80% of the difference in private bond market capitalization between Latin America and the advanced economies.[37] This same set of observable variables also explains 70% of the difference in the development of the financial institutions bond market and the entirety of the difference in the bonds of corporations between the two regions.

If we take these 22 country characteristics and replace their average values for Latin America with their average values for the industrial countries, we would presumably find that the two regions would have

Table 9.4
Differences-in-Differences Analysis: Emerging Market Countries

	(1) Government bonds as excluded interaction		(2) Financial bonds as excluded interaction		(3) Corporate bonds as excluded interaction	
CORP	23.856 (1.69)*		22.308 (1.58)			
FIN	1.548 (0.11)				−22.308 (1.58)	
GOV			−1.548 (0.11)		−23.856 (1.69)*	
	CORP	FIN	CORP	GOV	FIN	GOV
GDP	−5.925 (1.80)*	−2.440 (0.78)	−3.485 (1.06)	2.440 (0.78)	3.485 (1.06)	5.925 (1.80)*
GDP2	1.169 (1.99)**	0.888 (1.58)	0.280 (0.48)	−0.888 (1.58)	−0.280 (0.48)	−1.169 (1.99)**
GDP_PC	2.402 (3.55)***	1.484 (2.20)**	0.918 (1.37)	−1.484 (2.20)**	−0.918 (1.37)	−2.402 (3.55)***
GDP_PC2	−0.008 (0.25)	0.020 (0.67)	−0.027 (0.88)	−0.020 (0.67)	0.027 (0.88)	0.008 (0.25)
EXP	−0.119 (1.69)*	−0.061 (1.04)	−0.057 (0.83)	0.061 (1.04)	0.057 (0.83)	0.119 (1.69)*
PRSAV	46.472 (2.61)***	45.112 (2.62)***	1.360 (0.08)	−45.112 (2.62)***	−1.360 (0.08)	−46.472 (2.61)***
FIX	−4.635 (2.04)**	−3.767 (1.72)*	−0.868 (0.38)	3.767 (1.72)*	0.868 (0.38)	4.635 (2.04)**
INT	0.232 (0.12)	1.437 (0.78)	−1.205 (0.65)	−1.437 (0.78)	1.205 (0.65)	−0.232 (0.12)
IRATE	0.202 (3.13)***	0.191 (2.97)***	0.011 (0.17)	−0.191 (2.97)***	−0.011 (0.17)	−0.202 (3.13)***
SD_IRATE	0.265 (1.27)	0.128 (0.62)	0.137 (0.66)	−0.128 (0.62)	−0.137 (0.66)	−0.265 (1.27)
YR_PR	0.712 (2.06)**	0.826 (2.42)**	−0.114 (0.33)	−0.826 (2.42)**	0.114 (0.33)	−0.712 (2.06)**
RULEOFLAW	3.285 (4.08)***	3.291 (4.18)***	−0.006 (0.01)	−3.291 (4.18)***	0.006 (0.01)	−3.285 (4.08)***
INVPROT	−3.867 (3.42)***	−1.460 (1.32)	−2.407 (2.13)**	1.460 (1.32)	2.407 (2.13)**	3.867 (3.42)***
CRIGHT	−1.476 (1.04)	−1.266 (0.92)	−0.210 (0.15)	1.266 (0.92)	0.210 (0.15)	1.476 (1.04)
CONTR_C	0.172 (3.19)***	0.124 (2.35)**	0.048 (0.89)	−0.124 (2.35)**	−0.048 (0.89)	−0.172 (3.19)***
DOMCR	−32.319 (3.05)***	−32.430 (3.17)***	0.111 (0.01)	32.430 (3.17)***	−0.111 (0.01)	32.319 (3.05)***

Table 9.4
(continued)

	(1) Government bonds as excluded interaction		(2) Financial bonds as excluded interaction		(3) Corporate bonds as excluded interaction	
DOMCR2	9.267	8.205	1.062	−8.205	−1.062	−9.267
	(1.79)*	(1.63)	(0.21)	(1.63)	(0.21)	(1.79)*
CONC	17.311	19.496	−2.185	−19.496	2.185	−17.311
	(1.79)*	(2.22)**	(0.23)	(2.22)**	(0.23)	(1.79)*
SPREAD	−0.815	−0.411	−0.404	0.411	0.404	0.815
	(0.85)	(0.43)	(0.42)	(0.43)	(0.42)	(0.85)
LATITUDE	−91.006	−82.140	−8.867	82.140	8.867	91.006
	(7.20)***	(6.56)***	(0.71)	(6.56)***	(0.71)	(7.20)***
KAPCON	−3.388	−2.201	−1.187	2.201	1.187	3.388
	(2.05)**	(1.34)	(0.73)	(1.34)	(0.73)	(2.05)**
PUBLICDEBT	−0.223	−0.213	−0.010	0.213	0.010	0.223
	(7.47)***	(7.14)***	(0.34)	(7.14)***	(0.34)	(7.47)***
FRENCH	−28.315	−15.800	−12.515	15.800	12.515	28.315
	(4.73)***	(2.72)***	(2.09)**	(2.72)***	(2.09)**	(4.73)***
SOC	2.261	8.643	−6.382	−8.643	6.382	−2.261
	(0.50)	(1.92)*	(1.41)	(1.92)*	(1.41)	(0.50)
GER	22.569	30.512	−7.943	−30.512	7.943	−22.569
	(3.68)***	(5.18)***	(1.30)	(5.18)***	(1.30)	(3.68)***
Constant	23.297		3.808		3.306	
	(51.01)***		(8.40)***		(7.04)***	
Observations	662		662		662	
R-squared	0.89		0.89		0.89	

Note: Absolute value of *t* statistics in parentheses. *, **, *** denote significance at 10%, 5%, and 1% levels, respectively.
Source: Authors' calculations.

private bond markets of similar size. This follows from the fact that the coefficients are constrained to be equal across regions and the explanatory power of the estimated equations is relatively high. Does this, therefore, mean that rapid improvements in policies and institutions would quickly close the gap? Unfortunately not. Improvements in policy take time to work their effects. In addition, our statistical analysis shows that a quarter of the difference in private bond market capitalization between industrial countries and Latin America is due to country size (measured by aggregate GDP) and the level of development (measured by GDP per capita). About 15% of difference is attributable to the development of the financial system (measured by bank credit to the private sector) and another 15% is related to historical and geographical factors (such as the origin of the legal code and other measures of institutional inheritance). Policy variables that play an important role include macroeconomic stability (proxied by the volatility of the interest rate), openness (proxied by exports over GDP), investor protection, the cost of enforcing a contract, and pension privatization, but these factors can explain at most one quarter of the difference between the Latin America and the industrial countries. Policy variables like the exchange rate regime, the presence or absence of capital controls, the level of public debt, bank concentration, and banking spreads are sometimes statistically significant in the empirical analysis but play only a small role in explaining differences in the development of bond markets in the industrial countries and Latin America.

While this does not mean that policies and institutions do not matter, it clearly means that there is no convenient shortcut. By implication, the same policies that are necessary for economic development in general are also necessary for the development of domestic bond markets.

Appendix: Data Sources

CONC   Bank concentration. Source: Micco, Panizza, and Yañez (2006).

CONTR_COST   Cost to enforce a contract. Source: Doing Business database (http://www.doingbusiness.org) (accessed September 15, 2006).

DOMCR   Bank credit to the private sector. Source: World Bank (2006) and IMF (2006).

EXP   Exports over GDP. Source: World Bank (2006).

FIX   Fixed exchange rate dummy. Source: Levy Yeyati and Sturzenegger (2005).

FRENCHLAW   Dummy variable taking value 1 for countries with French civil law. Source: La Porta et al. (1998).

GBOND/GDP,   All measures for amount of outstanding bonds are
CBOND/GDP,   from the BIS securities statistics, tables 16a and 16b.
FBOND/GDP   Available at http://www.bis.org/statistics/secstats
                  .htm (accessed January 15, 2007). The ratios were
                  computed using data in current dollar GDP from
                  the World Bank's World Development Indicators
                  (World Bank 2006).

GDP_PC	GDP per capita in current purchasing power parity-adjusted dollars. Source: World Bank (2006).
GERSCANLAW	Dummy variable taking value 1 for countries with German or Scandinavian legal origin. Source: La Porta et al. (1998).
INTER	Intermediate exchange rate dummy. Source: Levy Yeyati and Sturzenegger (2005).
INVPROT	Investor protection. Source: Doing Business database (http://www.doingbusiness.org) (accessed September 15, 2006).
IRATE	Interest rate (average between lending and deposit rate). Source: World Bank (2006) and IMF (2006).
KAPCON	Capital controls. Source: Brune (2006).
LATITUDE	Latitude. Source: La Porta et al. (1998).
PRSAV	Private savings over GDP. Source: World Bank (2006).
PUBLICDEBT	Central government debt over GDP. Source: Jaimovich and Panizza (2006).
RULEOFLAW	Index of law and order. Source: ICRG (2006).
SD_RATE	Standard deviation of IRATE. Source: authors' calculations.
SOCLAW	Dummy variable taking value 1 for countries with socialist legal origin. Source: La Porta et al. (1998).
SPREAD	Bank spread (lending rate minus deposit rate). Source: World Bank (2006) and IMF (2006).
YR_PR	Number of years since privatization of the pension system. Source: www.fiap.cl (accessed September 15, 2006).

Notes

1. Germany is a partial exception, where a reasonably deep and liquid bond market has coexisted with a well-developed banking system.

2. In fact, when we scale the bond market by domestic credit and use weighted averages, we find that in 2004 Latin America was the region with the largest bond market.

3. Although in practice this seems to be more the case in the advanced economies and in East Asia than in Latin America. In addition, banks in many countries hold a large share of short-term government debt to meet statutory liquidity requirements.

4. Banks may do this by limiting access to the payment system and by supporting the maintenance of regulations that increase the cost of underwriting and issuance (Schinasi and Smith 1998; Rajan and Zingales 2003a; Eichengreen and Leungnareumitchai 2004).

5. To measure firm size, we compute the assets of the largest 100 firms as a share of GDP and regress this on GDP (as a way of acknowledging the fact that, by construction, this ratio is negatively correlated with country size). We use the residual of this regression as our measure of adjusted firm size. This correlation is particularly strong when we measure corporate bonds as a share of M2, indicating that given the size of the financial system countries with larger firms are more likely to develop a corporate bond market.

6. We analyze comparative bond market development in Latin America and East Asia in a companion paper (Eichengreen, Borensztein, Panizza 2006).

7. The fact that this relationship is stronger for total saving than private saving is another hint that chronic government budget deficits (public dissaving, in other words) are not especially good for bond market development, the advantages of public issuance for the creation of a liquid benchmark asset notwithstanding.

8. These exercises use BIS data and partial out the effect of pension privatization using a variety of controls. We find that the effect of years since pension privatization is stronger on the capitalization of government bond markets than corporate bond markets, however, perhaps because pension funds often operate subject to restrictive mandates that limit their ability to hold speculative credits.

9. A by-product of these prudential regulations that may limit the participation of pension funds and insurance companies in the domestic corporate bond market is that such funds and companies are precluded from holding bonds rated below BBB. In turn, this limits the demand for the bonds of smaller and riskier firms. However, institutional investors in Chile are able to circumvent this constraint to some extent by utilizing the market for credit derivatives. It is also argued that competition between the three mandatory pension funds is not particularly intense; hence, they have relatively little incentive to compete for yield by purchasing higher-yielding instruments and utilizing costly credit derivatives (see chapter 6). This constraint binds even more tightly in countries like Colombia where credit derivatives do not exist; instead, six mandatory pension funds are allowed to invest only in corporate bonds with investment-grade ratings, which is a large part of the explanation for why firms only issue bonds if they are investment grade.

10. IMF (2002) notes, however, that institutional investors—insurance companies in particular—have an incentive to trade more actively to raise the yield on their investment portfolios in periods when interest rates are low.

11. The discussion here focuses on foreign purchases of local issues by residents. The other way of involving nonresidents is by encouraging them to issue domestically. Some emerging Asian countries have gone a considerable way down this road. Thus, as of the end of 2004, issues by nonresidents accounted for 56% of corporate bond issuance in Hong Kong (admittedly, a special case), 36% in Singapore, and 13% in the Philippines (see Gyntelberg, Ma, and Remolona 2006). In Latin America this practice is still all but nonexistent, aside from a few local issues by the IADB.

12. Thus, the Brazilian authorities moved in February 2006 to reduce taxes on foreign investment in local government bonds, though not yet also on corporate issues.

13. Note that the figure for East Asia does not include China. In constructing these estimates we follow the practice of Burger and Warnock (2003) and Claessens, Klingebiel,

and Schmukler (2003) in assuming that all domestic issuers are residents and that all domestic issues are in local currency.

14. Data on foreign investors' positions in local markets are incomplete. Among other things, foreign investors participate through total return swaps where the bonds themselves are registered with local banks (see IMF 2002).

15. The data for Asia are from Takeuchi (2005) while data for other countries are from IMF (2005).

16. With the few exceptions (Uruguay, Hungary, Poland) noted previously in the text.

17. The literature on whether foreign listing of equity claims discourages domestic trading of the same stocks points in this direction. Again, we explore this further in our companion paper (Eichengreen, Borensztein, Panizza 2006).

18. That these instruments received preferential treatment under the Brazilian tax code and bankruptcy law seems to have been a major factor in their development. See chapter 7 for further discussion.

19. As in the survey returns for Colombia reported in chapter 5.

20. The authors also find that GDP per capita as a measure of general economic and financial development has a positive effect in their benchmark regressions, although this effect weakens when they also include the vector of institutional controls mentioned in the previous paragraph, and the effect is relatively unstable when they disaggregate government and corporate bonds.

21. Contrary to arguments emphasizing either crowding out or the advantages of a benchmark government bond.

22. This is consistent with the emphasis in De la Torre and Schmukler (2004) who argue that Latin American countries have smaller bond markets because of weaker enforcement of creditor rights.

23. Questions can be raised about these results in particular, given the data set's limited coverage of short-term bonds.

24. Further results from this study are reported in De la Torre and Schmukler (2004).

25. In regressions using BIS data for 40-plus countries, we find that the exchange rate regime has no differential effect (with respect to government bonds) on the currency composition of private (corporate and financial) bonds. When we drop industrial countries, we find that, with respect to the government sector, private issuers tend to issue more foreign currency bonds in presence of floating regimes. In the next section, we analyze in detail how the exchange rate regime affects the size of different segments of the domestic bond market.

26. Finally there are studies taking international capital flows via the bond market as their dependent variable. Ghosh and Wolf (2000) study debt flows using the basic gravity model and data on outflows from Germany, the United States, and Italy. They include only the standard gravity variables. Interestingly, these do not work very well, except in the case of the United States. Buch (2000) uses IMF data on debt securities for 1997 only. In this study the basic gravity variables are well behaved and look similar to those in regressions for bank claims (suggesting in turn that the relatively poor results in the study by Ghosh and Wolf reflect the very limited nature of their sample). The impact

of having a larger domestic banking system is ambiguous, varying by source country. Finally, coefficients on the ratio of bank loans to total debt finance suggest that the relative importance of bond finance rises with the development of the host country, while country (population) size is otherwise insignificant, suggesting minimal economies of scale.

27. A possible problem with some of the studies quoted above is that, in measuring the size of the local currency bond market, the authors are forced to accept the BIS' assertion that all local currency bonds included in the BIS data are denominated in local currency. However, contrary to the case of international bonds, BIS does not build its tables on domestic bonds from bond-level data and hence cannot guarantee that all domestic bonds are indeed in local currency. Comparing the data for Argentina and Peru with the tabulations published by the BIS shows clearly for these two countries that the BIS data include local-market debt denominated in foreign currencies as well (in fact, the BIS website notes that "The domestic data for Argentina and Peru include local issues in foreign currency" [www.bis.org/publ/quarterly.htm: BIS Quarterly Review, Statistical Annex, September 2007, p. A112]). We suspect that the same may be true for other countries. For instance, we know that in the build-up to the 1994–1995 crisis, Mexico was retiring domestic debt denominated in currency (Cetes) and issuing a large amount of domestic debt indexed to the dollar (Tesobonos). However, the BIS data does not show any clear decreasing trend in the amount of domestic debt in domestic currency. The amount of Mexican domestic government bonds went from US$39 billion in March 1994 to US$42 billion in September 1994 and only dropped to US$32 billion after the devaluation of December 2004.

28. Relative to Eichengreen and Luengnaruemitchai, we have data for three additional years (2002–2004) and for as many as 14 additional countries. The appendix to this chapter includes a complete list of our sources. The sample differs across columns because, in order to control for outliers, we drop all observations for which the dependent variable takes values which are 3 standard deviations above the sample mean. By doing so, we drop 5 observations for government bonds (2 for Japan and 3 for Lebanon), 12 for corporate bonds (2 for Iceland, 3 for Korea, and 7 for Malaysia), and 22 for financial bonds (16 for Denmark, 3 for Iceland, and 3 for the United States).

29. We censor IRATE at 100%.

30. Eichengreen and Luengnaruemitchai (2004) found no significant relationship in both cases.

31. When we focus on government and corporate bonds, we find no significant effect of DOMCR.

32. There are two differences between our definition of SPREAD and that of Eichengreen and Luengnaruemitchai (2004). First, we define spread as the difference between lending and deposit rate a bit differently. Second, we scale the spread by the deposit interest rate in order to remove the effect of the average interest rate (see appendix to this chapter for details).

33. We compute the interaction by subtracting from PUBLICDEBT and KAPCON their mean values, so that including the interaction has no effect on the estimates of the main coefficients.

34. This result is driven by the fact that we control for several variables that are correlated with legal origin. If we run a regressions without controls, we find that countries

with the French and Socialist legal code have the smallest private bond market and that latitude is positively correlated with the size of the private bond market.

35. Clearly the results of the three columns are symmetrical and they could all be obtained by algebraic manipulations of any two columns; by presenting them separately, however, we are able to directly test for differences between various types of bond market.

36. We also find the same puzzling results we found before with the relative size of the government bond market being positively associated with higher levels of investor protection and lower cost to enforce a contract.

37. However, this set of variables only explains one third of the difference in the capitalization of the government bond market.

References

Bolton, Patrick (2003). "Towards a Statutory Approach to Sovereign Debt Restructuring: Lessons from Corporate Bankruptcy Practice around the World." *IMF Staff Papers* 50: 41–71.

Braun, Matías, and Ignacio Briones (2006). "The Development of Bond Markets around the World." Unpublished manuscript, Universidad Adolfo Ibáñez (February).

Brune, Nancy (2006). "Capital Account Liberalization Policy in Developing Countries." Mimeo, Yale University.

Buch, Claudia (2000). "Information or Regulation: What Is Driving the International Activities of Commercial Banks?" Kiel Working Paper No. 1011. Kiel Institute of World Economics.

Burger, John, and Francis Warnock (2003). "Diversification, Original Sin, and International Bond Portfolios." International Finance Discussion Paper No. 755 (January). Washington, D.C.: Board of Governors of the Federal Reserve System.

Burger, John, and Francis Warnock (2004). "Foreign Participation in Local-Currency Bond Markets." International Finance Discussion Paper No. 794 (February). Board of Governors of the Federal Reserve System.

Burger, John, and Francis Warnock (2006). "Local Currency Bond Markets." *IMF Staff Papers* 53 (special issue, September): 133–146.

Claessens, Stijn, Daniela Klingebiel, and Sergio Schmukler (2003). "Government Bonds in Domestic and Foreign Currency: The Role of Macroeconomic and Institutional Factors." CEPR Discussion Paper No. 3789 (February).

De la Torre, Augusto, and Sergio Schmukler (2004). *Whither Latin American Capital Markets?* Washington, D.C.: World Bank.

Demirgüç-Kunt, Asli, and Ross Levine (1999). "Bank Based and Market Based Financial Systems: Cross-Country Comparisons." World Bank Policy Research Working Paper No. 2143.

Eichengreen, Barry (2000). "The Euro One Year On." *Journal of Policy Modeling* 22: 355–368.

Eichengreen, Barry, Eduardo Borensztein, and Ugo Panizza (2006). "A Tale of Two Markets: Bond Market Development in East Asia and Latin America." Hong Kong Institute for Monetary Research, Occasional Papers No. 3.

Eichengreen, Barry, and Pipat Luengnaruemitchai (2004). "Why Doesn't Asia Have Bigger Bond Markets?" NBER Working Paper No. 10576 (May).

Ghosh, Swati, and Holger Wolf (2000). "Is There a Curse of Location? Spatial Determinants of Capital Flows to Emerging Markets." In Sebastian Edwards (ed.), *Capital Flows and the Emerging Economies*. Chicago: University of Chicago Press, 137–158.

Gyntelberg, Jacob, Guonan Ma, and Eli Remolona (2006). "Developing Corporate Bond Markets in Asia." In "Developing Corporate Bond Markets in Asia." BIS Paper No. 26 (February), 13–20.

Hausmann, Ricardo, and Ugo Panizza (2003). "On the Determinants of Original Sin: An Empirical Investigation." *Journal of International Money and Finance* 22: 957–990.

ICRG (2006). International Country Risk Guide. CD-ROM. East Syracuse, NY: PRS Group.

International Monetary Fund (2002). "Emerging Local Bond Markets." *Global Financial Stability Report*, 48–66.

International Monetary Fund (2005). "Development of Corporate Bond Markets in Emerging Economies." *Global Financial Stability Report* (September), 103–141.

International Monetary Fund (2006). *International Financial Statistics* (December). Washington, DC: International Monetary Fund.

Jaimovich, Dany, and Ugo Panizza (2006). "Public Debt around the World." Working Paper No. 561, Research Department, Inter-American Development Bank; forthcoming in *Applied Economics Letters*.

La Porta, Rafael, Florencio López-de-Silanes, Andrei Shleifer, and Robert Vishny (1998). "Law and Finance." *Journal of Political Economy* 106: 1133–1155.

Levy Yeyati, Eduardo, and Federico Sturzenegger (2005). "Classifying Exchange Rate Regimes: Deeds vs. Words." *European Economic Review* 49: 1603–1635.

Ma, Guonan, Eli Remolona, and He Jianxiong (2006). "Developing Corporate Bond Markets in Asia: A Synopsis of the Kunming Discussions." In "Developing Corporate Bond Markets in Asia." BIS Paper No. 26 (February), 1–6.

Mehl, Arnaud, and Julien Reynaud (2005). "The Determinants of 'Domestic' Original Sin in Emerging Market Economies." Working Paper No. 560 (December). European Central Bank, Frankfurt.

Micco, Alejandro, Ugo Panizza, and Monica Yañez (2006). "Bank Ownership and Performance: Does Politics Matter?" *Journal of Banking and Finance* 31(1): 219–241.

Nierop, Erwin (2006). "Developing Corporate Bond Markets: A European Legal Perspectives." In "Developing Corporate Bond Markets in Asia." BIS Paper No. 26 (February), 61–73.

Rajan, Raghuram, and Luigi Zingales (2003a). "Banks and Markets: The Changing Character of European Finance." NBER Working Paper No. 9595.

Rajan, Raghuran, and Luigi Zingales (2003b). "The Great Reversals: The Politics of Financial Development in the Twentieth Century." *Journal of Monetary Economics* 69: 5–50.

Schinasi, Gary, and Todd Smith (1998). "Fixed Income Markets in the United States, Europe and Japan: Some Lessons for Emerging Markets." IMF Working Paper No. 98-173.

Takeuchi, Atsushi (2005). "Study of Impediments to Cross-Border Bond Investment and Issuance in Asian Countries." www.asianbondsonline.com (December).

World Bank (2006). World Development Indicators. CD-ROM. Washington, DC: World Bank.

List of Material Included in the Web Appendix

The Web Appendix (http://mitpress.mit.edu/9780262026321/webappendix) includes six folders (one for each country study) and a summary document. The summary document presents detailed information on the data available in each of the six folders and a table that summarizes the available data. The material in the folders is divided into four parts:

1. Supplementary tables, which include information on the structure of the domestic bond market that was not included in the text in order to save space.

2. Bond- (or bond/firm)-level data, which include all bond-level (and firm-level) information used in the statistical analyses of the country studies.

3. Responses to the firm survey, including the template used in each country.

4. Responses to the institutional investor survey, including the template used in each country.

The country folders also include README documents with detailed lists of all the information included in each country study. The README files include:

1. A list of all tables and datasets included in the country folder.

2. A brief description of the survey (number of respondents for each survey; date when the surveys were administered; how the survey was administered; and other relevant information that is not included in the paper). This description is not available in all README files.

3. Templates used for the survey, including both the original version (in Spanish or Portuguese) and an English translation of the questions

that are not included in the common templates (which are in the appendix of the summary document).

4. Contact information for the authors of the papers.

The list below covers all the data included in the Web Appendix.

Argentina

1. Supplementary tables
   1.1. Level and composition of bonds issued by: (1) central government, (2) local governments, (3) central bank, (4) private sector
      1.1.1. Domestic bonds: domestic and foreign currency, nominal and indexed, short- and long-term
      1.1.2. Foreign bonds: domestic and foreign currency, nominal and indexed, short- and long-term
   1.2. Level and composition of asset-backed securities
2. Security-level data. This includes security-level data for corporate bonds, asset-backed securities, and checks of deferred payment
3. Firm survey
4. Investor survey

Brazil

1. Supplementary Tables
   1.1. Level and composition of bonds issued by: (1) central government, (2) local governments, (3) central bank, (4) private sector
      1.1.1. Domestic bonds: domestic and foreign currency, nominal and indexed, short- and long-term
      1.1.2. Foreign bonds: domestic and foreign currency, nominal and indexed, short- and long-term
   1.2. Level and composition of asset-backed securities
   1.3. Average term (in years) of federal debt
      1.3.1. Internal federal debt: fixed and floating interest rate bills, inflation- and U.S. dollar-adjusted notes
      1.3.2. External federal debt: Brady bonds, global bonds, Eurobonds
   1.4. Issues of: (1) stocks, (2) debentures, (3) commercial paper

1.4.1. Number and volume for (1), (2), and (3)

1.4.2. Debenture volume and turnover in the secondary market

1.4.3. Issues of debentures by industry, 1995–2005: number of issues, amounts, percent of total

2. Bond-level data: includes the following information: type of firm; type of bond; currency; interest rate; issued volume; issued quantity; outstanding quantity; actual volume; traded volume; traded quantity; price; issue date; maturity date; original term (years); remaining term (years); collateral; convertible; rating

3. Firm survey

4. Investor survey

Chile

1. Supplementary tables

1.1. Level and composition of bonds issued by: (1) central government, (2) local governments, (3) central bank, (4) corporate private sector

1.1.1. Domestic bonds: domestic and foreign currency, nominal and indexed, short- and long-term

1.1.2. Foreign bonds: domestic and foreign currency, nominal and indexed, short- and long-term

1.2. Level and composition of asset-backed securities

1.3. Amount outstanding and yield of corporate and central bank bonds

1.3.1. Central bank bonds by years to maturity

1.3.2. Corporate bonds by sector, years to maturity, risk classification

1.4. Traded and turnover

1.4.1. Transactions

- Volume traded (million US$)

- Share of corporate bonds

- Share of central bank bonds

- Share of mortgage bonds

- Share of banking bonds

- Share of leasing bonds
- Share of recognition bonds

1.4.2. Turnover

- Corporate bonds
- Mortgage bonds
- Central bank bonds
- Recognition bonds

1.5. Corporate bonds detail

1.5.1. Uses of funds: declared uses of funds of companies having issued bonds

1.5.2. Economic sector detail

1.5.3. Corporate bonds issued abroad (1993–2005)

- Total amount issued abroad
- Number of issuances
- Number of different indebted companies
- Average amount per bond issued abroad
- Average amount per bond issued domestically

2. Bond-level data, corporate bonds: includes the following information: issuance date; ticker symbol; sector; time to maturity; risk rating; amount outstanding; date; company; date of issuance; currency; face value; series; coupon; floating rate; maturity date; years to maturity; industry sector; rating FITCH; rating HUMPHREYS; rating FELLER; rating CCR; aggregate rating

3. Firm Survey

4. Investor Survey

Colombia

1. Supplementary tables

1.1. Level and composition of bonds issued by: (1) central government, (2) local governments, (3) central bank, (4) private sector

1.1.1. Domestic bonds: domestic and foreign currency, nominal and indexed, short- and long-term

1.1.2. Foreign bonds: domestic and foreign currency, nominal and indexed, short- and long-term

1.2. Level and composition of asset-backed securities (*fideicomisos*)

1.3. Disaggregation of the amounts outstanding of domestic public bonds

1.4. Characteristics of issuers of bonds in domestic and international markets

2. Firm survey

3. Investor survey

Mexico

1. Supplementary tables

1.1. Level and composition of bonds issued by: (1) central government, (2) local governments, (3) central bank, (4) private sector

1.1.1. Domestic bonds: domestic and foreign currency, nominal and indexed, short- and long-term

1.1.2. Foreign bonds: domestic and foreign currency, nominal and indexed, short- and long-term

1.2. Level and composition of asset-backed securities

2. Firm survey (data only available at the aggregated level)

3. Investor survey

Uruguay

1. Supplementary tables

1.1. Level and composition of bonds issued by: (1) central government, (2) local governments, (3) central bank, (4) private sector

1.1.1. Domestic bonds: domestic and foreign currency, nominal and indexed, short- and long-term

1.1.2. Foreign bonds: domestic and foreign currency, nominal and indexed, short- and long-term

1.2. Level and composition of asset-backed securities

2. Firm survey

3. Investor survey

Index

The letter f after a page number indicates a figure; n with a following number indicates a note; t indicates a table.